VICKI SMITH BERDIT

Where the

River

Flows

**ENJOYING THE CURRENT OF GOD
IN AND THROUGH YOUR LIFE**

Contents

This work is dedicated to all the great men and women of God who took the time to teach, to preach, and to share the love of God with so many people over the years. I am one of the least of those who benefitted from your sacrifices. The credit for this book is yours; the glory of it belongs to our God. Thank you for leading me through the waters and into the depths of the River of God.

A Word about the Author

from Dr. Errol Mustafa

I AM HONORED TO TELL YOU ABOUT DR. VICKI Berdit, whom I have known for over twenty years. On pondering the qualities I have seen in her over the years, I can truly say that she lives what she believes. Vicki is a woman of integrity and is sincere in her love for the people that God brings to her for ministry.

She has grown in experience and knowledge on subjects that pertain to transformation and freedom, and is passionate about seeing people living in victory. Vicki is committed to coming alongside those who are hurting and wounded, and is effective in helping them pursue a journey of complete restoration.

The revelations Vicki has received are tremendous. As God has taught her and given her insight that carries the inherent potential to bring freedom, hope, and transformation to the reader. Her books take you on a journey of self-discovery, and challenge you to seek all that God has for you. As you come on this journey with her, it will be the start to a life of fulfillment and joy in receiving what God has for you.

Dr. Errol Mustafa
Founder and Senior Pastor
City Bible Church Int.
Jacksonville, Florida

Foreword

by Pastor Wendell Knight

THE THIEF COMES NOT BUT FOR TO STEAL, AND TO KILL, AND TO DESTROY: I AM COME THAT THEY MIGHT HAVE LIFE, AND THAT THEY MIGHT HAVE IT MORE ABUNDANTLY. (JOHN 10:10)

THESE WORDS OF JESUS PRESENT TO US A comparison of two very different kingdoms, God's kingdom and Satan's kingdom. At the forefront of God's kingdom is His love for us and His plan for our lives with instruction on how to live a godly Christian life. Satan's kingdom, however, wants to take from us all that God wants for us. He is the thief of John 10:10. These two opposing forces, with man in the middle, clash in battle to win the souls of men.

God's plan for us is that we be imitators of Him, speaking like Him, thinking like Him, and acting the way He would have us act. We learn how to do this through His Word and through our love relationship with Him. We have, however, through our thoughts and life experiences, listened to Satan and his kingdom without even realizing it, thus enabling him to hold us captive to his plan for our lives.

This book by Vicki Smith Berdit reveals in great detail these two plans. Holy Spirit-inspired teaching brings forth truth and revelation knowledge to the reader, the one who studies to show himself approved, rightly dividing the Word of God. Facts are backed up by Scripture, and many prayers are offered throughout the book for the reader's personal deliverance and freedom.

This study is one that can be used over and over again, not only for your own personal deliverance and freedom, but also as a tool to minister to the needs of others. I highly recommend that you add this to your personal library!

Pastor Wendell Knight (1942–2022)
Pathway to Health, Inc.
Orlando, Florida

Introducing "Where the River Flows"

A word from the author

IF YOU ARE LOOKING FOR A BOOK WRITTEN by someone with lots of academic degrees and certificates, or a person who is interested in the psychology of the mind, or even world views of therapy and counseling, keep looking. That's not me. But if you have finally come to the realization (as I did) that you can't fix yourself, and that the world and no one in it can fix you, either, then keep reading. Get a highlighter and a pen and don't be afraid to write in this book! Take your time absorbing and reabsorbing the principles and practicalities the Lord God Himself will reveal to you, the truths about Him and about yourself that will free you from bondages of your mind, negative influences of your past, and ungodly subjection to your emotions.

Maybe that seems to be an unbelievable claim, that God Himself will reveal Himself to you, and reveal YOU to you, through these pages. Who am I to say such a thing? Do I presume to speak for God? Who gave me such authority? Who told me I could? What are my qualifications? Admittedly, I have none, neither from, nor in, this world! Ah, but praise be to God who is faithful to pour out His anointing and wisdom through His saints, and to use the foolish things of the world to confound the wise!

Which begs yet another confession – the insights and observations compiled here did not all originate with me; some have been gleaned from the thoughts of great men and women of God. While many are direct revelations by the Holy Spirit to me personally, some come from teachings I've read or messages I've heard over many years of study and growth. The Lord has granted me the ability to put it all together into what I hope is a simple and understandable way that will free you from misery and tormenting doubts and position you to free others as well.

Jesus said all authority, all power, in heaven and earth and under the earth, was given to Him— "Now, You go!" He is the one who gave His followers the authority and the power of Heaven. I simply yield to Him and allow Him to teach, to make disciples, to free His precious people from all hindrances and limitations and move in resurrection power that is only available through His Holy Spirit. I am fully qualified in Him, because God is faithful—and He loves you.

Where the River Flows is the title given to this work by the Holy Spirit, as are all the parts of it that penetrate your heart and change your thinking. I was a few months into the writing of it before I knew the title, an unusual switch for me, as God had always given me the title of other books first, and then the content. Then one day as we were reading in Ezekiel chapter 47, I knew what to call this book. I heard its title clearly in my spirit. Following are the Scriptures through which the Holy Spirit of God spoke.

AFTERWARD HE BROUGHT ME AGAIN UNTO THE DOOR OF THE HOUSE; AND, BEHOLD, WATERS ISSUED OUT FROM UNDER THE THRESHOLD OF THE HOUSE EASTWARD: FOR THE FORE-FRONT OF THE HOUSE STOOD TOWARD THE EAST, AND THE WATERS CAME DOWN FROM UNDER FROM THE RIGHT SIDE OF THE HOUSE, AT THE SOUTH SIDE OF THE ALTAR. THEN HE BROUGHT ME OUT OF THE WAY OF THE GATE NORTHWARD, AND LED ME ABOUT THE WAY WITHOUT TO THE OUTER GATE BY THE WAY THAT LOOKS EASTWARD; AND, BEHOLD, THERE RAN OUT WATERS ON THE RIGHT SIDE. AND WHEN THE MAN THAT HAD THE LINE IN HIS HAND WENT FORTH EASTWARD, HE MEASURED A THOUSAND CUBITS, AND HE BROUGHT ME THROUGH THE WATERS; THE WATERS WERE TO THE

ANKLES. AGAIN HE MEASURED A THOUSAND, AND BROUGHT
ME THROUGH THE WATERS; THE WATERS WERE TO THE KNEES.
AGAIN HE MEASURED A THOUSAND, AND BROUGHT ME
THROUGH; THE WATERS WERE TO THE LOINS. AFTERWARD HE
MEASURED A THOUSAND; AND IT WAS A RIVER THAT I COULD
NOT PASS OVER: FOR THE WATERS WERE RISEN, WATERS TO
SWIM IN, A RIVER THAT COULD NOT BE PASSED OVER. AND
HE SAID TO ME, SON OF MAN, HAVE YOU SEEN THIS? THEN
HE BROUGHT ME, AND CAUSED ME TO RETURN TO THE BRINK
OF THE RIVER. NOW WHEN I HAD RETURNED, BEHOLD, AT THE
BANK OF THE RIVER WERE VERY MANY TREES ON THE ONE SIDE
AND ON THE OTHER. THEN SAID HE TO ME, THESE WATERS
ISSUE OUT TOWARD THE EAST COUNTRY, AND GO DOWN INTO
THE DESERT, AND GO INTO THE SEA: WHICH BEING BROUGHT
FORTH INTO THE SEA, THE WATERS SHALL BE HEALED. AND IT
SHALL COME TO PASS, THAT EVERY THING THAT LIVES, WHICH
MOVES, WHITHERSOEVER THE RIVERS SHALL COME, SHALL LIVE:
AND THERE SHALL BE A VERY GREAT MULTITUDE OF FISH,
BECAUSE THESE WATERS SHALL COME THERE: FOR THEY SHALL
BE HEALED; AND EVERY THING SHALL LIVE WHERE THE RIVER
COMES. (EZEKIEL 47:1–9)

Having lived most of my life on or near a river, I understand the flow of water pretty well. This enhanced my ability to discern the spiritual implications of this River of God flowing from His temple. If you go down to a river, you will usually find a shallow stretch of water near the river bank, gradually deepening toward mid-stream. You can wade around in the water, and enjoy the coolness and the refreshing feeling of getting your feet wet. As you venture farther out, you begin to feel the flow of the river, at first a gentle nudge, and then as you walk deeper, a stronger pull that can feel a bit un-settling. As you wade deeper, there comes a point where you can no longer stand because of the strength of the current and the depth of the river. At this point you realize that you are no longer in control, you can't simply walk back to shore, and that in order to live, you must swim in harmony with the flow of the current which pulls you.

In the river that issues from the throne of God the current is Faith, Love, Obedience, and Willingness.

As you step into the river with me, remember there is healing wherever the river goes. Each chapter will take you deeper into revealed understanding of who you are and the power you possess through the sacrifice of our Lord Jesus Christ. When you reach the end of this book, you will be in the middle of the river. I encourage you to lay back, kick up your feet, and enjoy the ride.

Vicki Smith Berdit

Section One

AND WHEN THE MAN
THAT HAD THE LINE IN HIS HAND
WENT FORTH EASTWARD,
HE MEASURED A THOUSAND CUBITS,
AND HE BROUGHT ME THROUGH THE WATERS;
THE WATERS WERE TO THE ANKLES.
(EZEKIEL 47:3)

Chapter One

You Already Belong

W E ALL WANT TO FEEL THAT WE BELONG, don't we? Yet, many of God's people spend too much of our lives searching for love and acceptance, hoping to experience a sense of belonging. At times, our families don't seem to accept us. Perhaps we think we don't "fit in" in social circles, or that we can't find a church where love is. Some people find that loving relationships don't seem to last. Others are plagued with rejection around every corner. We may begin to think, "What's the point?" and allow confusion to rule our lives. Conflict seems impossible to avoid, and defeat seems to be the day's offering once again. The only hope to find genuine belonging lies in discovering your true identity, and there is real opposition to uncovering that truth. Let's get some understanding to recognize Satan's maneuvers to falsely establish our identity.

Yes, there is a devil; and yes, he would assign a false identity to you. The devil is real. If you don't believe that, if you think, "It's just me" or "I'm this way because this is the way I am," you will have a very difficult time coming out of the trap of religious-minded thinking Satan has built for you. Why? Because God's Word tells us to

COME OUT FROM THE UNCLEAN THING. (2 CORINTHIANS 6:17)

and YOU THAT LOVE THE LORD, HATE EVIL. (PSALM 97:10)

If you believe you are the evil one, or if you believe that you are the unclean one, there's a real problem, because you cannot separate you from you! Further, Jesus says we are to love our neighbor as we love ourselves. That being the case, if you hate evil, and you think you are evil, then you cannot truly love yourself or anyone else.

How in the world did this come about? Go back a couple of paragraphs to a very interesting thing you just read—"the trap of religious-minded thinking." Here is a bold truth: Religion as it is presented in today's world is actually anti-Christ! Before you close the book and call me a heretic, hear me out. Religion is man's formula of performance designed to make us believe we are acceptable to God because of the "good works" that we do. It is a form of self-righteousness which causes our focus to be on, "How can I look good to you and in the world?" It also focuses us on "What's wrong with me and how did I get this way?" rather than, "What's right with Jesus and how can I express that?" Religion is a harsh task master which ignores, neglects and even opposes personal relationship with the Lord Jesus. You may have found that true in your own life.

Religion teaches us this formula: First of all, religion teaches you must believe. Then it proceeds to tell you what to believe, which happens to be whatever creed or doctrine the particular person or church body has decided is correct and righteous. Because it sounds good, and because you want to fit in, you agree to believe what you are told. This is a mental assenting that usually has very little to do with the personal experience you may have had, or still long to have, with the Lord Jesus Christ.

Next, religion teaches that after you've confessed your "belief" to be what you've been told, you must behave. You are now expected to adhere to a certain standard of "Christian" behavior. There is a definite set of rules laid out before you, as well as threats or actual punishments or persecutions for failures to abide by the set standard. For example, in some denominations or sects of Christianity, if you are divorced, then you are tainted, persecuted, prevented from serving or growing into leadership, and perhaps even shunned or asked to leave the church. You can never marry again, your friends cease to be your friends, and you are left with the distinct impression that God Himself is angry with you. You begin to believe you are not truly forgiven because you've been taught that divorce is unforgivable, whether you're the victim or the initiator. Maybe it isn't a divorce, but some other fault, transgression, or hidden sin of your past or present that has been discovered and exposed to the world. Now the door is opened for shame to rule in your life.

This thinking stems from hell itself, causing you to doubt God's love. Satan's primary goal is to speak to us in such a way that we become uncertain about ourselves, and about God. The truth is this: Nothing you've done is unforgivable. God's love and mercy was poured out on you through His judgment on sin, and the punishment for all sins of all people was taken by the Lord Jesus Christ. Nothing you've done is unforgivable.

Finally, after you believe and after you behave, religion teaches that now you can belong. You can belong to the church, you can belong to the group, you can belong to the family, you can belong to God. Believe, Behave, Belong—that is the order of religion. First you must believe, next, you must behave, and then you can belong. No wonder God's people have such a hard time trusting and such a miserable time living. We are all striving to belong, to be accepted, and many of us remain constantly in fear that we don't measure up.

Now, let's look at the truth of relationship, the antithesis (opposing force) to religion. God says, "Guess what, precious child? You already belong! Belonging is first in God's order, not last. YOU belong to ME," says the Lord God. Most Christians will agree that we are God's creation. His Word tells us so in the beginning of the Book.

> So God created man in his own image, in the image of God created he him; male and female created he them. (Genesis 1:27)

You are either going to believe the Word of God or you're not. It's your choice. If you choose to believe this word, then you must know and accept that you are created by God. You are not an accident of your mommy and daddy. You did not crawl up from the slime.

You aren't a product of nature or someone's lustful activity. You are created by God.

As you consider this, also ask yourself, "Does a man make something for no reason?" The answer, of course, is NO! There is always a purpose for whatever is created. Whether it's a major feat of engineering to make life easier or a batch of cookies to enjoy, there's a reason it is made. Take this line of obvious truth a little bit further, and ask yourself this, "If I create something, craft it, design it, make it, or otherwise cause it to come into being, does it belong to me?" The answer, obviously, is YES! You made it, it's yours.

Now, let's say that God is smarter than man. Would you agree? If not, we REALLY need to talk! I think maybe a lot of people actually believe they are as smart as, or smarter, than God. Otherwise, why would they continually tell Him how He should do things? It's like the old joke about the scientist who was going to have a showdown with God. He said, "Hey God! We are just as smart as you. You made man, and now we can, too. I can make a man, just like you did."

"Go ahead," answered the Father. So the man bent down and scooped up a handful of dirt, at which point God gently wagged His finger and said, "No, no. Get your own dirt."

There are two very important points in knowing we are God's creation. First of all, by virtue of our creation, we each have purpose. Again, not even man creates something which has no use. The second point is simply that we belong to God. By virtue of our creation, we already belong. We are God's because He made us.

And He made us with everything inside us to fulfill the particular purpose for which we each were created. We each are specially crafted, unique, and valuable. Perhaps you don't yet recognize what your purpose is … it's okay if you don't. Perhaps you don't really understand God's plan for you … it's okay if you don't. Once you realize you don't have to understand God's plan in order to agree with it, you will begin to come into a place of true freedom.

Knowing that you already belong to God is the first truth to receive in your heart of hearts, not just in your mind! Jesus said,

> You shall know the truth, and the truth will make you free. (John 8:32)

It is truth that you KNOW that makes you free, not truth that you simply hear or read about and then file away in your brain so that you can go on with your mundane little existence. Jesus wants you to live an abundant life, not a get-through-the-day-and-hope-for-a-better-one-tomorrow life. To have the kind of life Jesus wants for you, start by knowing you belong to your Father in Heaven who loves you.

Remember, when Adam knew Eve, she conceived and bore him a son. That is an intimate knowledge, and that is the kind of knowing we need of this truth, a knowing that impregnates us to birth our freedom. There are two basic understandings of knowledge. The Greek understanding of knowledge was that of compiling all the information, gathering the data and storing it away. It's similar to a file cabinet in your brain which holds all your notes. It's intellectual knowledge. The Hebrew understanding of knowledge is altogether different. In the Hebrew understanding of knowing something, you gather the information and then you apply it so that there is a change, and it becomes a part of you. It's experiential knowledge.

Which surgeon do you choose to operate on you? The one who read the books and passed the exam or the one who has had the scalpel in his hand and used it successfully? Do you want to fly in a small plane with the guy who studied the instrument panel and read the manual or the one who has flown the aircraft and is a pilot? Here's a relatable example of intellectual and experiential knowledge: You know the brake pedal in your vehicle is designed to stop the car. You have knowledge of that, and the fact of the brake's purpose is filed away in your brain. But until that big truck turns in front of you and you purposely stand on the brake, the knowledge you have of the brake pedal is simply intellectual. Once you use the truth of the brake pedal's purpose to make a change—and perhaps even save your life—you now have experiential knowledge of the brake pedal and its purpose.

My ardent desire is for you to have experiential knowledge of your belonging to God, and to that end, it is time for you to take a stand against the lie of hell that you don't belong! Stand against the lie that you have to perform a certain way, or strive to do everything right, or wear yourself out on good works. Many of our good works are actually dead works because of the motivation of fear or obligation or self-righteousness that set them in motion. When we perform some work for God because we are afraid we won't be accepted if we don't, what we've done means nothing in the eternal picture. A feeling of obligation is often a form of fear. According to God's holy Word, fear is not an emotion or a way of life, it is a spirit that He did not give you.

> FOR GOD HAS NOT GIVEN US A SPIRIT OF FEAR;
> BUT OF POWER AND LOVE AND A SOUND MIND.
> (2 TIMOTHY 1:7)

God wants to separate you from religious thinking that has bound you. He wants to release you into truth and love that brings freedom from the bondage of your mind and your past. He wants to strip away the labels of outcast, outsider, unwanted, unloved, unlovely, not good enough—and all the other labels put on you by people and experiences in the world.

You already belong to God! He owns you, and you are His. Every person is His creation, both the saved and the unsaved; it's just that most people in the world don't know that, just as those of us who are born again did not know that before we "found" Jesus. (How anyone ever thought He was lost, I don't know!) Before we became born again, we were wandering around in the world as lost souls. The devil started walking along with us, and took us into some dangerous and ungodly places and situations. We suffered at the hands of the cruel and unjust, the merciless and arrogant, the dominating and intimidating, the abusive and uncaring. We learned how to control and manipulate, how to lie and steal and cheat, and how to seek comfort and escape through things of the world. Then one day, when the devil had exacted all he could get from us, he walked us into the pawn shop and sold us into misery and depression, into poverty and pain. We were stuck, with no way out. "Who would want me?" we may have thought. "Just look at my condition! I'm a mess. Nobody is ever going to want me."

The One who created you is the One who wants you, that's who! Your Father in Heaven who loves you looked down and saw you in your misery and pain and said, "Holy Spirit, there is my beloved child! Go tell Jesus to redeem that child for me!"

> AND WHEN I PASSED BY YOU, AND SAW YOU POLLUTED IN YOUR OWN BLOOD, I SAID TO YOU WHEN YOU WERE IN YOUR BLOOD, LIVE; YES, I SAID TO YOU WHEN YOU WERE IN YOUR BLOOD, LIVE. (EZEKIEL 16:6)

Our Savior, the Lord Jesus Christ of Nazareth, Yeshua Hamashiach (Hebrew for "Jesus the Anointed One"), our Redeemer, our Risen Lord, came and bought us back with His own precious blood. Now we are DOUBLY owned by God! We are His precious possessions by virtue of our creation, and by virtue of our buy-back.

From before the foundation of the world, God's plan was to have a family—and you and I are included in it. He even told us time and again in His Word that we would be HIS people and He would be our God. In ancient Jewish culture, the adoption process was verbal. Called in Latin *verba solemnia*, or solemn declaration, an adoptee would publicly identify the adopter with the words, "You are my father," and the adopter would say, "You are my son." Scripture calls Israel the son of God, His people.

> WHEN ISRAEL WAS A CHILD, THEN I LOVED HIM, AND CALLED MY SON OUT OF EGYPT. (HOSEA 11:1)

> YOU ARE THE CHILDREN OF THE LORD YOUR GOD. (DEUTERONOMY 14:1)

Then, God went further and adopted the Gentiles—people not of Jewish descent—as well. In doing so, He demonstrated that all are His creation, as well as His chosen. Not only are you redeemed from a life of misery and pain, you are adopted into the family of God through the blood of Jesus Christ and the Spirit of the Living God!

> AND I WILL SAY TO THEM WHICH WERE NOT MY PEOPLE, YOU ARE MY PEOPLE; AND THEY SHALL SAY, YOU ARE MY GOD. (HOSEA 2:23)

> AS HE SAYS ALSO IN HOSEA, I WILL CALL THEM MY PEOPLE, WHICH WERE NOT MY PEOPLE; AND HER BELOVED, WHICH WAS NOT BELOVED. AND IT SHALL COME TO PASS, THAT IN THE PLACE WHERE IT WAS SAID UNTO THEM, YOU ARE NOT MY PEOPLE; THERE SHALL THEY BE CALLED THE CHILDREN OF THE LIVING GOD. (ROMANS 9:25–26)

> BUT YOU HAVE NOT RECEIVED THE SPIRIT OF BONDAGE AGAIN TO FEAR; BUT YOU HAVE RECEIVED THE SPIRIT OF ADOPTION, BY WHICH WE CRY, ABBA, FATHER. THE SPIRIT ITSELF BEARS WITNESS WITH OUR SPIRIT, THAT WE ARE THE CHILDREN OF GOD. (ROMANS 8:15–16)

God's choice to adopt both Jews and Gentiles was never about our earning adoption or being deserving of it. It was not about merit; it was about His amazing love and astounding mercy.

> AND SO ALL ISRAEL SHALL BE SAVED: AS IT IS WRITTEN, THERE SHALL COME OUT OF SION THE DELIVERER, AND SHALL TURN AWAY UNGODLINESS FROM JACOB: FOR THIS IS MY COVENANT UNTO THEM, WHEN I SHALL TAKE AWAY THEIR SINS. AS CONCERNING THE GOSPEL, THEY ARE ENEMIES FOR YOUR SAKES: BUT AS TOUCHING THE ELECTION, THEY ARE BELOVED FOR THE FATHERS' SAKES. FOR THE GIFTS AND

CALLING OF GOD ARE WITHOUT REPENTANCE. FOR AS YOU
IN TIMES PAST HAVE NOT BELIEVED GOD, YET HAVE NOW
OBTAINED MERCY THROUGH THEIR UNBELIEF: EVEN SO HAVE
THESE ALSO NOW NOT BELIEVED, THAT THROUGH YOUR
MERCY THEY ALSO MAY OBTAIN MERCY. FOR GOD HATH
CONCLUDED THEM ALL IN UNBELIEF, THAT HE MIGHT HAVE
MERCY UPON ALL. (ROMANS 11:26–32)

We never deserved to be included in the family. We didn't earn it
or buy it; in fact, we deserved to be excluded. But by the sure mer-
cies of God, we who were wretched and pitifully poor in spirit and
understanding are made royal heirs together with Christ the King
of Glory. We who once were wayward sinners are now given the
opportunity to become the sons of God. We have been adopted!

---

*You belong. Never, never again, doubt
this: You belong.*

When you receive the truth that you already belong, and establish
that truth in your heart, it frees you from fear of not pleasing God,
and fear of not being perfect. This truth frees you from feeling compelled to do everything right, and from fear of failing or looking bad
to others. You will know it's okay to do your best, that you no longer
have to be the best, and it's okay to fail and to try again. You will
know that God's not mad at you.

You will know God is with you to pick you up when you fall
down, to dry your tears of disappointment when you fail at something, and to encourage you to give it another go! You will know
that He is not going to leave you in the street if you're a little slow
at something, or put you on the shelf to gather dust, or abandon you
or give up on you. You will know that because you are His precious
possession, He's going to take care of you, and meet your needs.

Once belonging is established in your heart, you can now truly believe God! You can trust Him because you know you are His, you know He created you with purpose, and He will see that the purpose He put within you is fulfilled.

> BEING CONFIDENT OF THIS VERY THING, THAT HE WHICH HAS BEGUN A GOOD WORK IN YOU WILL PERFORM IT UNTIL THE DAY OF JESUS CHRIST. (PHILIPPIANS 1:6)

What day is that? It is the day in the life of each individual in which we yield ourselves completely to the Lordship of Jesus.

> THEN JESUS SAID TO HIS DISCIPLES, IF ANY MAN WILL COME AFTER ME, LET HIM DENY HIMSELF, AND TAKE UP HIS CROSS, AND FOLLOW ME. (MATTHEW 16:24)

It is the day when we truly turn over our thoughts to God's control and think with the mind of Christ He has given us.

> FOR WHO HAS KNOWN THE MIND OF THE LORD, THAT WE MAY INSTRUCT HIM? BUT WE HAVE THE MIND OF CHRIST. (1 CORINTHIANS 2:16)

It is the day when we give up our own will and our own ways to conform to the will and ways of our Father in Heaven, as Jesus did.

> O MY FATHER, IF IT BE POSSIBLE, LET THIS CUP PASS FROM ME: NEVERTHELESS, NOT AS I WILL, BUT AS YOU WILL. (MATTHEW 26:39)

It is the day in which we stop allowing our emotions to rule us, when we discover and line up with God's emotions. The day when we trade our desires for what the Lord desires for us to have. It is the day when Christ is fully formed in us. More of you, Lord, and less of me; more of you and less of me; more of you and less of me; all of you, and none of me. As John the Baptist said,

> HE MUST INCREASE BUT I MUST DECREASE. (JOHN 3:30)

Your mind, will, emotions, and desires are in your own control, and so the day of Christ becomes your choice.

MY SOUL IS CONTINUALLY IN MY HAND. (PSALM 119:109)

So you see, in order for belief to be real and true, it has to move from your head, which is mental assenting, to your heart, which is true agreement. That comes through knowing you belong to God, that you are His precious possession, created with purpose and placed lovingly into His perfect plan for all eternity. This knowing creates the spiritual atmosphere in which you can believe and breathe in the love of God which created you, the mercy of God which adopted you, and the grace of God which saved you. You can at last receive and live in the truth of our Almighty God, the wisdom and authority of our Lord Jesus Christ, and the awesome resurrection power and sweet discernment of the Holy Spirit. You belong, therefore you can believe, and now you will find that your behavior changes.

That's right, you discover a wonderful, freeing truth that you no longer have to strive to do everything right, to be perfect, to never fall or fail. The Holy Spirit of the Living God works in you from the inside out to perfect you, to direct you, and to correct you! It is a work of the Holy Spirit inside you. You simply agree with Him and cooperate in the process. It's no longer your own work from the outside, striving and "trying" to be good. You simply find that you are good, that the ungodly desires you carried are falling away in the light of His glory. That your greater desire is to please the Lord and not yourself, to prefer others over yourself, to forgive as you have been forgiven, to love as you are loved.

Can you now see why the devil wants to keep you in religion and religious thinking? Once you're out of that prison, you are truly dangerous to darkness! Your light begins to emanate from within, blinding the enemies of your soul and chasing the rulers of darkness back to hell. Jesus is the light that came into the world, and if you have received Him as your Lord and Savior, He is now IN YOU. If you have not, and you want to begin to come out of the darkness of misery, poverty, fear, depression, rejection, and the hundreds of other hindering spirits that torment you, then pray this simple prayer and mean it from your heart:

Father God, I've not fully understood who I am, because I've not really known You. But I want to know You, Father, and I do believe that You sent Your Son, Yeshua, Jesus, to take the punishment for all my sins and to restore me to the person You created me to be. I do believe that He was crucified, died and was buried, and was resurrected by Your Holy Spirit. Jesus is alive today and seated at Your right hand in Heaven. I confess my sins before You, and I receive the sacrifice of Jesus on my behalf. I ask Jesus to come into my heart to reign as my Lord, and I thank You for Your forgiveness and cleansing. Wash me and cleanse me in the blood of Jesus as I yield myself to You. I thank You, Lord, and I declare today that I belong to YOU. I am Your precious child and I am now ready to grow up in You. Amen.

The light that has now come into you is eternal, and it is glorious. You are a glory carrier!

ARISE, SHINE; FOR YOUR LIGHT IS COME, AND THE GLORY OF THE LORD IS RISEN UPON YOU. (ISAIAH 60:1)

FOR YOU WERE SOMETIMES DARKNESS, BUT NOW YOU ARE LIGHT IN THE WORLD: WALK AS CHILDREN OF LIGHT. (FOR THE FRUIT OF THE SPIRIT IS IN ALL GOODNESS AND RIGHTEOUSNESS AND TRUTH;) PROVING WHAT IS ACCEPTABLE UNTO THE LORD. (EPHESIANS 5:8–10)

YOU ARE ALL THE CHILDREN OF LIGHT, AND THE CHILDREN OF
THE DAY: WE ARE NOT OF THE NIGHT, NOR OF DARKNESS.
(1 THESSALONIANS 5:5)

The differences in religious-minded thinking and true, loving
relationship with the Living God are vast and yet clear. Religion's
formula of Believe, Behave, Belong is upside down, backward, and
opposite of God's simple truth of Belong, Believe, Behave. Religion's
harsh punishments and persecutions were erased through the
sacrifice of our Lord Jesus—the One who took all the punishment
meant for us, so we don't have to. To continue to feel unworthy,
blameworthy, worthy of punishment, immoral, indecent, inadequate or incompetent, is actually to deny the cross and the sacrifice
of Jesus Christ. That attitude of self-focus and self-abasement is
the same as saying to the Lord, "What You did for me just wasn't
enough. I have to punish myself for a while now because I was
wrong. I did the wrong thing. I committed a sin. I am a terrible
person."

There's not a person on the planet who has arrived at perfection, one who has actually risen to the level of our intended creation. None of us is yet spiritually or naturally perfect; but there is
a process. It begins with rejecting our warped, religious thinking
and agreeing with our Father in Heaven who loves us and with His
wonderful Word. We must start saying what God says about us and
others. We must begin, and continue, to remove the negative "back-
talk" from the enemy that echoes in our thoughts. We must continue
to deny ourselves and allow the Lord to conform us to His image,
from glory to glory and faith to faith.

Let this prayer be your starting point. Read it through, then
pray it aloud, from your heart, engaging every fiber of your being
in agreement with the Word and truth of God. The reason we pray
aloud is because only God knows your thoughts and what's in your
mind. Angels are listening for an audible word that agrees with

God, so that they can be released to perform that word, to minister to our needs and strengthen us in our commitments. Psalm 103 tells us angels hearken to the voice of the Word of God—they need to hear it voiced! Neither can demons/fallen angels read your mind. They should hear your agreement with God's Word, so that they will tremble and be prepared to leave you alone.

Father God, thank You for telling me the truth. Thank You for giving me courage to believe this truth that I belong to You and You are not against me. You are not mad at me. You are not punishing me. Thank You for giving me courage to separate myself from religious thinking that condemns me at every turn. Thank You for giving me courage to trust You, to give You my heart, knowing You will not break it—You will heal it. I admit I am already broken, and I have been afraid to let go of my life to You. I admit I have felt left out and unwanted, and just not good enough. I have disagreed with everything You say about me. I have lined my thoughts up with the enemy of my soul. I am sorry, Lord, and I ask Your forgiveness. Father, if there is any place in me which is unwilling to believe You, I declare right now that I am willing to be made willing. Work in my mind to rid me of the lies of hell that have been reinforced by my experiences in the world. Work in my emotions to heal the unmet needs and wounds of my past, to compel me to truly forgive my abusers and accusers and walk in love. Work in my will so that I will not allow deception and misery to enter and so that I will be open to Your Holy Spirit guidance and correction at all times, not simply when it seems necessary or convenient. Give me ears to hear Your love, Your truth, and the conviction of Your Holy Spirit and not the condemnation of the enemy. I want more of You, Lord Jesus, and less of me. Help me die daily, take up my cross, and follow You. Amen.

Chapter Two
Being a Child of God

EVEN THOUGH WE ARE ESTABLISHED IN THE TRUTH of belonging to God, secure in the knowledge of our acceptance, and are no longer striving for inclusion in His family, there may yet be a lingering question. Am I truly a child of God? Within the Body of Christ, there are conflicting understandings of what it means to be a child of God or a child of the devil. Some scholars, churches, and denominations teach that only those born again are children of God. Some teach that only the Jewish people are children of God. Some teach replacement theology, meaning that born-again believers have taken the place of the Jewish people. They say that only those spiritually born again are God's children, and that the Jews are no different from the heathen or pagan.

Another area of confusion pertains to our new nature as opposed to what the Bible calls our "old man." Some scholars, churches, and denominations teach that all are sinners, both the unsaved and the born-again believers. Some teach that only those who do righteous things are righteous. Some teach that once you accept Jesus, you are righteous and there is no need for repentance, since the sacrifice of Jesus covered all sin. Perhaps the words you read here will clear some of the confusion brought on by these different points of view.

Each of these positions has a thread of truth in it, but there is little or no overall balance. Balance is a key to life itself. Without balance, it doesn't matter how healthy you are, or how strong you are, or how intelligent you are, you will fall. Balance is also the key that opens us to understanding the heart of God. As we read in the first chapter of Isaiah, the Lord says, "Come now, and let us reason together." How do we tell the difference between being a child of God or a child of the devil? Clearly, the Bible speaks of both.

> JESUS SAID UNTO THEM, IF GOD WERE YOUR FATHER, YOU WOULD LOVE ME: FOR I PROCEEDED FORTH AND CAME FROM GOD; NEITHER CAME I OF MYSELF, BUT HE SENT ME. WHY DO YOU NOT UNDERSTAND MY SPEECH? EVEN BECAUSE YOU CANNOT HEAR MY WORD. YOU ARE OF YOUR FATHER THE DEVIL, AND THE LUSTS OF YOUR FATHER YOU WILL DO. HE WAS A MURDERER FROM THE BEGINNING, AND ABODE NOT IN THE TRUTH, BECAUSE THERE IS NO TRUTH IN HIM. WHEN HE SPEAKS A LIE, HE SPEAKS OF HIS OWN: FOR HE IS A LIAR, AND THE FATHER OF IT. AND BECAUSE I TELL YOU THE TRUTH, YOU BELIEVE ME NOT. (JOHN 8:42–45)

Jesus was speaking here to Jewish people, His own people, the natural Jews! Not only were they of the nation of Israel, God's chosen people whom He Himself called His children; but they loved God and did their best to serve Him and to keep His laws. Admittedly, though, they had become rather self-righteous in their attitudes and actions. They had turned from worshiping the God of the law to worshiping the law of God. But does this mean they were thrown out of the family, disowned, and no longer His children?

The child of God/child of the devil question seems to be intertwined with the two natures issue, the image and likeness of God or that of the "old man." Let's consider. First of all, if the "old man" were actually who you are, then when you accepted Christ's sacrifice on your behalf and became born again, therefore a "new creature" with a brand-new nature, there would no longer be any "old man." This would hold true particularly if "new creature" meant brand-new as in never having existed before. Compare this to evolution, if you want to—if man evolved from monkeys, why are there still monkeys? If new means brand-new, then why are we who believe not already perfected and totally holy in every way? Better yet, why were we not immediately translated, instantly taken from the physical realm and into the spiritual one, as Enoch was for his confession that he pleased God?

> BY FAITH ENOCH WAS TRANSLATED THAT HE SHOULD NOT SEE DEATH; AND WAS NOT FOUND, BECAUSE GOD HAD TRANSLATED HIM: FOR BEFORE HIS TRANSLATION HE HAD THIS TESTIMONY, THAT HE PLEASED GOD. (HEBREWS 11:5)

> THEREFORE IF ANY MAN BE IN CHRIST, HE IS A NEW CREATURE: OLD THINGS ARE PASSED AWAY; BEHOLD, ALL THINGS ARE BECOME NEW. (2 CORINTHIANS 5:17)

When you look up the word new, you find something interesting —it doesn't necessarily mean never having existed before. In the Greek, it refers to "freshness." The dictionary tells us it also means, "made, introduced, or discovered recently for the first time." Another definition is "already existing but seen, experienced, or acquired recently or now for the first time." Apparently then, new is not always brand-new. This makes sense, considering that since Eve's deception and Adam's disobedience, mankind has had both the holy nature of God, His image and likeness, and the sin-nature of Satan, what we call the flesh or the "old man." Our true nature was shanghaied, bound, gagged, and hidden away while the nature of the accuser, the enemy of God and all things good took over rulership of our lives. We became slaves to sin.

> KNOW YOU NOT, THAT TO WHOM YOU YIELD YOURSELVES SERVANTS TO OBEY, HIS SERVANTS YOU ARE TO WHOM YOU OBEY; WHETHER OF SIN UNTO DEATH, OR OF OBEDIENCE UNTO RIGHTEOUSNESS? (ROMANS 6:16)

Surely, Scripture is clear about ALL having fallen short of the glory of God, and about ALL being born sinners because of the sin-nature in us. Of course that is true, otherwise there would be no need of a Savior! Not one of us, Jew or Gentile, can separate himself from the sin-nature apart from the sacrifice of Yeshua, our Messiah, Jesus

Christ. What does this really have to do with being a child of God? Jesus Himself made a distinction in answering the "Who's your Daddy?" question, a distinction that is often overlooked, when He taught His disciples to pray.

> AFTER THIS MANNER THEREFORE PRAY YOU: OUR FATHER WHICH ART IN HEAVEN, HALLOWED BE THY NAME. (MATTHEW 6:9)

In this very first line of what we call *The Lord's Prayer*, Jesus taught us two very important things. First of all, He said "our" Father. He did not say "my" Father or "the" Father, or just "Father;" He said "OUR Father." That tells us that God is the creator of all people, and therefore the Father of all living. By His Spirit, His characteristics are in us, just as our natural, biological fathers' traits are inherent in us by the flesh. We understand Jesus was fathered by the Holy Spirit; but that same Holy Spirit put each one of us together. With these first two words, Jesus brought all of us into the knowledge that God is OUR Father, not just His own Father.

In the King James Version of Scripture, the third word of the prayer is the other invaluable lesson to learn from its beginning — "which." Which denotes a choice. Which do you want, this or that? Which appeals to you, one of these or one of those? Which of these three or four or more will you take? Where there is a "which," there is a choice, always. Obviously, then, there is more than one father in our lives. Jesus wants us to direct our prayers, our spiritual communication, to our true Father, the one in heaven, and not to the illegitimate substitute father from hell, Satan, who is the father of lies, or the earthly, biological, or adopted father from the world.

> AND IN THAT DAY YOU SHALL ASK ME NOTHING. VERILY, VERILY, I SAY UNTO YOU, WHATSOEVER YOU SHALL ASK THE FATHER IN MY NAME, HE WILL GIVE IT YOU. HITHERTO HAVE YOU ASKED NOTHING IN MY NAME: ASK, AND YOU SHALL RECEIVE, THAT YOUR JOY MAY BE FULL. THESE THINGS HAVE

I SPOKEN UNTO YOU IN PROVERBS: BUT THE TIME COMES,
WHEN I SHALL NO MORE SPEAK UNTO YOU IN PROVERBS, BUT I
SHALL SHOW YOU PLAINLY OF THE FATHER. AT THAT DAY YOU
SHALL ASK IN MY NAME: AND I SAY NOT UNTO YOU, THAT I
WILL PRAY THE FATHER FOR YOU: FOR THE FATHER HIMSELF
LOVES YOU, BECAUSE YOU HAVE LOVED ME, AND HAVE BE-
LIEVED THAT I CAME OUT FROM GOD. (JOHN 16:23-27)

You may ask, "Why would we choose any other father? Why would
Jesus have to tell us that?" He was showing us that we have within
us both the traits and nature of God, which is our true identity, and
the traits and nature of the devil, which is the flesh or "old man." We
get to choose which nature we will exhibit, which father we will follow. Your creation in the mind and heart of God was accomplished
from before the foundation of the world. He knows everything
about you because He is the one who designed everything about
you. His design of you was, and is, a perfect design. When God
finished creating the world and everything in it, He looked at the
whole of His creation and pronounced it not just good, but VERY
good. Everything He made, God judged to be good.

AND GOD SAW THE LIGHT, THAT IT WAS GOOD: AND GOD
DIVIDED THE LIGHT FROM THE DARKNESS.

AND GOD CALLED THE DRY LAND EARTH; AND THE GATHER-
ING TOGETHER OF THE WATERS CALLED HE SEAS: AND GOD
SAW THAT IT WAS GOOD.

AND THE EARTH BROUGHT FORTH GRASS, AND HERB YIELDING
SEED AFTER HIS KIND, AND THE TREE YIELDING FRUIT, WHOSE
SEED WAS IN ITSELF, AFTER HIS KIND: AND GOD SAW THAT IT
WAS GOOD.

AND GOD MADE TWO GREAT LIGHTS; THE GREATER LIGHT TO
RULE THE DAY, AND THE LESSER LIGHT TO RULE THE NIGHT: HE
MADE THE STARS ALSO. AND GOD SET THEM IN THE FIR-
MAMENT OF THE HEAVEN TO GIVE LIGHT UPON THE EARTH,
AND TO RULE OVER THE DAY AND OVER THE NIGHT, AND TO

DIVIDE THE LIGHT FROM THE DARKNESS: AND GOD SAW THAT
IT WAS GOOD.

AND GOD CREATED GREAT WHALES, AND EVERY LIVING
CREATURE THAT MOVES, WHICH THE WATERS BROUGHT FORTH
ABUNDANTLY, AFTER THEIR KIND, AND EVERY WINGED FOWL
AFTER HIS KIND: AND GOD SAW THAT IT WAS GOOD.

AND GOD MADE THE BEAST OF THE EARTH AFTER HIS KIND,
AND CATTLE AFTER THEIR KIND, AND EVERY THING THAT
CREEPS UPON THE EARTH AFTER HIS KIND: AND GOD SAW
THAT IT WAS GOOD.

SO GOD CREATED MAN IN HIS OWN IMAGE, IN THE IMAGE
OF GOD CREATED HE HIM; MALE AND FEMALE CREATED HE
THEM. (GENESIS 1:4, 10, 12, 16–18, 21, 25, 27)

Then at the end, when He was closing up shop, so to speak, God looked everything over again and proclaimed this: "And God saw everything that he had made, and, behold, it was very good. And the evening and the morning were the sixth day" (Genesis 1:31).

We all know that in the beginning Adam, like Jesus, was a sinless human. You were the same in the heart of God when you were created, a sinless individual, perfect from before the foundation of the world. What happened? The nature of God in you became corrupted through the blood line of Adam, because of his disobedience. Sin entered mankind in the form of Satan's rebellious and prideful nature. However, Satan discovered that he could not remove the nature of God which was already in you, because that's who you were created to be. What he could do was separate man from God and disconnect you from your true nature. Mankind lost touch with our true, godly identity, and forgot who we are. The other nature took over. Even though Satan was able to separate you from God because of sin, he could not separate you from you. Instead, his spirit came to dwell in you, in competition with God's Spirit. Mankind became double-minded, which actually means, "two-spirited."

> A DOUBLE MINDED MAN IS UNSTABLE IN ALL HIS WAYS.
> (JAMES 1:8)

Double-minded in this verse translates to two-spirited, as referred to above. Its root words in the Greek mean "twice" and "breath." Consider this: Because God breathed His Spirit into the dust of the earth which He had formed into human shape, man became a living soul. When Adam sinned, the devil brought his breath, his spirit, into man and he became a dead soul. Every person born through the bloodline of Adam was born dead! That's why Jesus said we must be born again.

> MARVEL NOT THAT I SAID TO YOU, YOU MUST BE BORN
> AGAIN. (JOHN 3:7)

Death is separation from God. Adam did not physically die immediately, but he did immediately die spiritually. Adam knew immediately that he had been separated from God. He was thrown out of the garden where everything had been provided for him, where all his days were pleasant and all he knew was the goodness of God. He was evicted from the place where he could commune one-on-one with God, walking with the Lord in the cool of the day, feeling the love and power of the Almighty, and seeing His awesome hand in everything. Suddenly, after disobeying the word given to him by the Lord—BAM! Adam was displaced, stripped of God's presence and authority and made to work the land for a living.

Adam experienced the consequences of sin, but he could remember that time of oneness with God, of having a single-minded focus. The understanding of subsequent generations was shrouded in deception, pride, and fear. The traits of Satan had so concealed God's traits that we became unaware of the love, truth, and humility of God within us. If we are ever to rise to the level of our intended creation, to become not only the children of God, but SONS of God, fully mature, we must know what that looks like—what our true identity is. Clearly defining the nature of God and the nature of the devil enables us to make the right choice of father, <u>and it is our choice.</u> Satan's nature was never meant to be our nature; it's not who we are created to be. Once we are born again, this knowledge empowers us to separate ourselves from every evil spirit that attempts to deceive us into accepting Satan's nature as our own.

If we are ever to know who we truly are, we must know who God is. First and foremost, God is love. This is the very core of God's nature. He doesn't simply love us, He IS love. This is the most important thing to know—

God cannot NOT love you, because He is love.

That's who He is, not what He does. All love comes from God and <u>love is a primary aspect of the nature of God.</u>

> BELOVED, LET US LOVE ONE ANOTHER: FOR LOVE IS OF GOD; AND EVERY ONE THAT LOVES IS BORN OF GOD, AND KNOWS GOD. HE THAT LOVES NOT KNOWS NOT GOD; FOR GOD IS LOVE. (I JOHN 4:7–8)

> AND WE HAVE KNOWN AND BELIEVED THE LOVE THAT GOD HATH TO US. GOD IS LOVE; AND HE THAT DWELLS IN LOVE DWELLS IN GOD, AND GOD IN HIM. (I JOHN 4:16)

Scripture tells us that even evil people know how to give good gifts to their children. We can see the truth of this in the world. There are many unsaved people in the world who are nice people, nicer than many Christians we know. There are unsaved people who conduct their businesses with integrity, and there are unsaved people who are loving and generous. Even the worst among us loves someone and is loved by someone. That aspect of God's nature is in every individual, the saved and the unsaved alike, because God essentially made us the same—we were all created with the same heart.

> THE LORD LOOKS FROM HEAVEN; HE BEHOLDS ALL THE SONS OF MEN. FROM THE PLACE OF HIS HABITATION, HE LOOKS UPON ALL THE INHABITANTS OF THE EARTH. HE FASHIONS THEIR HEARTS ALIKE; HE CONSIDERS ALL THEIR WORKS. (PSALM 33:13-15)

This tells us that we truly are God's creation, no matter what we believe, and that His love is in our hearts, no matter how corrupted and twisted the devil has caused that love to become.

What else do we have that Satan has hidden in his attempt to clothe us in his evil nature? There seem to be three major aspects of the nature of God. Love, of course, is primary (Let the main thing be the main thing, and the main thing is love!). Then we have truth and humility, in no particular order of importance. Both are vital to life. Jesus clearly told us He is truth, and that the Holy Spirit is our witness to truth. <u>Truth is another primary aspect of God's character.</u>

> JESUS SAYS UNTO HIM, I AM THE WAY, THE TRUTH, AND THE LIFE: NO MAN COMES TO THE FATHER, BUT BY ME. (JOHN 14:6)

> BUT WHEN THE COMFORTER IS COME, WHOM I WILL SEND TO YOU FROM THE FATHER, EVEN THE SPIRIT OF TRUTH, WHICH PROCEEDS FROM THE FATHER, HE SHALL TESTIFY OF ME. (JOHN 15:26)

Also, and equally notable, Jesus was the epitome of humility. Everything about Him was humble. He never sought reputation or glory in the world. He never defended Himself or His position; but rather, He humbled Himself in every way, even to His death on the cross. We know, have read and heard, that this death was the most horrific punishment that could be inflicted on a man; but we can't really understand the depth of what that means. This selfless act of the Lord is the pinnacle of true love, to humble yourself to death for the sake of others, all the while trusting in the plan of God. What Jesus endured on our behalf can never truly be measured or understood. <u>Humility is the third primary aspect of God's nature.</u>

> LET THIS MIND BE IN YOU, WHICH WAS ALSO IN CHRIST JESUS: WHO, BEING IN THE FORM OF GOD, THOUGHT IT NOT ROBBERY TO BE EQUAL WITH GOD: BUT MADE HIMSELF OF NO REPUTATION, AND TOOK UPON HIM THE FORM OF A SERVANT, AND WAS MADE IN THE LIKENESS OF MEN: AND BEING FOUND IN FASHION AS A MAN, HE HUMBLED HIMSELF, AND BECAME OBEDIENT UNTO DEATH, EVEN THE DEATH OF THE CROSS. (PHILIPPIANS 2:5–8)

Knowing the nature of God to be primarily love, truth, and humility, we can then say, "That is the level of my intended creation. That is who I was created to be in the heart of God from before the foundation of the world." We can now say, "The nature of God is my true nature. As God is love, I am love. As God is truth, I am truth. As God is humility, I am humility. My identity is not in the flesh, which is the other nature and what I mistakenly thought was just my old man. I <u>can</u> separate myself from that other nature, from the flesh called 'old man,' because it's NOT ME!" Praise God!

Take a look now at the nature of Satan, the arch enemy of God and good, who breathed death into mankind, instilling in us the aspects of his nature. The primary aspects of the nature of the devil are the exact opposite of God's. There's no surprise there. The surprise comes as we realize these things are not who we are. Many people have become so comfortable with one or more of these characteristics that they believe, "It's just who I am," or "This is how God made me." Many people have been patterned and programmed by their families, upbringing, or experiences to believe the lies of false identity rather than the truth of God's identity in us. If that's you, it is time to develop a new comfort zone, one with benefits from heaven and not curses from hell disguised as blessings. It's time to break the programming of past twisted thinking and emotional traumas, and reprogram your minds and hearts to peace and stability.

First, and perhaps of greatest importance in his schemes, Satan brought us fear, which is the opposite of love. According to the Word of God, fear is not an emotion, it is a spirit! It finds its easiest entry through your emotions and works diligently to stir them up. The spirit of fear disguises itself as emotion, when in reality what you experience is a demonic spirit of pure evil that never came from God.

> FOR GOD HAS NOT GIVEN US THE SPIRIT OF FEAR; BUT OF POWER, AND OF LOVE, AND OF A SOUND MIND. (2 TIMOTHY 1:7)

Over the years, we've had many people tell us fear is a good thing, that if people didn't have fear, they would be getting themselves in all kinds of painful or dangerous situations. No, it is not fear that keeps us safe, it is caution and prudence which keep us from being foolish or foolhardy. Caution and prudence are traits of wisdom, not fear. Fear is a preventer, not a protector. If God wanted you to fear, would He have said 331 times in His Word, "Fear not?" Would He have told you 30 times, "Be not afraid," or 175 times, to "Not be afraid?" It is vital that you know fear is not a part of you and you can therefore separate yourself from it.

That being said, there is a bit of a qualifier in this explanation, in that there are two types of fear. One is built in, designed by God to help us escape from life-threatening circumstances. It creates a rush of adrenaline that is, in and of itself, not a harmful thing to our bodies. Adrenaline is the chemical that allows people to lift cars off other people, and to accomplish other "supernatural" feats of physical prowess. Then, there is the fear that stems from the flesh, the nature of Satan. His core nature is fear. He, of all creatures, is fearful. Satan is full of fear. He has been judged and he knows his time is short. The difference between this fear and godly fear is that godly fear does not hang around after the crisis is past, and Satan's fear lingers to torment you, and to steal your peace and your health.

The other aspects of Satan's core nature are pride and deception, in no particular order of importance—both are deadly. It was pride that got Lucifer thrown out of heaven, and it is one of those evils "that so easily beset us." As you may have been taught, Lucifer was God's worship leader, an archangel of great beauty and talent. Perhaps because of his beauty and talents, he began to worship himself, and to think that he, not God, should be the exalted one. Satan believed he was the one to be worshiped and obeyed.

> YOUR HEART WAS LIFTED UP BECAUSE OF YOUR BEAUTY, YOU HAVE CORRUPTED YOUR WISDOM BY REASON OF YOUR BRIGHTNESS: I WILL CAST YOU TO THE GROUND, I WILL LAY YOU BEFORE KINGS, THAT THEY MAY BEHOLD YOU. (EZEKIEL 28:17)

> HOW ARE YOU FALLEN FROM HEAVEN, O LUCIFER, SON OF THE MORNING! HOW ARE YOU CUT DOWN TO THE GROUND, WHICH DID WEAKEN THE NATIONS! FOR YOU HAVE SAID IN YOUR HEART, I WILL ASCEND INTO HEAVEN, I WILL EXALT MY THRONE ABOVE THE STARS OF GOD: I WILL SIT ALSO UPON THE MOUNT OF THE CONGREGATION, IN THE SIDES OF THE NORTH: I WILL ASCEND ABOVE THE HEIGHTS OF THE CLOUDS; I WILL BE LIKE THE MOST HIGH. (ISAIAH 14:12–14)

Most of us read these verses and think, "Well, I've never done that. That doesn't apply to me!" But, when you think it through, you may find that it does. For example, the first thing Lucifer said was "I will ascend." You could put it this way—"I will climb up. I will climb up socially. I will climb up financially. I will climb up spiritually. I can do it myself!" This causes us to be fiercely independent, self-sufficient, self-preserving, and self-protecting—all of which are anti-Christ.

Next, he said, "I will exalt my throne above the stars of God." In today's terminology and environment, this would be the same as saying (or thinking), "I have to be the best." It is an attitude that sends us into perfectionism, ungodly competition, striving, and performance-oriented behaviors. These ultimately backfire, resulting in self-rejection and abasement, and in resentment and bitterness.

Third, Lucifer said, "I will sit … in the sides of the north." The "sides of the north" refers to a place of special favor, appointed to someone for a particular purpose at a particular time. This aspect of pride causes us to begin to think, "That should be me up there doing that! Why wasn't I chosen? I can do it better." It sets us up for murmuring and complaining, envy and jealousy, and rejection and disappointment.

Next, he said, "I will ascend above the heights of the clouds." This aspect of pride refers to spiritual matters. These are times when we think we are farther along, more spiritual than others, and should be recognized for our amazing spiritual prowess. We should not be expected to serve the practical needs of our brothers and sisters. We resent serving, because we are the ones who should be served. At the same time, many with pride will boast about their service and how much they do and how hard they work. God Himself will resist us and bring us low when we have this attitude of spiritual superiority.

Finally, Lucifer said in his heart, "I will be like the Most High." We put ourselves on the throne, judging the actions and attitudes of others, because "I'm right, you're wrong. You can come to me and apologize. I don't have to make it right with you; you have to make it right with me by admitting your error and asking my forgiveness." This sets us up for a life of offense, broken and unhealed relationships, and misery.

The other aspect of Satan's nature (the "old man") is deception. Deception has many faces, just as do pride and fear. It doesn't always appear as what my grandmother would have called "a bald-faced lie." It can present itself very innocently in manipulation and control, in enchantment, in spiritual bewitchment, in many healing modalities, in occult practices, in false religions, and hundreds of other ways.

Deception is a huge and extremely fluid aspect of Satan's nature in us. Know this: if we choose the lie, God will surely let us have it. We also need to know that Satan will lie to us as often as we will listen.

> HE WAS A MURDERER FROM THE BEGINNING, AND ABODE NOT IN THE TRUTH, BECAUSE THERE IS NO TRUTH IN HIM. WHEN HE SPEAKS A LIE, HE SPEAKS OF HIS OWN: FOR HE IS A LIAR, AND THE FATHER OF IT. (JOHN 8:44)

> STAND NOW WITH YOUR ENCHANTMENTS, AND WITH THE MULTITUDE OF YOUR SORCERIES, WHEREIN YOU HAVE LABORED FROM YOUR YOUTH; IF SO BE YOU SHALL BE ABLE TO PROFIT, IF SO BE YOU MAY PREVAIL. YOU ARE WEARIED IN THE MULTITUDE OF YOUR COUNSELS. LET NOW THE ASTROLOGERS, THE STARGAZERS, THE MONTHLY PROGNOSTICATORS, STAND UP, AND SAVE YOU FROM THESE THINGS THAT SHALL COME UPON YOU. (ISAIAH 47:12–13)

> AND WITH ALL DECEIVABLENESS OF UNRIGHTEOUSNESS IN THEM THAT PERISH; BECAUSE THEY RECEIVED NOT THE LOVE OF THE TRUTH, THAT THEY MIGHT BE SAVED. AND FOR THIS CAUSE GOD SHALL SEND THEM STRONG DELUSION, THAT THEY SHOULD BELIEVE A LIE. (2 THESSALONIANS 10:11)

That should clear the confusion a bit as to why we do some of the ungodly things we do! It explains why we continue to commit sins, even though we've been born again and are believers. What have we seen so far? Let's recap:

- Scripture tells us there are two fathers.
- All of mankind has the traits of two natures.
- The unsaved (those who don't believe and accept the sacrifice of the Lord Jesus) and the saved (those who do) are all created by God.
- God's core nature is characterized by love, truth, and humility.
- Satan's core nature is characterized by fear, pride, and deception.

- The nation of Israel, the Jewish people, are clearly called God's children, as are those who have been adopted through God's grace and mercy because of faith.

  FOR YOU ARE ALL THE CHILDREN OF GOD BY FAITH IN CHRIST JESUS. (GALATIANS 3:26)

God's Word speaks of three people groups in the world, the Jews, the Gentiles, and the Church of God, the collective Body of Christ.

  GIVE NONE OFFENCE, NEITHER TO THE JEWS, NOR TO THE GENTILES, NOR TO THE CHURCH OF GOD:
  (1 CORINTHIANS 10:32)

The Jews are the nation of Israel, the Jewish people. The church of God are the believers in Christ Jesus. The Gentiles are those who either refuse to believe the gospel, or have not yet had the opportunity to hear it. Those in this last group are the only ones not named somewhere in Scripture as children of God. But several questions remain unanswered: why Jesus called those Jewish religious-minded people children of the devil, why there are other references to being a child of God as conditional, and why John said this:

  HE THAT COMMITS SIN IS OF THE DEVIL; FOR THE DEVIL SINS FROM THE BEGINNING. FOR THIS PURPOSE THE SON OF GOD WAS MANIFESTED, THAT HE MIGHT DESTROY THE WORKS OF THE DEVIL. WHOSOEVER IS BORN OF GOD DOES NOT COMMIT SIN; FOR HIS SEED REMAINS IN HIM: AND HE CANNOT SIN, BECAUSE HE IS BORN OF GOD. IN THIS THE CHILDREN OF GOD ARE MANIFEST, AND THE CHILDREN OF THE DEVIL: WHOSOEVER DOES NOT RIGHTEOUSNESS IS NOT OF GOD, NEITHER HE THAT LOVES NOT HIS BROTHER. (1 JOHN 3:8–10)

  BUT I SAY UNTO YOU, LOVE YOUR ENEMIES, BLESS THEM THAT CURSE YOU, DO GOOD TO THEM THAT HATE YOU, AND PRAY FOR THEM WHICH DESPITEFULLY USE YOU, AND PERSECUTE YOU; THAT YOU MAY BE THE CHILDREN OF YOUR FATHER WHICH IS IN HEAVEN: FOR HE MAKES HIS SUN TO RISE ON THE

EVIL AND ON THE GOOD, AND SENDS RAIN ON THE JUST AND
ON THE UNJUST. (MATTHEW 5:44–45)

The answer to the question of who can be a child of God is simple—it's your choice! It's your choice as to which nature, which father, you will follow. Will we choose our true nature, which is the same as our Father's in heaven, and reveal love, truth, and humility in our actions and attitudes? Or will we choose the flesh and follow our old man, the nature of our father the devil, and reveal fear, pride, and deception in our actions and attitudes? It's a sobering question, and carries a great responsibility to continually separate ourselves from any thought or feeling that is not God's nature and our true identity—the higher level of our intended creation. God's love for us is unconditional. Is our love for Him the same? Make the commitment with this prayer. God will help you fulfill it.

Father God, You are my Father. I choose to separate myself from all other fathers and cling to You and to You alone. I am Your child and You are my Father. Thank You for showing me my true nature, so that I can free myself from the flesh, that nature of the enemy which has corrupted and deceived me into believing that the old man is me, and that I cannot be free of the old man. Christ in me is my hope of glory, and because of Jesus I have hope each day to overcome the enticements, the seductions, the enchantments, and the deceptions of hell. Thank You for showing me I have a choice, and empowering me to make the choice to walk as Your child every day. Help me recognize when any of my thoughts or feelings begin to sway away from love, truth, and humility, and bring me back into perfect balance, so that my heart and mind are always fixed on You. Make me quick to recognize assignments of hell designed to bring out the fear, deception, and pride of the flesh belonging to the devil's nature in me. Make me quick to submit to You and resist the devil, so that he flees from me. Father, help me see those times and situations where I've failed to do this, and to repent to You, turning my thoughts, my heart attitude, and my direction back to You and into my true identity. I declare today, I am an overcomer, created by You for good works. I am forgiven of all my sins by the sacrifice of Jesus Christ. His blood has cleansed me, and I am a child of our Father in heaven. I have His nature inside me. I am love, I am truth, I am humility; and I am learning to look in the mirror and see Jesus as I am transformed from glory to glory and from faith to faith. Amen.

Chapter Three

Truth about Saints and Sinners

In order to explore the subject of saints and sinners, the definitions and differences, the expectations and exhibitions, and the heart of God regarding both groups, we need to put aside what we think we know and dive into the Scriptures for fresh revelation. As a starting point, perhaps we should define sin and sinner according to what God Himself had to say about it, and not what we've been taught or told. In the Book of Genesis, the Father had a very interesting conversation with Cain about sin. This is what God had to say:

> And in process of time it came to pass, that Cain brought of the fruit of the ground an offering unto the LORD. And Abel, he also brought of the firstlings of his flock and of the fat thereof. And the LORD had respect unto Abel and to his offering: But unto Cain and to his offering he had not respect. And Cain was very wroth, and his countenance fell. And the LORD said unto Cain, Why are you wroth? and why is your countenance fallen? If you do well, shall you not be accepted? and if you do not well, sin lieth at the door. And unto you shall be his desire, and you shall rule over him. (Genesis 4:3–7)

Let me paraphrase this for you for a little more understanding: After a while, Cain brought an offering from the field to the Lord, crops he had grown with his own hands. His brother Abel brought a first-born lamb, chosen for its excellent appearance and health. The Lord accepted Abel's sacrifice, but not Cain's, which made Cain very angry. So, the Lord spoke to Cain, questioning his attitude in order to cause

Cain to examine his own heart and motivations. God said to Cain, "Why are you so upset, Son? If you agree with me and do what you know to be right, things will be well with you; but if you don't agree with me and follow my directives, sin is waiting at your door. Sin wants to pounce on you, to attack you and capture you, desiring eventually to take your life. However, you have the ability within you to overcome sin and take dominion over him."

In God's Words to Cain, He personified sin. In other words, He gave form and human characteristics to something non-human. He gave a physical form to a concept or attribute of evil. The word "lieth" used in the King James Version of the Bible means "crouches on all fours, like an animal." Well, you can't crouch if you don't have a body. When God told Cain sin desired to have him, He was also saying sin has some form of intelligence, since you can't have a desire if you can't think. Basically, God said sin is some form of intelligent being. It has a body, even if it's a spirit body, and it has desires, which means it has a mind of some kind. It can think.

In Hebrew, the word "sin" in this passage of Scripture means both the offense and the offender; in other words, it encompasses not simply the action, but also the being behind the action. When you get to the New Testament, the Greek translation of sin leaves out the "offender" piece of the definition and becomes simply the offense. This new definition is founded on Jesus' teachings, and has profound implications for His followers. However, we've been taught that sin is only bad things that bad people do. No wonder so many of God's people cannot seem to separate themselves from sin. They are convinced that they are bad people, sinners who continually "miss the mark." Is that the case? Jesus addressed the definition of sin and a sinner, even as God had done so long ago.

> NEVERTHELESS I TELL YOU THE TRUTH; IT IS EXPEDIENT
> FOR YOU THAT I GO AWAY: FOR IF I GO NOT AWAY, THE
> COMFORTER WILL NOT COME UNTO YOU; BUT IF I DEPART, I

WILL SEND HIM UNTO YOU. AND WHEN HE IS COME, HE WILL
REPROVE THE WORLD OF SIN, AND OF RIGHTEOUSNESS, AND
OF JUDGMENT: OF SIN, BECAUSE THEY BELIEVE NOT ON ME.
(JOHN 16:7–9)

In this verse, Jesus Himself says that a sinner is one who does not
believe on Him! If a sinner is a non-believer, what are you when
you come into the saving knowledge of the Lord Jesus Christ?
Throughout the New Testament Scriptures, believers are called
"saints." This word derives from a Greek adjective with only one
meaning, which is "sacred." The explanation of sacred is "physically
pure, morally blameless, ceremonially consecrated." Let's work our
way through each part of that definition.

Through being born again, we are physically pure, like a new-
born babe is physically pure. "Seeing you have purified your souls
in obeying the truth through the Spirit unto unfeigned love of the
brethren, see that you love one another with a pure heart fervently:
Being born again, not of corruptible seed, but of incorruptible, by
the Word of God, which lives and abides for ever" (1 Peter 1:22–23).

Perhaps this is why the Scripture refers to believers as "vir-
gins," a group whom we consider to be physically pure. The blood
of Jesus cleanses us of our past and all unrighteousness, so that we
are morally blameless. He took the punishment for our crimes of
sin against God and others, so we who believe on Him are un-con-
demned. "There is therefore now no condemnation to them which
are in Christ Jesus, who walk not after the flesh, but after the Spirit"
(Romans 8:1).

To consecrate means "to make or pronounce clean."
Ceremonially consecrated refers to our setting ourselves apart to
God, usually by a public declaration of our faith in accepting Jesus
as both Lord and Savior. Ceremonial consecration may also be
through baptism, which is generally thought of as the "outward
sign of God's inward work" in us. We can also be ceremonially

consecrated, or set aside, for a specific spiritual purpose or ministerial calling or vocation within the structure of our churches and the Body of Christ. Basically, to be consecrated means you have made a heart commitment to follow on to know the Lord, and to serve Him as He wills without murmur or complaint.

> BE YOU NOT UNEQUALLY YOKED TOGETHER WITH UNBELIEVERS: FOR WHAT FELLOWSHIP HAS RIGHTEOUSNESS WITH UNRIGHTEOUSNESS? AND WHAT COMMUNION HAS LIGHT WITH DARKNESS? AND WHAT CONCORD HAS CHRIST WITH BELIAL? OR WHAT PART HAS HE THAT BELIEVES WITH AN INFIDEL? AND WHAT AGREEMENT HAS THE TEMPLE OF GOD WITH IDOLS? FOR YOU ARE THE TEMPLE OF THE LIVING GOD; AS GOD HAS SAID, I WILL DWELL IN THEM, AND WALK IN THEM; AND I WILL BE THEIR GOD, AND THEY SHALL BE MY PEOPLE. WHEREFORE COME OUT FROM AMONG THEM, AND BE YOU SEPARATE, SAYS THE LORD, AND TOUCH NOT THE UNCLEAN THING; AND I WILL RECEIVE YOU. (2 CORINTHIANS 6:14–17)

Therefore, if you are a believer, you have been born again and are considered by God to be physically pure.

If you are a believer, you have been cleansed by the blood of Jesus and are morally blameless. If you are a believer and have publically responded to the call of God to set yourself apart to His service and benefits, you are consecrated. By definition, then, you are not a sinner, you are a saint, one of the sacred group!

Undoubtably, this truth resonates with your spirit and the Spirit of God within you. Still, there remains the question of sin. We know we are born of God because we are born again, yet John says if we are born of God, we cannot sin! At the same time, we know that— oh, yes, we can commit sins. John didn't just say we won't sin, or that we can say no to sin, or we don't sin, or that we no longer have to sin or are compelled to sin. He says we CANNOT sin. "Whosoever is born of God does not commit sin; for his seed remains in him: and he cannot sin, because he is born of God" (I John 3:9).

Because we don't understand the realities of the spirit world, this is one of those Scriptures that can confuse us into thinking, "Maybe I'm not really born again. Maybe I'm not saved. I thought it was real, but now I'm not so sure." Remember, the devil wants to cause you to doubt—to doubt yourself, and to doubt God. Since he couldn't keep you from getting saved, he now tries to throw you into doubt, confusion, and ineffectiveness. This is one of those verses Satan uses to cause people to become religious and works-oriented, always striving to do more and more. He's delighted if you get caught up in self-doubt and fear of not doing enough, not pleasing God, not making it into heaven, always wondering if you're "good enough" to get there.

Let's look at something else John said, and then allow the apostle Paul to bring some clarity to what we've read. "If we say that we have no sin, we deceive ourselves, and the truth is not in us. If we confess our sins, he is faithful and just to forgive us our sins, and to cleanse us from all unrighteousness" (1 John 1:8–9).

These verses show both Hebrew understandings of "sin" —the offense and the offender. "If we say we have no sin" —this speaks of the offender, that personified being of evil, a spirit not of God. "If we confess our sins" —this speaks of our actions that manifest this same evil being, for which actions we are clearly responsible to correct through repentance and forgiveness. John understood spirit world reality, which is why he could say, "He that commits sin is of the devil; for the devil sins from the beginning. For this purpose the Son of God was manifested, that he might destroy the works of the devil" (I John 3:8).

This same truth is what Paul explained in the seventh chapter of Romans. Religion has taught us that we sin because of our "old man" or the flesh. The old man is considered our soulish realm, and the flesh is often believed to be simply our physical bodies. First, let's get that thought out of the way—your body cannot act independently of your mind, even in functions like breathing. There must be impulses from the brain. Your physical flesh does not have a mind of its own. That leaves the soul, your mind, will, emotions, and desires, as the reasons we sin. Yet these are the areas of our being which Paul addressed in speaking of his own soul and concluding that sin is "not me." Look what this great man who wrote much of our New Testament had to say:

> FOR WE KNOW THAT THE LAW IS SPIRITUAL: BUT I AM CARNAL, SOLD UNDER SIN. FOR THAT WHICH I DO I ALLOW NOT: FOR WHAT I WOULD, THAT DO I NOT; BUT WHAT I HATE, THAT DO I. IF THEN I DO THAT WHICH I WOULD NOT, I CONSENT UNTO THE LAW THAT IT IS GOOD. NOW THEN IT IS NO MORE I THAT DO IT, BUT SIN THAT DWELLS IN ME. FOR I KNOW THAT IN ME (THAT IS, IN MY FLESH,) DWELLS NO GOOD THING: FOR TO WILL IS PRESENT WITH ME; BUT HOW TO PERFORM THAT WHICH IS GOOD I FIND NOT. FOR THE GOOD THAT I WOULD I DO NOT: BUT THE EVIL WHICH I WOULD NOT, THAT I DO. NOW IF I DO THAT I WOULD NOT, IT IS NO MORE I THAT DO IT, BUT SIN THAT DWELLS IN ME. I FIND THEN A LAW, THAT, WHEN I WOULD DO GOOD, EVIL IS PRESENT WITH ME. BUT I SEE ANOTHER LAW IN MY MEMBERS, WARRING AGAINST THE LAW OF MY MIND, AND BRINGING ME INTO CAPTIVITY TO THE LAW OF SIN WHICH IS IN MY MEMBERS. O WRETCHED MAN THAT I AM! WHO SHALL DELIVER ME FROM THE BODY OF THIS DEATH? I THANK GOD THROUGH JESUS CHRIST OUR LORD. SO THEN WITH THE MIND I MYSELF SERVE THE LAW OF GOD; BUT WITH THE FLESH THE LAW OF SIN. (ROMANS 7:14–25)

Paul was giving us an understanding of how the spirit world works in our lives, how evil spirits cause us to sin against God and others, and how the problem is not in our minds, or wills, or emotions, or even desires. Those are the four strengths of our soul, representing the four horns of the altar on which we are to lay down our lives.

> GOD IS THE LORD, WHICH HATH SHOWN US LIGHT: BIND THE SACRIFICE WITH CORDS, EVEN UNTO THE HORNS OF THE ALTAR. (PSALM 118:27)

> I BESEECH YOU THEREFORE, BRETHREN, BY THE MERCIES OF GOD, THAT YOU PRESENT YOUR BODIES A LIVING SACRIFICE, HOLY, ACCEPTABLE UNTO GOD, WHICH IS YOUR REASONABLE SERVICE. (ROMANS 12:1)

In the book of Romans chapter seven, Paul clearly delineated and addressed each area of our souls to eliminate any mistaken idea that we are the evil motivators of our sins. Don't get the wrong idea that I am saying we are not responsible for our actions and attitudes—we are clearly responsible when we commit a sin against God or others. Yes, we are held accountable. Yes, we must repent, changing our hearts and minds and direction. In fact, we become even more accountable when we have this truth, because now we must also recognize what evil spirit we have allowed to manifest its nature through us, and remove it!

When Paul wrote, "For that which I do, I allow not," he was saying, "It's not my will to sin." Our will is the decision-making faculty which determines what we allow in our lives, and what we don't. When the doorbell rings, you are the one who decides whether or not you will allow that person in your home. You are the one who decides the standard by which you will live, and the standards to which those around you must adhere if they wish to stay around you. That is your will. Paul said, "I'm doing things I do not allow!" Therefore, Paul says it is not the will which is the problem.

In the area of desire, Paul wrote, "For what I would, that do I not; but what I hate, that do I." By this he meant, "I'm not doing what I want to do; I'm actually doing things that are detestable to me." His desire was to love and serve God, and not to be perverted or rebellious or whatever it was he was doing. Many of us have a heartfelt desire to do the right thing, yet we continue to fall short of our own good intentions, and often don't even realize why. Paul was saying the problem is not in the area of desire.

As for his emotions, Paul had more than one thing to say. First of all, he said he hated what he was doing, as stated above. We consider hatred to be an emotion, and certainly it is at times, although sometimes it is an evil spirit which works to stir up your emotions and take you off-track, steal your peace, and destroy your health. Paul also mentioned this aspect of his soul, his emotions, when he said, "For I delight in the law of God after the inward man," because feeling delight is certainly an emotion. Therefore, the problem is not in the emotions.

In his mind, his intellect, Paul was also sold out to God. He said, "So then with the mind, I myself serve the law of God." That is the final strength of the human soul, our thought life. Paul said his mind was for God, not against God; but that there was something else present that warred against "the law of my mind." His conclusion? "It's not me!" Clearly, according to these Scriptures, the problem was not in the mind. Repeatedly, Paul stated, "Now then it is no more I that do it, but sin that dwells in me … Now if I do that I would not, it is no more I that do it, but sin that dwells in me." Paul clearly said, there is something in me that is not me. It's not my mind, it's not my emotions, it's not my will, it's not my desires—it is flesh. Well, if your flesh—your physical body—can't think or perform without your mind, then flesh is not you, either! It is the carnal nature of Satan. This would explain what John was saying when he stated that if you are born of God you cannot sin. John was also telling us—it's not you.

Let's go on with what Paul was teaching us. "O wretched man that I am! who shall deliver me from the body of this death?" What an interesting thing to say—the body of this death. He also earlier in the passage referred to a war in his "members." These references call to mind other places in Scripture which speak of a body—the Body of Christ. Most Christians are aware that the Bible teaches that each person who is born again becomes a part, a member, of the Body of Christ, which is constructed by God and intended to bring life into the world.

> FOR AS THE BODY IS ONE, AND HAS MANY MEMBERS, AND
> ALL THE MEMBERS OF THAT ONE BODY, BEING MANY, ARE
> ONE BODY: SO ALSO IS CHRIST. FOR BY ONE SPIRIT ARE WE
> ALL BAPTIZED INTO ONE BODY, WHETHER WE BE JEWS OR
> GENTILES, WHETHER WE BE BOND OR FREE; AND HAVE BEEN
> ALL MADE TO DRINK INTO ONE SPIRIT. FOR THE BODY IS
> NOT ONE MEMBER, BUT MANY ... BUT NOW HAS GOD SET
> THE MEMBERS EVERY ONE OF THEM IN THE BODY, AS IT HAS
> PLEASED HIM. AND IF THEY WERE ALL ONE MEMBER, WHERE
> WERE THE BODY? BUT NOW ARE THEY MANY MEMBERS, YET
> BUT ONE BODY... NOW YOU ARE THE BODY OF CHRIST, AND
> MEMBERS IN PARTICULAR.
> (1 CORINTHIANS 12:12–14, 18–20, AND 27)

Think of this Body and its varied members. We all have different names, and many of us share the same name (John, Mary, Joe, Alice, etc.). We all have different personalities and character traits. We all have different gifts, talents, and abilities. We all have different functions and different assignments in the Body. Our various assignments come from the head, who is Jesus; but our mission is the same—to bring life. As God breathed into man and man became a living soul, we are meant to breathe life into situations, circumstances, and people, to see hearts and bodies healed, relationships restored, and brokenness mended.

As is his pattern, Satan has done his best to imitate God by constructing the body of sin, designed and meant to bring death into the world. "For the wages of sin is death; but the gift of God is eternal life through Jesus Christ our Lord" (Romans 6:23). The wages of sin is death. The body of sin is the body of death to which Paul referred.

Just as is the body of Christ, the body of sin is made up of members in particular. They all have different names, and some share the same name (there are many spirits of fear, rejection, accusation, etc.). They all have different gifts, talents, and abilities. They all have different functions and different assignments in their body. Their assignments come from their head, who is Satan, but their mission is a common one—to bring death. Again, as God breathed into man His spirit and nature, and man became a living soul, the "wanna be" god, Satan, came into man with his spirit and breathed his nature into man, and man became a dead soul. As previously stated, this is why Jesus said, "You must be born again." The function and goal of evil spirits is to breathe death into situations, circumstances, and people, to see hearts and bodies wounded and diseased, relationships destroyed, and brokenness abound on every side.

We can conclude, then, that "sin" is not simply bad things that bad people do, and therefore if you commit a sin you are by definition a bad person. Despite our failures and transgressions, our faults and shortcomings, our missing the mark of the high calling of God repeatedly in our lives, if we are true believers in the Lord Jesus Christ and His finished work on the cross of Calvary, we are saints and not sinners. We may be considered sinners in the natural world because of our sins, but in the spirit world, we are made righteous by the blood of Jesus.

With this new perspective, we can now begin to "come out from the unclean thing" as we have been commanded. Our love of God and His love for us empower us to do exactly that. The infilling of the Holy Spirit enables us to discern the evil spirits (those spirit realm sinners, often called the workers of iniquity) which want to rise up within our hearts and cause us to commit sin.

HIDE ME FROM THE SECRET COUNSEL OF THE WICKED; FROM
THE INSURRECTION OF THE WORKERS OF INIQUITY:
(PSALM 64:2)

Insurrection is an uprising that comes from within. Once identified, these evil things can be removed from us by our deliverer Jesus
Christ, the Word of the Living God. They can be cast down and out
of our lives, our thoughts, our feelings, and our desires so that they
can no longer manipulate and control our wills.

AND THE SERVANT OF THE LORD MUST NOT STRIVE; BUT
BE GENTLE UNTO ALL MEN, APT TO TEACH, PATIENT, IN
MEEKNESS INSTRUCTING THOSE THAT OPPOSE THEMSELVES;
IF GOD PERADVENTURE WILL GIVE THEM REPENTANCE TO
THE ACKNOWLEDGING OF THE TRUTH; AND THAT THEY MAY
RECOVER THEMSELVES OUT OF THE SNARE OF THE DEVIL, WHO
ARE TAKEN CAPTIVE BY HIM AT HIS WILL.
(2 TIMOTHY 2:24–26)

THERE ARE THE WORKERS OF INIQUITY FALLEN: THEY ARE CAST
DOWN, AND SHALL NOT BE ABLE TO RISE. (PSALM 36:12)

No one likes to think we carry evil spirits around in us. After all,
once we are born again and the Holy Spirit of God comes into us,
no other evil spirit can be there, right? And doesn't the Word of
God tell us that Jesus bore our curses, so there is no more curse? We
will make two brief points in answer now, then further explore these
doctrines in later chapters.

First of all, Jesus Himself explained what Paul and John later
attempted to teach. Evil enters our hearts and is within us. It doesn't
just float around in the atmosphere waiting to jump on us and at-
tach itself.

AND HE SAID, THAT WHICH COMES OUT OF THE MAN, THAT
DEFILES THE MAN. FOR FROM WITHIN, OUT OF THE HEART OF
MEN, PROCEED EVIL THOUGHTS, ADULTERIES, FORNICATIONS,
MURDERS, THEFTS, COVETOUSNESS, WICKEDNESS, DECEIT,

LASCIVIOUSNESS, AN EVIL EYE, BLASPHEMY, PRIDE, FOOLISHNESS: ALL THESE EVIL THINGS COME FROM WITHIN, AND DEFILE THE MAN. (MARK 7:20-23)

Reminiscent of the conversation between God and Cain, isn't it? God said, "Hey, Cain, if you open the door, sin comes in. Sin has a desire to have you." It isn't a question of whether or not a Christian can have a demon; it's a question of whether or not a demon can use a Christian to manifest its nature. Obviously, the answer is "yes."

As for curses, it is absolutely true that Jesus is our curse bearer, and that He made a way through His stripes and crucifixion for us to be completely free of sin, sickness, poverty, and death. Those are the four strengths of the curse. Now that Jesus has finished His work, we have a responsibility to appropriate what He accomplished. We are the ones who must recognize the curses over our own lives and families, renounce and break them in the power of the Holy Spirit and the blood of Jesus Christ of Nazareth.

Think of it this way—if Jesus did it all with no responsibility on our part, then we would all have been born saved after the Lord Jesus sacrificed His life for ours. If the curses were automatically eliminated at His death, not one person would ever suffer from mental illness or physical disease. But no! We had to acknowledge and accept what He did by recognizing, confessing, and repenting of our sins in order to be saved and have eternal life. We must do the same thing in order to be free of the curses of our generations and the doors we have opened to the devil through our own iniquities. The way we entered the kingdom is the way we go forward in it and gain its benefits.

Being released out of error and spiritual bondage is being released into truth and deeper relationship with God. The Lord never releases us to our own ways, because the way of man has a snare. The snare is set by the devil, and without properly understanding our freedom and its responsibilities we can easily fall into the devil's trap. Ask the Lord to seal these truths in your heart and in your mind so that you won't be guided by a broken compass as you navigate through life's challenges.

Father God, thank You for showing me the difference between saints and sinners. Thank You that I am a believer and therefore, in the group called "saints," I am sacred to You. Help me know deep in my heart that You are my righteousness, Jesus, and that I can love with Your love because You are within me. Because of You, I can keep a pure heart and right motives. Help me, Lord, to walk in love so that I can be always morally blameless. Make me quick to repent to You when I fail to recognize the snare of the devil and fall into his trap of sin, and to know that when I repent of my daily sins, I am forgiven and cleansed of all unrighteousness; and help me, Lord, to forgive myself. My desire is to continually set myself apart to You and to Your purposes and plans, so that everyone will know that I am consecrated to the Living God and to no other. My desire is to appropriate my full salvation package so that I can break all curses over my life by Your power in me, and rid myself of all uncleanness in my heart. As I grow in Your love and in Your power, never let me think of myself more highly than I should, or to think of myself as less than Your best. I want to agree with You and what You say about me and others, so that I can recognize myself as sacred—physically pure, morally blameless, and set apart to You Lord God and to Your purpose—a saint, and not a sinner. I declare that the blood of Jesus Christ is all powerful and effective to see this prayer accomplished in my life. Amen.

Chapter Four

Truth about Salvation and Reward

NOW THAT THE QUESTION OF SAINTS AND SINNERS is resolved, does that settle the issue of "once saved, always saved?" Many people often ask, "Can we lose our salvation?" They wonder, "Am I really saved?" Much of the confusion as to whether or not we're going to hell centers in self-righteous ideas and self-focused guilt. Much of the confusion comes directly from our churches which seem to teach us we have to DO-DO-DO for God, always striving to please Him and ever falling short of the mark. Much of the confusion comes from what others say. Things like, "If you're still doing THAT thing, you must not really be saved." Or "If you're acting this way, you need to question your salvation, brother!" And much of the confusion is manufactured in our own minds as we attempt to understand and accept the simplicity of the gospel.

We're going to explore the question of salvation, because the religious church has been busy since its beginning trying to complicate the matter; and it has created great fear in people about whether or not they are going to heaven when they die. Even those who are obviously walking close to God, those who hear His voice regularly, and who are doing their best to live a life pleasing to the Lord can (and do) fall for this lie of hell. *Maybe* they are not really saved, *maybe* God doesn't really love them, *maybe* they are just not good enough. The truth is that the gospel is so simple it takes help to misunderstand it. Unfortunately, there's a lot of help out there. In our exalted opinions and intelligence, we fail to recognize its simplicity. We think, "It just can't be that simple!"

Let's see what the Word has to say about salvation. First, we are going once again down the old Roman's Road:

> THAT IF YOU SHALL CONFESS WITH YOUR MOUTH THE LORD
> JESUS, AND SHALL BELIEVE IN YOUR HEART THAT GOD HAS
> RAISED HIM FROM THE DEAD, YOU SHALL BE SAVED. FOR
> WITH THE HEART MAN BELIEVES UNTO RIGHTEOUSNESS; AND
> WITH THE MOUTH CONFESSION IS MADE UNTO SALVATION.
> (ROMANS 10:9–10)

According to these verses, when we believe in our hearts that God raised Jesus from the dead (which means we know He is alive today), and we speak out that Jesus Christ is Lord (which means He is the One in authority over all things, especially our own lives), then we are saved. Our righteousness, our salvation, can never be of ourselves; it is only by Jesus Christ and what He did, not by anything more or anything less, that we can do. The perfect blood sacrifice made by Yeshua Hamashiach, Jesus the Messiah, is the only way into the Holy of Holies, into the very presence of the Living God.

It was always true that blood had to be shed for the remission of sins, even before Jesus was born into the world. There are numerous references to the sacrifice that is acceptable to the Father. We discussed one example earlier: When Cain brought the works of his own hands to sacrifice to the Lord, his offering was not accepted. Yet his brother Abel's sacrifice of the lamb without spot or blemish was acceptable and received. The blood of Jesus, applied by faith in His blood, His finished work of sacrifice on our behalf, is our righteousness and the only way anyone enters into God's heaven.

Look a little deeper into this truth. Again, in the book of Romans, Paul gives us an example: "For what says the Scripture? Abraham believed God, and it was counted unto him for righteousness" (Romans 4:3). Now skip down a few verses:

> HE STAGGERED NOT AT THE PROMISE OF GOD THROUGH
> UNBELIEF; BUT WAS STRONG IN FAITH, GIVING GLORY TO

GOD; AND BEING FULLY PERSUADED THAT, WHAT HE HAD
PROMISED, HE WAS ABLE ALSO TO PERFORM. AND THEREFORE
IT WAS IMPUTED TO HIM FOR RIGHTEOUSNESS. NOW IT WAS
NOT WRITTEN FOR HIS SAKE ALONE, THAT IT WAS IMPUTED TO
HIM; BUT FOR US ALSO, TO WHOM IT SHALL BE IMPUTED, IF
WE BELIEVE ON HIM THAT RAISED UP JESUS OUR LORD FROM
THE DEAD. (ROMANS 4:20–24)

The "it" Paul is talking about here is righteousness—the righteousness of God which is the only thing that carries us into heaven.
When you study the Hebrew meaning of this word "imputed," it
means "interpenetrated," literally woven into.

When we believe God, His righteousness is woven into the very fabric of our being.

In other words, it is not something that is layered onto our lives,
it is something that is a part of our lives. You cannot "unweave" a
garment. You can cut it up, you can burn a hole in it, you can wear
it down until it is threadbare. But you cannot unweave it. Here's another comparison. If you are an artist mixing oils and you put yellow
into blue, you're going to get green. You will never again be able to
separate the yellow from the blue. The yellow pigment has interpenetrated the blue and become inextricably a part of it, resulting in a
new color altogether.

That is what belief does for us! It weaves the righteousness of
God, Jesus Christ Himself, into our lives. The righteousness inter-
penetrates us, like the yellow paint that transforms the blue paint
into an entirely different color. His righteousness changes our lives.
Our efforts do not change our lives. Think of this: the reverse of a
truth is also a truth. If our good works cannot get us into heaven,
then our bad works cannot keep us out of it.

Every Christian I know will say he or she can do nothing to save himself or herself. And yet, here we are, falling into the trap of works—doing, doing, doing—to prove ourselves "worthy," or to insure our place in glory. We fret and worry whether we're doing enough for God, if we're really going to heaven, if we have somehow messed up so much He's going to change His mind about us and send us to hell instead. Many Christians, good, God-fearing souls who believe in Jesus with their whole hearts, live in a constant state of anxiety and tension about their personal salvation. Why? I believe the reason for our uncertainty lies in the fact that so many well-meaning men and women of God continue to teach and preach that we can "lose" our salvation if we don't toe the line for God. These people seem to know what they're talking about, don't they?

After all, what about all those Scriptures in James that say man is justified by works AND faith? Don't I have to prove myself to God? Actually, no. Do you honestly think God doesn't already know all about you? What the book of James tells us is that when we believe God, our faith creates in us the desire to do good works. We can have good works without faith, and many people do; but we cannot have faith without good works. It isn't doing "good works" that makes us righteous, it is righteousness that makes us do good works. Don't allow the devil to deceive you about this.

WHAT DOES IT PROFIT, MY BRETHREN, THOUGH A MAN SAY HE HAS FAITH, AND HAVE NOT WORKS? CAN FAITH SAVE HIM? IF A BROTHER OR SISTER BE NAKED, AND DESTITUTE OF DAILY FOOD, AND ONE OF YOU SAY UNTO THEM, DEPART IN PEACE, BE YOU WARMED AND FILLED; NOTWITHSTANDING YOU GIVE THEM NOT THOSE THINGS WHICH ARE NEEDFUL TO THE BODY; WHAT DOES IT PROFIT? EVEN SO FAITH, IF IT HAS NOT WORKS, IS DEAD, BEING ALONE. YES, A MAN MAY SAY, YOU HAVE FAITH, AND I HAVE WORKS: SHOW ME YOUR FAITH WITHOUT YOUR WORKS, AND I WILL SHOW YOU MY FAITH BY MY WORKS. (JAMES 2:14-18)

There are also those who use the Scripture in Galatians about the works of the flesh in their attempt to prove we can lose our salvation.

> NOW THE WORKS OF THE FLESH ARE MANIFEST, WHICH ARE THESE; ADULTERY, FORNICATION, UNCLEANNESS, LASCIVIOUSNESS, IDOLATRY, WITCHCRAFT, HATRED, VARIANCE, EMULATIONS, WRATH, STRIFE, SEDITIONS, HERESIES, ENVYINGS, MURDERS, DRUNKENNESS, REVELLINGS, AND SUCH LIKE: OF THE WHICH I TELL YOU BEFORE, AS I HAVE ALSO TOLD YOU IN TIME PAST, THAT THEY WHICH DO SUCH THINGS SHALL NOT INHERIT THE KINGDOM OF GOD. (GALATIANS 5:19–21)

Let me tell you, if the works of the flesh could take us into hell, then we're all going. There is not one single person sitting in any church or standing behind any pulpit in this land or any other who has not done something or other from this list since their born-again experience! Now you'll say, well, it means "habitually do," not just once in a while. Really? That doesn't change anything you just read. If you take a closer look down this list, I am quite certain you will find something that applies to you habitually.

For those who may not know what some of these words mean: "variance" means quarreling, contention, or debate; "emulations" means jealousy, malice, or indignation; "seditions" means disunity, dissension, or division; and "murders" includes gossip, character assassination, slander, criticism, and judgments. Ever told (or listened to) a dirty joke since you got saved? Do you slip over into profanity occasionally when you are angry or hurt? Would that not fall into the category of uncleanness? Have you stayed away from church and the presence of God to go to a football game or fishing or a concert or social event, or maybe just felt like sleeping in? Have you compromised righteousness to be around unrighteous people (even family members) and be accepted by them? Would that not be idolatry? Many of us live in constant strife at home or in our workplaces. We Christians are known for our hypocrisy, aren't we?

Obviously, we're either all going to hell and the Word of God lied to us about being saved by grace, or "inherit the kingdom of God" does not mean going to heaven. I prefer the latter explanation, and you likely feel the same way. The kingdom of God refers to God's authority. It is rulership. When we choose to agree with the enemy and manifest Satan's nature through these works of the flesh (remember, flesh means the carnal nature of Satan, not you) then we find ourselves without the authority to combat the enemy. Lots of times we accuse God of not answering our prayers about this or that, when in fact we have given up our authority in Christ. You can't use the name of Jesus in power when you aren't standing in His character. Again, the gospel is so simple, it takes help to misunderstand it and unfortunately, there is still a lot of help out there!

There's another infamous verse that is grossly misinterpreted and has put extreme fear in God's people, and that is the one in Hebrews about repentance being impossible after having come to Christ. Perhaps you are familiar with this passage. You may even have experienced some spiritual abuse because of it.

> FOR IT IS IMPOSSIBLE FOR THOSE WHO WERE ONCE ENLIGHT-
> ENED, AND HAVE TASTED OF THE HEAVENLY GIFT, AND WERE
> MADE PARTAKERS OF THE HOLY GHOST, AND HAVE TASTED
> THE GOOD WORD OF GOD, AND THE POWERS OF THE WORLD
> TO COME, IF THEY SHALL FALL AWAY, TO RENEW THEM AGAIN
> UNTO REPENTANCE; SEEING THEY CRUCIFY TO THEMSELVES
> THE SON OF GOD AFRESH, AND PUT HIM TO AN OPEN SHAME.
> (HEBREWS 6:4–6)

Religious people want to control you and keep you in line with them by instilling the belief that if you ever sin after you're saved, you're done. It's over. If you are truly born again, then you should know better; and if you sin after you are born again, then you're going to hell. End of story. I can't tell you the number of people who agonize over this, trying to get back in God's good graces, all the time believing in their inmost heart there is truly no hope for them.

Usually, these are people who "hold on to their lives," who are consumed with personal health issues, always observing symptoms and running to doctors at the slightest little thing. It's because they fear death, and that is because they think in their hearts they're going to hell. Christians are not to fear death, we are to overcome it!

> FOR HE MUST REIGN, TILL HE HAS PUT ALL ENEMIES UNDER HIS
> FEET. THE LAST ENEMY THAT SHALL BE DESTROYED IS DEATH.
> (1 CORINTHIANS 15:25–26)

So, if these verses in the book of Hebrews do not mean we lose our salvation, what do they mean? First of all, to "fall away" doesn't mean to commit a sin. It means to renounce Jesus completely. It doesn't mean you are lost forever if you get angry at God in your deception and the lies of hell, shake your fist and even curse God! "Fall away" means to consciously, intentionally, and completely reject the truth of God's love and His expression of that love by sending Jesus to die in your place.

Because of a personal experience in my own life, I seriously doubt that once you are born again, you could ever do that. Here's what happened. I received Jesus in a little country church when I was only eleven years old, visiting grandparents, aunts, and uncles who required church attendance. But I wasn't really taught anything at all about relationship with God, only church. Growing up, I was not close to the Lord, and really didn't know much about Him; and so like most people, I went my own way and the devil starting walking along with me. Looking back on my life, I can see many, many times and situations where the Lord protected me; but I certainly didn't consider any of that to be happening at the time. I figured I was just "lucky."

The devil made me feel unimportant in my family, no matter what I did or accomplished; and so as a child I felt very much like an outcast. The "church" did the same thing. I simply did not fit in, which is what I wanted more than anything. When I got older, I had a few Jewish friends who seemed to enjoy a real sense of community, and I decided that's what I wanted. They were devout, lived good lives, and were always there for one another. It was very attractive, since I didn't think anyone was there for me. After carefully considering these things, I made the decision to convert to Judaism. I wanted to have a family that would be there for me.

So I started attending Hebrew classes and meeting regularly with the rabbi, who continually questioned why I would want to do such a thing, and repeatedly asked, "Are you sure?" He told me I'd be persecuted, and in some ways, I was already. Everyone I knew thought I was crazy. But I was determined to stick it out and become a Jew, eventually marry a Jewish man and live happily ever after in a Jewish community. After about two years of regular meetings and training, the day finally approached when I was to be officially and ceremoniously accepted into the congregation, a Jew at last!

Then, at our last meeting before the big day, the rabbi said to me, "You do know you'll have to renounce Jesus, don't you?"

"What do you mean?" I responded.

"You'll have to publicly declare that Jesus is not the Messiah. He is not the Son of God and He is not God. He did not die for your sins and He was not resurrected. You must declare this before everyone," the rabbi said. "You must renounce Him completely."

Something turned over in my stomach with such a force, it almost brought me to my knees. I began to question this mighty man of God. "Why? Why can't I have both? What if you're wrong?" The Spirit of God inside me, the precious breath of the Holy Spirit would not allow me to reject the Christ I had received as a child! All my worldly hopes and dreams of family, community, and safety were dashed in a heartbeat. "I can't," was all I could say to the rabbi, and I walked out of his office, out of the synagogue, and out of Judaism. I was totally unable to fall away.

"Fall away" means you steadfastly refuse to accept or believe that Jesus Christ is your Savior, that He was resurrected and is alive today. That this verse in Hebrews doesn't mean what you thought it meant is good news. And here's the even better news: Even if you rejected Christ at some time in your life, if you are now worried about going to hell, then you did not ever completely renounce Him! If you had, you wouldn't even think about a place or condition called hell, other than what you've been living right here on earth.

Maybe it's time we all simply get over our self-focus and get on with our lives. Jesus didn't die for us to have eternal life just so we could worry about whether or not He's going to take it away from us! "For the gifts and calling of God are without repentance" (Romans 11:29). That means He doesn't change His mind.

"For by grace are you saved through faith; and that not of yourselves: it is the gift of God: Not of works, lest any man should boast" (Ephesians 2:8–9). Salvation is a gift of God. He doesn't change His mind, and He doesn't take back the gift. Your salvation does not depend on your works, it depends on your belief.

Previously, we explained some of the other verses that cause us to doubt, like the ones in 1 John about a born-again believer being unable to commit sin. Explaining difficult verses and clarifying confusing arguments strengthens us in our faith. But real experiential knowledge comes through our personal encounter with Jesus, the born-again experience, no matter our age, the awakening of God's Spirit in us. No one can take that away from us or argue us out of it. A man with an experience is never at the mercy of a man with an argument. Even at the early age of eleven, I had an encounter with the Living God. Maybe it wasn't as dramatic as Paul's on the road to Damascus, but it was real nonetheless. I. Do. Believe. We all know that being born again does not mean we cannot choose to sin. Again, sin is an expression of evil brought on by a demonic manifestation. The workers of iniquity dwell within us until we recognize them and kick them out. They hide and work, and hide their work.

An evil spirit, let's say a spirit of anger, rises up from within and uses your body to bring evil to pass—maybe you take a swing at someone and land a punch that breaks a nose or a jaw. Now that evil thing withdraws back into its hiding place within your heart and you are left with a mess to clean up. Maybe you're arrested for assault, maybe you've lost a friend, or ruined a relationship; maybe it becomes even more serious. But, as Paul did his best to teach us in Romans 7—"It's not me, it's the sin that dwells within."

Are you responsible? Yes, you agreed with that spirit and allowed it to manifest its nature. Are you a sinner? No, you are a sinning saint. Again, it is at this point that you realize you are doubly responsible—you must account for the action itself, and you must recognize and remove the spirit that caused it. Don't begin to doubt your born-again experience or the truth that you are going to heaven and not to hell. Every one of us has the love of God in us—we're just busy removing all the junk that has smothered and covered it!

Nothing we do in the way of good works will ever get us into heaven, and nothing we do in the way of evil can keep us out! Does that give us a license to sin? As Paul says, God forbid! It is our love for God and His love for us that works in us to bring us to perfection, and to accomplish the good things He calls us to do, and to live the righteous life of abundance He desires us to live.

Where does that leave us as far as good works are concerned? Look at these verses found in 1 Corinthians 3:8–15 for the answer to the question of "once saved always saved."

"Now he that plants and he that waters are one: and every man shall receive his own reward according to his own labor." This verse tells us plainly that there is a reward coming for our works. "For we are laborers together with God: you are God's husbandry, you are God's building." This verse tells us that God builds us, and we cooperate with Him in the process, working right alongside Him.

"According to the grace of God which is given unto me, as a wise masterbuilder, I have laid the foundation, and another builds thereon. But let every man take heed how he builds thereupon." This verse tells us that we help lay the foundation in other people by demonstrating the love of God and introducing them to Christ. Then it is up to that person to work with God to build his life in a way pleasing to the Lord.

"For other foundation can no man lay than that is laid, which is Jesus Christ." This verse tells us there is no other sure foundation for our lives than the Lord Jesus. Everything starts with Him and our born-again experience.

"Now if any man build upon this foundation gold, silver, precious stones, wood, hay, stubble." Gold, silver, and precious stones represent the works that we do which are motivated out of love for God and for His people. Wood, hay, and stubble represent the works we do which are motivated by a desire to look good to others, to show ourselves to be great Christians, to prove our worth or value, or out of fear, obligation, guilt, or some other heavy religious yoke.

"Every man's work shall be made manifest: for the day shall declare it, because it shall be revealed by fire; and the fire shall try every man's work of what sort it is." In this verse we see that whatever we do, every action and attitude after our born-again experience, is going to be revealed for what it truly is.

"If any man's work abide which he has built thereupon, he shall receive a reward." We are told in this verse that we will all be judged, and the good works we do, the ones which are done out of love, become the jewels in our crowns, and the works that were done from some other motivation will be burned away.

"If any man's work shall be burned, he shall suffer loss: but he himself shall be saved; yet so as by fire." Here is the answer! Our works won't send us to hell, but they can cause us to lose reward. All we have done will be judged, and that judgment will determine the extent of our heavenly reward.

These are some of the Scriptures that tell us there is more to going to heaven than simply making it in; and that we are not all going to be the same, or receive the same reward. When we stand before the judgment seat of Christ, we are not going to be there for punishment, we are going to be there for reward. The Scripture clearly says some will suffer loss; but the loss is not the loss of salvation, it's loss of reward.

What is the reward? We may not know exactly everything, but there are some passages that tell us, at least in part, what we may expect. In the book of Revelation, first look at chapter 3 verse 21. Jesus is speaking here and He says: "To him that overcomes will I grant to sit with me in my throne, even as I also overcame, and am set down with my Father in his throne."

Then move over to chapter 7. First, we see the 144,000. As you read the book of Revelation, keep in mind that this is the greatest single parable in the Bible. Those who read, hear, and keep the prophecy of it are blessed, according to the third verse in the first chapter. This book has also been said to be a divorce decree of the apostate church and a love letter to the Bride. With that in mind, and considering the law of first reference in identifying symbolism in Scripture, as well as meanings of numbers and names, we will do our best to show you who the 144,000 are, and that they are the overcomers to whom Jesus referred. 144,000 is not a literal number; it is a symbolic number.

AND AFTER THESE THINGS I SAW FOUR ANGELS STANDING ON THE FOUR CORNERS OF THE EARTH, HOLDING THE FOUR WINDS OF THE EARTH, THAT THE WIND SHOULD NOT BLOW ON THE EARTH, NOR ON THE SEA, NOR ON ANY TREE. AND I SAW ANOTHER ANGEL ASCENDING FROM THE EAST, HAVING THE SEAL OF THE LIVING GOD: AND HE CRIED WITH A LOUD VOICE TO THE FOUR ANGELS, TO WHOM IT WAS GIVEN TO HURT THE EARTH AND THE SEA, SAYING, HURT NOT THE EARTH, NEITHER THE SEA, NOR THE TREES, TILL WE HAVE SEALED THE SERVANTS OF OUR GOD IN THEIR FOREHEADS. AND I HEARD THE NUMBER OF THEM WHICH WERE SEALED: AND THERE WERE SEALED AN HUNDRED AND FORTY AND FOUR

THOUSAND OF ALL THE TRIBES OF THE CHILDREN OF ISRAEL.
(REVELATION 7:1–4)

First, understand that "sea" and "trees" are both words which are
symbolic of people. Next, John tells us that the 144,000 are a com-
posite of 12 tribes, and he then names the tribes. From a symbolic
interpretation of the numbers, we see that 12 is the number of
government—12 patriarchs/12 apostles, and 12 times 12 would be
144, or the number for godly government in the earth. The number
144 is followed by three zeroes. The word from which we derive our
word zero is "zera," which means seed. The seed of Abraham, on
whose shoulders the government is placed, is Jesus Christ. Three is
God's number for completion or fullness. Knowing these symbol-
isms, we can see that 144,000 is the fullness of the seed of Abraham,
seated in godly government in the earth. In other words, the ones
who are ruling and reigning with the Lord Jesus Christ are the
overcomers.

As if that explanation isn't enough, we will now see the same
thing from the meanings of the names given in verses 5–8. The
first thing to note is that these names of the tribes are not listed
here in birth order. Next, notice that the name of the tribe of Dan
is not listed at all. First, we look at the names and their individual meanings, and then put them in order as they are listed here in
Revelation. Judah means "praise;" Reuben means "behold, a son;"
Gad means "army;" Aser means "blessing;" Napthali means "wrestling;" Manasseh means "forgetting;" Simeon means "obedience;"
Levi means "unity or united;" Issachar means "reward;" Zebulon
means "Dwelling place or habitation;" Joseph represents Christ; and
Benjamin is "son of my right hand."

By putting them together in the order they are named, this is
the picture that results: "His praise in the earth, revealing His Son,
becoming a mighty army gathered together and being a blessing to
creation. Their lives came through wrestling, overcoming carnality

and the flesh, forgetting those things that are behind and stretching forward in obedience to the Holy Spirit. They united together in one accord to receive the greatest reward, and that was becoming a dwelling place and habitation for Christ, the many-membered church that is the right hand of God in the earth!"

Here then, are the overcomers. The tribe of Dan, which means "judge," is not mentioned because this entire group, the overcomers, collectively become the judge. After describing the overcomers, Revelation 7:9 goes on with a picture of the throne room in Heaven: "After this I beheld, and, lo, a great multitude, which no man could number, of all nations, and kindreds, and people, and tongues, stood before the throne, and before the Lamb, clothed with white robes, and palms in their hands."

Here before the throne is a great multitude of people that no man can number. Even though 144,000 is a symbolic number, not a literal one, it is a number nonetheless. But this crowd can't be numbered, which would indicate its magnitude.

AND ONE OF THE ELDERS ANSWERED, SAYING UNTO ME, WHAT ARE THESE WHICH ARE ARRAYED IN WHITE ROBES? AND WHENCE CAME THEY? AND I SAID UNTO HIM, SIR, YOU KNOW. AND HE SAID TO ME, THESE ARE THEY WHICH CAME OUT OF GREAT TRIBULATION, AND HAVE WASHED THEIR ROBES, AND MADE THEM WHITE IN THE BLOOD OF THE LAMB. THEREFORE ARE THEY BEFORE THE THRONE OF GOD, AND SERVE HIM DAY AND NIGHT IN HIS TEMPLE: AND HE THAT SITS ON THE THRONE SHALL DWELL AMONG THEM. THEY SHALL HUNGER NO MORE, NEITHER THIRST ANY MORE; NEITHER SHALL THE SUN LIGHT ON THEM, NOR ANY HEAT. FOR THE LAMB WHICH IS IN THE MIDST OF THE THRONE SHALL FEED THEM, AND SHALL LEAD THEM UNTO LIVING FOUNTAINS OF WATERS: AND GOD SHALL WIPE AWAY ALL TEARS FROM THEIR EYES. (REVELATION 7:13–17)

This great crowd of people all have their white robes, symbolizing they are now righteous through the blood of the Lamb. They have their palm fronds, which are a symbol of victory. They made it into heaven, but they are crying! You have to ask yourself, "Why are they crying?" If their tears were tears of joy, God wouldn't wipe them away. It has to be because they are before the throne, and they see— seated in the throne, in the place of authority, ruling and reigning with Jesus is another people group. Their tears are tears of regret for how they lived their lives, and the missed opportunities they were presented to show God's love. This multitude before the throne of God made it into heaven, but they missed their greatest reward!

Getting this one revelation will change the way you live your life. Now you won't be trying to perform for God out of fear of losing your salvation. Now you'll be producing all those good works from a true and deep love for God and a zeal to receive everything God has for you. This truth helps develop desire to sit with Jesus in His throne and rule and reign with Him forever, to know that special relationship of intimacy and purity and power. We don't get there until we realize the third piece of the overcoming puzzle, which is "loving not our lives unto the death." We give up our mind for the mind of Christ, our emotions for the emotions of God, our will for the will of the Father, and our desires for what He desires us to have.

Thank You, Father God, for this awesome truth. Settle it in my heart that once I received Jesus Christ as my Lord and Savior, I am saved. I don't want to miss the day of my visitation or miss my reward by focusing on myself; and so I pledge to You now that I will stop listening to the lies of the enemy that I'm going to hell or that I can mess up and lose my salvation. I will not give it up! Help me to recognize the lies, Lord, and to stop allowing the enemy to draw me off course and into performance-based relationship with You. I don't want to mix law and grace, Father, or slide down the slippery slope of "doing" for You rather than being who

You called me to be. Let all my good works be done out of faith, birthed from a pure heart of love for You and others, Lord, and not done out of obligation or fear or guilt or hope of recognition or reward from others. You've given me a choice, Lord, and I choose You. I choose life in You, Christ Jesus. I need Your mind, Your will, Your emotions, and Your desires and not my own. Jesus, You said, "Let not your heart be troubled. Neither let it be afraid." It's my choice, and so I choose to die to myself daily. Resurrect me in newness of life every day, God, that I may be the overcomer You have called me to be. Amen.

Chapter Five

Why God Loves Me

KNOWING WE BELONG TO GOD AND ARE HIS precious possession is amazing. Having the choice to be a child of the One who is King over all things is awesome. Being called sacred and considered pure, blameless, and consecrated is remarkable. Discovering that there are rewards waiting for us in heaven is wonderful. All these truths are astonishingly great, so why do we still doubt the truth of God's unending and unconditional love? Perhaps because we continue to judge ourselves and can't truly understand why God should, would, or even could, love us!

These words will change your life, if you receive their truth, because we are now going to answer the "why" in the question, "Why does God love me?" What you are going to read now is a part of my own journey—the message that began the turn-around in my own life from being a person of outward bravado and inner fear to one with the inner strength and outward confidence that result from a complete trust in God. It will give you a fresh perspective—a view from God's eyes—about who you are. There is an identity crisis in the church today, and it's been there for a long time. God's people just don't realize who we truly are, why we were created, and the delightful destiny we face.

If you have struggled with receiving the love of God, or the truth that GOD IS LOVE, then this was written for you. If you have struggled with your own sense of worthiness, if you have listened to the lies of hell that you are a failure, and if your life seems to reinforce those lies, then this was written for you. If you have wondered why Jesus just won't leave you alone, and through the Holy Spirit keeps on pointing out things in your life that need adjustment, then this was written for you.

When the Lord quickened this word in me once more, I let it simmer for a while, thinking that by this point in the book, you, Dear Reader, must be somewhat tired of yet another chapter about your identity. Sometimes in ministry, the truths we work to instill just don't seem to "stick" with people. It's like we all hear truth—GOD LOVES ME! —and somehow can't believe it. We hear truth—I AM WONDERFUL! —and then deny it. We seem to easily fall into self-deprecation and self-abasement, and into warped perceptions of God.

Here is what most of us believe, on some level: God loves others but not me. God created others special and talented, but not me. God has a plan for others, but not for me. God wants and accepts others, but not me. That's a lot of wrong belief to overcome, but God reminded me of a truth I heard years ago which actually penetrated my spirit and began to expand inside me. I am passing it on to you, and I believe that this seed which is being planted in your hearts will germinate and begin to grow and flourish. It will take you into an amazing, confident life of abundant joy and peace. You will gain a blessed assurance that you didn't have—about yourself, about God our Father, and about Jesus Christ our Lord.

We're going to look at yet another picture of our true identity, this time from the perspective of eternal love. In order to do that, we need to lay a foundation. As they are presented, take time to meditate on these Scripture passages, since you may need to do that to really "get it." As previously stated, this is truth that will begin to expand in you and change you, and it will be a continuing and continual process of growth. I know that is true because it's still changing me. I'm not the same person I was ten years ago, or five years ago, or even last year; and I'm not yet the person I am destined to become. Every day is a day when this truth gets bigger in me, and it's amazing.

As you read, allow God to take you to a place from which you can never again go back into the old lies of worthlessness and failure that have led you in life for so long. Begin to absorb what you read, and carefully consider its truth. Position yourself and allow the Lord to prepare your heart to receive. "LORD, you have heard the desire of the humble: you will prepare their heart, you will cause your ear to hear" (Psalm 10:17).

We are first going to establish the truth about the eternal love affair between the Father and the Son, God Almighty, and Jesus the Christ. It's very important to understand this foundational truth: that from eternity past, for all time, and for all time before time God the Father has been passionately in love with God the Son. And from eternity past, forever and ever and ever, God the Son has been passionately in love with God the Father. This relationship existed before we ever were created. This is a pure love, undefiled, complete, never-ending, deeper than anything we can imagine, and absolutely true. It's a perfect love, a passionate love. God is a three-fold being; that's part of the mystery of God, and within the Godhead, we find God the Father, God the Son, and God the Holy Spirit. God the Father and God the Son have had a passionate love relationship, facilitated by the Holy Spirit, who holds them in this constant state of love. In the book of John, Jesus is speaking to His Father when He says this:

> FATHER, I WILL THAT THEY ALSO, WHOM YOU HAVE GIVEN ME,
> BE WITH ME WHERE I AM; THAT THEY MAY BEHOLD MY GLO-
> RY, WHICH YOU HAVE GIVEN ME: FOR YOU LOVED ME BEFORE
> THE FOUNDATION OF THE WORLD. (JOHN 17:24)

In this one verse, Jesus alludes to an eternal love. "You loved me! You gave me glory! From before the foundation of the world, You loved me! I want my disciples to see it!" There are other verses which give us insights into what was going on before the world ever was.

> AND NOW, O FATHER, GLORIFY YOU ME WITH YOUR OWN
> SELF WITH THE GLORY WHICH I HAD WITH YOU BEFORE THE
> WORLD WAS. (JOHN 17:5)

Jesus is sharing about this love—a perfect love, a pure love, exchanged within the Godhead, a love that is vibrant and constantly expanding. A love of glory and honor. There is another verse in John that makes it very plain.

> THE FATHER LOVES THE SON, AND HAS GIVEN ALL THINGS
> INTO HIS HAND. (JOHN 3:35)

It is established in the Scripture that the Father loves the Son, and He's been doing it since before the world was. "For the Father loves the Son, and shows him all things that (he) himself does: and he will show him greater works than these, that you may marvel" (John 5:20). This is another Scripture which gives us more undeniable evidence of this point, that the Father loves the Son. Jesus is speaking here to His disciples, just like He is speaking to you today as His disciples. Jesus says, "This is important! I want you to know this … my Father loves me."

The Father loves the Son and shows Him everything. He holds nothing back. That's the kind of love it is. It is pure and completely trusting, open. He shows Him everything and will even show Him more—and here's the reason for it—that you might marvel. Marvel at what? At this perfect love relationship that's going on between the Father and the Son and has been going on forever and ever and ever. God wants people, especially His disciples, to know about this kind of love, a love that is unspotted, passionate, and perfect in every way. Understanding this perfect love between the Father and the Son is a huge piece in our Christianity, and you'll see why as we go along. It's plain that the Father loves the Son and it's been going on forever. Now let's look at how the Son loves the Father.

YOU HAVE HEARD HOW I SAID UNTO YOU, I GO AWAY, AND
COME AGAIN UNTO YOU. IF YOU LOVED ME, YOU WOULD RE-
JOICE, BECAUSE I SAID, I GO TO THE FATHER: FOR MY FATHER
IS GREATER THAN I. AND NOW I HAVE TOLD YOU BEFORE IT
COME TO PASS, THAT, WHEN IT IS COME TO PASS, YOU MIGHT
BELIEVE. HEREAFTER, I WILL NOT TALK MUCH WITH YOU: FOR
THE PRINCE OF THIS WORLD COMES, AND HAS NOTHING IN
ME. BUT THAT THE WORLD MAY KNOW THAT I LOVE THE
FATHER; AND AS THE FATHER GAVE ME COMMANDMENT,
EVEN SO I DO. ARISE, LET US GO HENCE. (JOHN 14:28-31)

Here, Jesus is saying, "I want the world to know that I love the
Father." The context is, "I'm getting ready to go away"—boil that
down—"I'm getting ready to hang on a cross, make the ultimate
sacrifice, endure that which nobody has ever endured by taking on
the sins of the whole world, as well as all the illnesses, infirmities,
infections, injuries, you name it." We have no idea what it would be
like to bear what Jesus bore. Jesus said, "You should be happy for me,
because I go to the Father."

He essentially said, "I'm going to the cross to die for the sins
of the people not just because I love them, but because I love the
Father. And I want you to know how much I love the Father." Praise
God! We know that the Father passionately loves the Son, and we
also know the Son passionately loves the Father. We know that
because, first of all, He was willing to come here—that was His love
for the Father—and to die to fulfill what was in the Father's heart:
"For God so loved the world that He gave his only begotten Son"
(John 3:16a).

I CAN OF MY OWN SELF DO NOTHING: AS I HEAR, I JUDGE:
AND MY JUDGMENT IS JUST; BECAUSE I SEEK NOT MY OWN
WILL, BUT THE WILL OF THE FATHER WHICH HAS SENT ME.
(JOHN 5:30)

It was all about a love exchange between the Father and the Son.
They were passionately and forever in love with each other. If you

ever want a model of what true love looks like, you get it by looking at the love relationship between the Father and the Son. That's what real love looks like. As you ponder this particular truth, you will begin to see it everywhere—the Scripture will explode with love, and your understanding of it will expand.

"I'm here," Jesus said, "not to do my own thing, but to do the will of my Father." Jesus' obedience was an expression of His love. Don't you think our obedience should be an expression of our love, and not our fear? That we obey not because of some heavy religious thing hung on us, or out of worry that we're going to hell if we don't? The strength of our relationship with the Lord is that out of love, we obey. Obedience from a pure heart shows our earnest desire to please God because of our love for Him. John 18:11 is another witness to this truth. You'll find many as you search this out in the days and months and even years to come, because as we already said, this word will change you. Maybe that seems presumptuous; but we believe in our hearts that you are going to feel the Holy Spirit come down and work this truth of God's love into your heart and take you to a place you've never been—and you're not going back to your old worries and doubts.

Even on the night He was betrayed, Jesus was focused on His Father and the love He had for His Father. This shared love was a constant strength to Him. "Then said Jesus unto Peter, Put up your sword into the sheath: the cup which my father has given me, shall I not drink it?" (John 18:11)

"Should I not drink what He's given me? I love Him!"

The Bible says that for the joy that was set before Him, Jesus endured the cross. We say that the joy set before Jesus was us, fully restored and free in Him. Yes, that is true; but there is a bigger truth than that! It was for the Father that He endured. In another place, Jesus said, "Don't you know I can ask and my Father will send more than twelve legions of angels?" Jesus knew His Father loved Him so much that He would rescue Him; but He didn't want to be rescued, because He loved His Father so much, too!

It's plain; the Father and the Son are passionately in love. It's a pure love, a passionate love, a love without fault, without blemish, without spot. There is nothing this love won't do, one for the other. It's totally complete in every way; and it is here that we begin to see that we have come into the picture. It's interesting to consider that God the Father has given something to the Son, and that something is us.

THAT THE SAYING MIGHT BE FULFILLED WHICH HE SPOKE, OF THEM WHICH YOU GAVE ME, I HAVE LOST NONE. (JOHN 18:9)

Now the Father, who's in love with the Son, gave us to Him. We just read it. Let's further establish this idea that the Father has given something to the Son, and it's us.

I PRAY FOR THEM: I PRAY NOT FOR THE WORLD, BUT FOR THEM WHICH YOU HAVE GIVEN ME; FOR THEY ARE YOURS. (JOHN 17:9)

We've been given to Jesus, but we belong to the Father. Consider: the Father and the Son have had this passionate love relationship for all eternity, and out of that love relationship, we were created to be a gift—from God, to God—a gift, an expression of their love. This gets right up in the face of the voices that tell us we're worthless and have no purpose. God created us out of this eternal love relationship to give to each other. Each one of us is an expression of their love for each other. We are each a gift from One to the Other. You're a gift from Almighty God! Let that sink in—we're talking about God now! God Almighty, Creator of the universe and everything in it, created you to be a gift.

God the Father wanted to choose a gift for His Son, and He picked YOU!

That will put value back into your life. It means YOU ARE WORTH SOMETHING! If you're in love with somebody, and you want to give them something to express your love, you're not going to give them something cheap, something messed up or worthless. You're going to give the person that you love something meaningful, something valuable, to express your love. That is who you and I are—we are God's gift—from God, to God. Just like the gifts you give at Christmas time, they have little tags on them— from Mom to Mary, from Joe to Jill. You might as well put one on your forehead right now—From God To God. Hallelujah! That should give you a new perspective of yourself, and remove any negative, self-abasing thoughts. Praise the Lord! God is right now lifting us up. All those voices from hell that want to trash us are fading out, all that religious "I'm-just-a-no-good-sinner-saved-by-grace" stuff. NO! You are a gift—from God to God. That passionate love which He's held since eternity past is the same passionate love with which He created each of us to be a precious gift in His hand.

We know by the Scriptures that the Father loves the Son, and gave Him a gift. That gift is all of us. We also know that the Son loves the Father, and gives us back to Him, as shown in the book of Revelation.

> AND THEY SUNG A NEW SONG, SAYING, YOU ARE WORTHY TO TAKE THE BOOK, AND TO OPEN THE SEALS THEREOF: FOR YOU WERE SLAIN, AND HAVE REDEEMED US TO GOD BY YOUR BLOOD OUT OF EVERY KINDRED, AND TONGUE, AND NATION. (REVELATION 5:9)

Jesus paid for our redemption with His pure, precious blood, and will give us back to the Father—we have been caught up into this great love relationship! When you start to see yourself in this way, the old ways of thinking of yourself as less than the best begin to change. The bondages of fear, self-rejection, self-accusation, self-hatred, guilt, and shame will start falling off you. For the ages to come, we are to be God's expression of love that <u>never fails</u> because He takes us into His perfect love, which never fails. We're drawn up into it—God takes us up into the middle of who He is! At the end of the age, when death is finally slain (we encourage you to read 1 Corinthians 15), Jesus is going to deliver the kingdom to the Father. He'll say, "Of all You've given me, I've lost nothing. I'm giving them back to You; and I'm giving them back clean, washed, redeemed, perfect in every way." We become a gift that is without blemish and will never come up short again because the love of God has perfected us.

> YOU ARE WORTHY, O LORD, TO RECEIVE GLORY AND HONOR AND POWER: FOR YOU HAVE CREATED ALL THINGS, AND FOR YOUR PLEASURE THEY ARE AND WERE CREATED.
> (REVELATION 4:11)

We were created for the pleasure of God. Now when we understand that the very purpose we were created is for this great love exchange, something shifts in our lives. We begin to realize that our destiny is far greater than we've understood. We can now see why Jesus is so interested in us, why He broods over our lives. It's because we're a gift from the Father; and if you love the one who gave the gift, you love the gift.

My first grandchild is very, very dear to me. She gave me a painting she did when she was about seven or eight years old. I framed it and have it hanging in my house. I would never part with it, or damage it, or stick it away out of sight to be neglected or forgotten. I've had that picture for over twenty-five years. This young woman remains very, very dear to me, although she believes some things I don't believe, and has accepted a lifestyle I can't accept. I can't embrace her beliefs, yet I haven't thrown out the gift she gave me. No matter how I feel about what she does or believes, my love for her has not diminished. Just as I keep and care for the gift she gave me, God keeps and cares for her. He will never neglect or throw out the gift He created her to be.

The Lord is the same with each of us. We all have things in our lives—ways or thoughts or even beliefs—that do not please Him, yet we remain His treasured gift. The gift from the one you love is precious. You esteem it, and you protect it, because the one whom you loved before you got the gift gave it to you. Jesus is caring for us. He esteems us and protects us as the gift He received from His loving Father. The first love of Jesus is the Father, and now, we've been brought into that love because we were given as a gift to Jesus. The love which begins in God extends outward, and His very nature makes Him share this love.

When we understand we are gifts from God to God, it helps us understand why we are so often "handled" by Jesus, and why the Holy Spirit so often convicts us of our ungodly actions and attitudes. They just simply won't leave us alone. We think, "Give me a break, Lord! Why do You always have to work at polishing me up? Go work on somebody else for a change."

Jesus would answer, "Because you're my gift, and I love you. Because when we stand together, you by my side as my bride, all that was ever meant to be in this gift that you are will be seen and realized and honored."

That is why He is sanctifying His church (please read Ephesians, chapter 5). Jesus is making ready His bride. He's so passionate, so longing to stand before His Father with a perfected bride by His side, a bride without spot and without blemish. Jesus is longing to present His church, the gift from His Father, as a glorious completion of Himself. That's why we are so passionately pursued by

Jesus—because before we were ever here, Father and Son were passionately in love, and now we've been included in that passion. Don't be offended by it, be honored in it! Jesus treasures the gift He's been given. He treasures you, He loves you, He adores you, if you can hear it. Many of us can't hear it because we've been so trodden under. But I'm writing this to tell you today, "You are the gift of God." Open your heart to hear, to receive, and to believe these words.

This understanding breaks off fear from our lives. Fear of ever being rejected or abandoned. Consider: The Father whom Jesus passionately loves, gives Him a gift. That gift is you and me. Why would He ever reject, abandon, or neglect the gift of the Father? This understanding eliminates fear of abandonment. Why would He ever abandon you? He sees the value, the expression of the Father's love for Him. This truth rids us of fear of failure. Why would He let you fail, when His desire is to perfect You as His gift back to the Father? Jesus is able to keep us from falling. He is able to hold us up when we need it, which happens to be every day and in every way.

Now, we know that between the Father and the Son is a passionate love. We know that we were created for their pleasure and to be an expression of that love, which is faultless and blameless. Once we recognize this, it becomes the centerpiece of everything in life. It was going on before anything else, so it takes priority, it has more weight. But now that we're here, we can see it in an even bigger picture. Let me say again that in the days and weeks to come, this seed of truth is going to grow in you and you will begin to see yourself the way God sees you. Because of that, you will begin to walk out of every lesser thing. Glory to God! Here is a glimpse of the bigger picture in which we can see this amazing truth of God's love, and our part in it.

BEHOLD, WHAT MANNER OF LOVE THE FATHER HAS BESTOWED
UPON US, THAT WE SHOULD BE CALLED THE SONS OF GOD:
THEREFORE THE WORLD KNOWS US NOT, BECAUSE IT KNEW

> HIM NOT. BELOVED, NOW WE ARE THE SONS OF GOD, AND
> IT DOES NOT YET APPEAR WHAT WE SHALL BE: BUT WE KNOW
> THAT, WHEN HE SHALL APPEAR, WE SHALL BE LIKE HIM; FOR
> WE SHALL SEE HIM AS HE IS. AND EVERY MAN THAT HAS THIS
> HOPE IN HIM PURIFIES HIMSELF, EVEN AS HE IS PURE.
> (1 JOHN 3:1–3)

When we realize that the Father loves us—that we're being included in this eternal love relationship, it's overwhelming! John, the disciple who more than any other had the revelation of God's love, is overwhelmed at this truth. You may be experiencing that same feeling right now. Any of us who realizes this love, purifies himself because we see something greater than ourselves. The call of God is greater than any other, and we are broken free of the shackles of "self." We come out of ungodly stuff because of a compelling desire to be just like Him. Behold! What manner of love!

We can't begin to understand that love until we understand the amazing love relationship between the Father and the Son. It's perfect, it's pure, it's awesome, and they want the whole world to know and to see it! Then suddenly, Jesus says—"Now, I LOVE YOU!" Me? Enter into that kind of love? That kind of passion? YES! Any man that wants it, let him walk out of every other lesser thing.

> AS THE FATHER HAS LOVED ME, SO HAVE I LOVED YOU: CON-
> TINUE YOU IN MY LOVE. (JOHN 15:9)

It all begins with our realizing the passion between the Father and the Son; then we see "behold what manner of the love the FATHER has given to us" and now Jesus is saying, "the same way the Father loves me, I LOVE YOU!" The same exact thing the Father showed Jesus, Jesus is now showing us—love without fault, without blemish, perfect in all its ways. Perfect. Oh, listen to the voice of the Bridegroom in your heart—you are loved by God the Father, and God the Son, and God the Holy Spirit, who is the great facilitator and comes to open up these truths to us. To bring us into them forever and ever and ever. He will guide and lead us into these truths for us to enjoy. The abundant life spoken of in Scripture comes out of this truth: that the Father and the Son love each other and now that love is being pointed at you, and you are being beckoned into it.

What's really wonderful is that we now have opportunity to respond. It's part of the mystery that all persons in the Godhead are equal. Yet, within the Godhead, it was necessary that one be greater for love to exist. Jesus said, "My Father is greater than I." Love has to come from the greater to the lesser—He loves me, and now I, in response, love Him. The same thing is true about us now. He has now initiated love toward us, so that we may respond in love to Him. The book of Revelation tells us the elders fall down before Him and cast their crowns to Him. This gesture of honor and gratitude represents all our accomplishments, all our struggles, all the things we're believing for and hoping for and holding on to Him for—all those things become the expression of love we give back to Him in worship. If you're in love with somebody, you're always looking for something to give them, some way to bless them. In like fashion, God is giving us opportunity. What does that opportunity look like?

> LIFT UP YOUR EYES ROUND ABOUT, AND BEHOLD: ALL THESE GATHER THEMSELVES TOGETHER, AND COME TO YOU. AS I LIVE, SAYS THE LORD, YOU SHALL SURELY CLOTHE YOU WITH THEM ALL, AS WITH AN ORNAMENT, AND BIND THEM ON YOU, AS A BRIDE DOES. (ISAIAH 49:18)

God is talking to the bride here. He says people are coming to you—why? Because the love and the favor and the honor of God is going to be all over us. That's why people flocked to Jesus—He didn't hand out flyers or design a website—He was just in love with the Father. And out of that eternal love, such grace was on His lips, and such compassion in His life, that people were compelled to be with Him. They were drawn to Him. The same thing is going to be true of people who deeply, truly, completely, and forever love God.

There's something about the anointing of God that draws people. People will be gathered together around us; and as Isaiah prophesied, they will become like an ornament upon you. As a bride adorns herself, so shall you adorn yourself with them. Here's the idea—at the end of the age, when all is said and done, as Jesus is able to present us to the Father, we're going to be able to present those whose lives we've touched. We'll be wearing them as part of our crown. Now, we know they belong to God, as Jesus said—those whom You've given me are Yours—but God is entrusting people into our lives. Just as Jesus is zealous over us, we should be zealous (not jealous) over those in our care. We are zealous over the gifts God has brought to us, the lives He has entrusted into ours. Our families and friends are gifts, from God to us! At the end, we're going to be clothed with the souls of people whose lives we touched in meaningful ways that enrich them. That is truly the most beautiful thing we can wear, because that's the thing God cares most about. But it won't matter to us that we have the most beautiful garment of all—all that will matter is our love for God.

Let us never forget that the very love that God the Father and God the Son are enjoying, and have enjoyed forever past and into forever future, they have now extended to you and me. In the exact same way that the Father loves the Son, they both love you. May grace and mercy and peace be to you in the revelation that both God the Father and God the Son want you to have them; and the Holy Spirit is in you to facilitate their abundant blessings of love in your life.

Father God, thank You so much for this new perspective about myself, and about You. Thank You for showing me so clearly that I am a gift, an extension of who You are, an expression of Your love; and that I have been given into the hand of Jesus Christ, and He loves me, too! Help me grow in this understanding of Your great love for each other, and how I have been brought into that love. Show me daily how I can bring others into Your love as well. Forgive me, Lord, for doubting Your love for me. Now that I have this truth, I can never go back into doubting myself or doubting You and Your love. Forgive me for listening to and living in the lies of hell that I am a failure, not good enough, without purpose. I now know that I am a gift, precious and treasured. I am created for Your pleasure, with purpose and destiny that far exceed anything I've ever hoped for or imagined. Forgive me, Lord Jesus, for accepting You as Savior but not as Lord, for not wanting to listen to You or follow You as You polish and perfect me so that I can be presented back to our Father in glorious completion. Grow this seed of truth in me, Father. Take me into a place in the spirit where it can be watered and fed—and keep me there—so that it will flourish into the abundant life You mean for me to have. I declare that the pure, precious blood of Jesus Christ of Nazareth is all powerful and effective to see this pledge fulfilled in me. AMEN.

Section Two

AGAIN HE MEASURED
A THOUSAND,
AND BROUGHT ME
THROUGH THE WATERS;
THE WATERS
WERE TO THE KNEES.
(EZEKIEL 47:4A)

Chapter Six

Shame and Guilt

THE ENEMY OF OUR SOULS, THE ENEMY OF God and all things good—Satan himself—has unleashed a cadre of lies designed to keep us from believing the truths you have read here. This anti-Christ, former worship leader, and archangel of God, busily assigns his demonic host, those members of the body of sin, to plant lies in our hearts as children. No one is immune to his devious ways, and actually many of us are more open than we know due to our ancestry or early environments. Satan's most potent weapons to control mankind include the lies of shame. Shame is perhaps the greatest identity thief on the planet.

In this chapter, we want to reveal the way hell has used shame to hinder and limit us in practically every area of our lives, on some level. We want to expose shame for the lie that it is, bringing it into the light of the truth of God, so that every vestige of shame can be forever removed from our hearts and lives. Our identity, our true identity, not who we think we are, but who God created us to be, has been affected by shame to a greater or lesser degree for all our lives, and it's time to let go of shame and embrace the glory of God. In many ways, we have agreed with the enemy of our souls, and the Lord makes an appeal to us to STOP!

> O YOU SONS OF MEN, HOW LONG WILL YOU TURN MY GLORY
> INTO SHAME? HOW LONG WILL YOU LOVE VANITY, AND SEEK
> AFTER LEASING? SELAH. (PSALM 4:2)

God points out here that we who are created and meant to be God's glory in the earth have agreed with hell and allowed the glory of God to be smothered by shame, because we love and follow worthless opinions (vanity) and seek out the lies (leasing) of the world. He shows us that we have a choice to give up our agreement with hell, turn our love back toward Him and reject the lie of the devil. "How long are you going to allow this to go on?" asks the Lord. "Are you going to continue to believe worthless opinions and lap up lies?"

Unfortunately, without an understanding of who the thief is and how the thief operates, we will do exactly that! Until you gain, accept, and apply the knowledge you are about to get, you're going to be stuck in an endless cycle of allowing the spirit of the world and the lies of hell to define you. Hope is in your hands right now. In this book, you are holding truth that will set you on your way to recognizing and overcoming the lies you received as children, lies you have believed and have been living. Once you make the decision to accept and apply the truth of your identity and release all false identity back to hell, you can then become the shining expression of God's glory which you were created to be.

What you are about to learn will bring about the deep healing that we all must experience to become the complete overcomers God created us to be. Let's first get an understanding of what shame is and what it isn't, and how shame controls us to some degree. As we go on, we will see God's answer of healing from shame more thoroughly and gain deeper revelation of who we are.

For an initial and clearer understanding, let's define shame. Shame is not guilt, although many people, both within the church and outside the church, combine the two, or use these words interchangeably. Shame is not guilt. Guilt is the feeling we have when we know we've done something wrong. We feel guilty. Shame brings condemnation. Guilt brings conviction. Feeling guilty should bring Holy Spirit conviction into our hearts and turn us to God in repentance. Unfortunately, this turning to God doesn't always happen, and shame is often the reason it doesn't. Shame doesn't want us or our sin to be "exposed."

While guilt is what we feel when we've done something wrong, shame is a feeling of BEING something wrong.

It's an inner feeling that "there's something wrong with me." Not, "I did something wrong," but rather, "I am something wrong."

Hell isn't fair. At some time in our childhood, maybe even in the womb, we were shamed. Reproach and disgrace were brought into our spirits through some lie from hell against which we had no defense of truth. Then, by the time we were exposed to truth, the lie was so entrenched that many of us had become one with it. No one told us shame is not a part of us, that it isn't a "normal emotion" or a way of life. We weren't taught how to recognize or how to separate ourselves from shame. On the contrary, the church told us Jesus was shamed, and we would suffer shame, too, because it makes us good Christians.

Satan joined the church in the first century, bringing the religious, self-righteous, judgmental spirit of the Pharisees to sit right alongside us in the pews and speak from the pulpit to keep us in bondage to shame. Many times, leaders in the body of Christ have been used by the devil (without their full knowledge) to cause you to feel that you are a lesser being, or that there is something wrong with you. You may have been verbally abused and belittled; you may have been shunned and humiliated or otherwise made to suffer spiritual abuse. Right now, I appeal to you to forgive every religious person who shamed you in any way, and to release them into the hand of God. I ask that you forgive them and release them now so that the shame they brought into your life can be rooted out and burned in the consuming fire of the Living God!

The church is just one of many places where shame is alive and well. Our families are another, and perhaps our workplaces or social circles as well. It just seems impossible to get away from shame. That's because the shame is in us, and wherever we go, it comes along. As you gain understanding, you will begin to recognize different sources of shame, dig them up and remove them from your heart through repentance and forgiveness. In practically all our lives, we've seen and/or experienced shame in the church, shame in the family, shame in the culture and in the generations, and all kinds of situations, circumstances, and people who were used by this thief.

Remember, guilt is a feeling of "I made a mistake. I messed up," while shame is a feeling of "I am a mistake. I'm a messed-up mess-up." This thinking puts us into a self-focused mindset that magnifies everything about us through a warped looking glass and twists our thinking. If any behavior or appearance on our part seems inappropriate, wrong, or embarrassing, then the thought patterns flow immediately into a river of shame: "There's something wrong with me and everybody knows it." "I deserve this (whatever bad thing might be happening) because I am so bad." "I'm not good enough." "I am not worthy." Shame makes us unable to receive compliments or love or acceptance.

Here's a good definition of shame: a disturbed or painful feeling of blameworthiness, incompetence, or indecency.

Once shame is established in us, it becomes strengthened by guilt. When we actually mess up and do something wrong, we feel guilty about it and shame takes occasion of guilt to reinforce its control of the lie from hell, which has three primary categories:

1. The lie that we are worthy of punishment (this lie keeps us from repenting).
2. The lie that we are incompetent and inadequate (this lie keeps us from receiving compliments, acceptance, and love).

3. The lie that we are indecent and disgraceful (this lie keeps us from receiving the love of God and people and turns us into bitter balls of self-hatred and rejection).

Shame is a lie which is based on a lie that we believe about ourselves or God and which settles into our spirits. Then the devil works to create situations and circumstances in our lives to reinforce the lie he has planted. When we merge the lie we believe with the experience we have in the world, we can become unwilling to believe God's Word and what He says about us and others. Shame causes us to reject God's love and forgiveness, based on feelings of personal unworthiness. People who say "I can't forgive myself," or "It's hard for me to forgive myself," are usually shame-based individuals. If that's you, do not allow the feeling of shame to take you further into the pit of self-pity and self-abasement, now feeling ashamed that you feel ashamed! Rejoice that you are at last discovering truth that makes you free and that one of your most deeply entrenched root-issues is about to be uprooted!

Shame prevents us from being vulnerable, because it tells us we can't appear weak. We need to realize that without vulnerability, we can't be healed. In this way, shame prevents our healing, especially emotional healing. We believe on some level that we are not worth anything, that no one wants or loves us, that we have no purpose, that we should never have been born, and so forth. Allow me to share a vision and revelation God gave me one day about vulnerability.

I was deep in worship one morning, and I had my hands sort of cupped together, and was lifting myself, and my life, to the Lord. As I lifted my hands, I saw myself standing in His hands, and I began to shrink. I got smaller and smaller and smaller until I slipped down between His hands, and then I was scrambling back up to stand in one of His massive hands. As I continued to shrink, I became so tiny that I disappeared into a pore of His skin! I was completely consumed. There was no more me, only Him.

It was at that point that I heard the Lord say to me, "There is a tender vulnerability in love." I questioned Him in my mind, as if to say, "Please explain, I need to understand what You are telling me." He then gave me a vision. I clearly saw God the Father, Creator of the universe and all things in it, pouring Himself into the womb of the young virgin, Mary, and I realized that of all created beings, the most vulnerable of them all is a human baby in the womb.

Anything could have happened! Abortion didn't start with us, you know. Mary could have decided, "This is too tough. I can't have this baby. Everyone is going to judge me." Joseph could have decided not to listen to the angel or to heed the dream from God. He could have put Mary away, or even had her stoned! Even after a child is born, that baby cannot survive without help. Many creatures in the wild are born, get up, and walk away. Even turtles break through their shells and head for the sea. But a human baby has to be nurtured, cared for, and protected.

Then, as a child grows, he has to be taught. Think of it. Even Jesus Christ had to grow up. He had to learn who He is, just as we must learn who we are. When Jesus stayed behind after His parents left Jerusalem, He was busy learning about Himself. "And it came to pass, that after three days they found him in the temple, sitting in the midst of the doctors, both hearing them, and asking them questions" (Luke 2:46). The Word tells us Jesus did not come into the world having all wisdom. If that were the case, He wouldn't have had to learn anything! As Jesus grew up, He gained more and more wisdom, and even more favor with God.

AND JESUS INCREASED IN WISDOM AND STATURE, AND IN FAVOR WITH GOD AND MAN. (LUKE 2:52)

All this was brought into my mind during this amazing time of worship to the Lord, and I realized that the pattern of Jesus' life didn't start with His ministry; it started in the womb of Mary. It started with vulnerability! God Almighty, Creator of the universe and all things in it, made Himself vulnerable to His own creation. That is our pattern for life and living, to know the tender vulnerability in love. No wonder shame works so diligently to hide us, and to hinder us from honest emotions, to cause us to fear "being hurt." Does love hurt? Yes. Is it worth it? Yes.

Shame binds itself to other evil spirits, which many mental health people call "emotional defense mechanisms" or some other such psychological jargon. We all need to realize and admit that demons are demons. If it makes you feel better to call them "hindrances" or "limitations" or "mental problems" or "chemical imbalances" or "influences from hell," then fine. But know that as long as you believe it's just you, that it's just a part of who you are, or you accept it as a mental or physical issue you have to live with, you will not be able to separate yourself from it. When we accept something into our lives, or settle for something that did not come from God, we get to live with that thing. What we believe and speak, we will experience.

I BELIEVED, THEREFORE HAVE I SPOKEN: I WAS GREATLY AFFLICTED. (PSALM 116:10)

Shame and its buddies work in our emotions, which is one reason why people think, "It's just me." God gave us emotions so that we can relate to Him and to each other in godly ways, not so that we would be ruled by them. Emotions are not bad, but unfortunately what we experience as emotions are not emotions at all; they are evil spirits acting out their nasty natures and deceiving us into more shame. When we deny or repress our true emotions, then shame has dominion. Here's what I mean: let's say that as a child, you had a special doll, or a toy fire truck, or something that really meant a lot to you. In the overall scheme of things, it wasn't worth much, but to you it was a treasure. A neighbor kid, or your big sister or brother took your treasure and destroyed it. How did that make you feel?

You were hurt, angry, disappointed, and brokenhearted. Those are real emotions.

You probably cried and went running to mom; but instead of understanding the pain you were feeling, she shamed you. She may have said something like this: "For goodness sake! It's only a toy, don't be such a crybaby." You were made to feel there was something wrong with you because you hurt inside. When this type of situation comes about, shame enters your spirit and begins to repress godly emotions so that you become unable to grieve when you're in pain over a loss, and you lose touch with yourself and others. Disassociative behaviors begin to pattern themselves in your thinking. The truth is that we should all be able to grieve without feeling ashamed. Shame masks true emotions and makes us try to become what we think other people want or need us to be. We give up our true identity to be molded by the opinions of others rather than by God and His opinion of us. "Big boys don't cry." "If you don't stop crying I'll give you something to cry about."

Shame can also come in and repress good emotions, such as joy in a personal or corporate victory. There may be family members who are negative to the point that you don't even want to share good news with them. One of the biblical examples of shame stealing joy is when the nation of Israel wrought a great victory against her enemies, but King David was in such ungodly grief that the people felt they could not express their jubilation in the victory.

> AND THE VICTORY THAT DAY WAS TURNED INTO MOURNING UNTO ALL THE PEOPLE: FOR THE PEOPLE HEARD SAY THAT DAY HOW THE KING WAS GRIEVED FOR HIS SON. AND THE PEOPLE GOT THEM BY STEALTH THAT DAY INTO THE CITY, AS PEOPLE BEING ASHAMED STEAL AWAY WHEN THEY FLEE IN BATTLE. (2 SAMUEL 19:2–3)

When true emotions are repressed, fear sets in. We become afraid that we won't be able to hold our emotions in and our true feelings will break out. We may fear being out of control, we may fear losing control, we may fear being exposed or vulnerable, and any of that would cause us more shame. This takes us into self-rejection and self-hatred, low or no self-esteem, chronic unhappiness and depression. Perhaps you are beginning to understand what a thief and destroyer you are dealing with in this thing called shame.

Shame causes us to be totally self-focused as we go about our lives trying to hide our shame, so that no one discovers how bad we really are. Some people hide shame behind a prideful or arrogant exterior. This only brings about more shame.

> WHEN PRIDE COMES, THEN COMES SHAME: BUT WITH THE
> LOWLY IS WISDOM. (PROVERBS 11:2)

Some of us hide shame behind independence and self-reliance, making it impossible to ask anyone for help when we need it. Sometimes we can be moving in self-reliance even while we're giving lip service to God. This is really just another face of pride, and it piles on more shame. We should realize that God will often use people to meet our needs. Unfortunately, that can't happen when shame keeps us from letting others know our needs.

> FOR I WAS ASHAMED TO REQUIRE OF THE KING A BAND OF
> SOLDIERS AND HORSEMEN TO HELP US AGAINST THE ENEMY IN
> THE WAY: BECAUSE WE HAD SPOKEN UNTO THE KING, SAYING,
> THE HAND OF OUR GOD IS UPON ALL THEM FOR GOOD THAT
> SEEK HIM; BUT HIS POWER AND HIS WRATH IS AGAINST ALL
> THEM THAT FORSAKE HIM. (EZRA 8:22)

All people have certain common needs, put in us by God. We have a need to be loved unconditionally. We have a need to feel we possess intrinsic value. We have a need to feel a measure of power in our lives. We have a need to be acknowledged or known. We have a need for an avenue by which to be heard, so that we feel important, and a need to feel understood when we express ourselves. We have a need to feel we are protected by someone. The Lord may choose to allow others to meet our needs, but He lets us know in His Word that He is more than able to meet each of those needs Himself. When we become dependent on those around us to meet our needs, it usually leads to disappointment, discouragement, and despair.

Some people wall off their hearts and hide behind "boundaries" created to keep others at a distance. We fear both being touched and feeling other people's pain. We're afraid we'll be "found out" and so remain always focused on ourselves, our problems, our thoughts, our lives, our everything. Let me tell you, it is impossible to see God's plan for your life when you have a self-focused mindset.

In addition to the self-focused mindset that shame instills, there are some emotional indicators that shame has captured our thought life and is controlling us in some way. As long as shame is in place, our healing and deliverance will only be superficial, incomplete, or temporary, because shame is at the root of many of our "issues." Shame can cause automatic, ungodly responses to people and situations. It can also cause you to vacillate between neurotic be-havior and character disorder caused by the functionally automatic responses of being shame-bound. Neurotic behavior exhibits itself in the automatic assumption that we are at fault whenever there's a conflict, and character disorder automatically assumes the conflict is always someone else's fault. There's no balanced ability to assess a situation with an objective eye for true personal accountability. Balance is a key to godly living. Here are a few of those indicators, which are functionally automatic responses of being shame-bound.

Anger is an indicator of shame. We're not talking about normal anger, but anger that expresses itself in violent emotional outbursts and unreasonable overreactions, even bringing on a sort of uncon-trollable rage. Oddly, there seldom seems to be a known or apparent reason for the anger. We explode on people with little or no provo-cation. Anger is more often than not an automatic response when things don't go our way. This is common with shame-bound people because the fear of shame causes us to repress normal anger, and it is always pent up and just under the surface.

Sarcasm is also an indicator of shame. Sarcasm is a destroyer that wounds the spirit. When sarcasm is prevalent in conversations, shame is almost always the motivator behind it. People who continually keep striking back at their families and those they love are tied to shame.

Another prevalent indicator of shame is self-hatred. The forms of self-hatred are many and varied, but a common one is self-rejection. One of the most common expressions of self-rejection is our hating the way we look. "My nose is too big, my eyes are the wrong color, my hair's too curly or too straight, my ears stick out, I'm too fat, I'm too thin, whatever." Self-hatred and rejecting your body can take you into bulimia or anorexia or death wishes or risky behaviors and all sorts of ungodly stuff. The sad part is, changing your looks will not cause you to accept yourself. No change in your appearance, however radical, will make you happy with you.

The next indicator of being shame-bound is a victim mentality. This is "poor me" thinking. "Nobody has it as bad as I do. Nobody understands me. Nobody loves me. Nobody helps me. No one wants to be my friend. I'm always the last one picked for the team," and so on. There are people in our lives, and we all know them, who live in this kind of thinking. If you've been busy inviting people to your pity parties, you need to stop! Nobody wants to come.

You may have heard the expression, "misery loves company," and it is true. Miserable people want to bring others down with them into victim thinking. Victim mentality never sees a way out, doom and gloom prevail, and even when the "victim" is offered a helping hand, they will have a reason why the solution won't work. Is this you? When things go wrong, do you wallow in the failure or mistake? A person with victim mentality usually has an evil eye also, and can only see the negative in everything. "I already tried that. That won't work because...." Victims want you in the pit with them, and victims are bound in shame. Even biblical answers are rejected, and so God can't help, either. Blame shifting is often an outgrowth of the victim mentality in shame-bound individuals. "I'm this way because…."

Warped thinking is another indicator of shame. For example, when rejection comes (and all of us have the opportunity to be rejected every day), twisted thinking exaggerates the rejection to epic proportions. It causes us to believe no one likes us, and can even set up paranoia. Shame-bound people seldom see circumstances clearly, and their warped, twisted thinking is transferred toward God in accusation. "What did I do to deserve this, God?" This person has a warped perception about life and their place in it, a warped view of God, and of themselves.

Shame-bound people also experience a lack of vision. Most people with shame live their lives without much direction. They blame events and people in their past for the lack of progress in their lives. Shame makes us forget the Scriptures that tell us we have a future and that God has plan and purpose for us. It also causes us to be unwilling to remove the distorted glasses that cloud our vision. People who lack vision usually just go through life's motions as they sit around and wait to die.

Hopelessness is another indicator of shame. This usually stems from the belief that we are no longer (or perhaps have never been) useful to God. Shame convinces us that we have sinned too much or too badly to be used, forgiven, or loved by God.

Shame-bound people also often believe they are marked for punishment. God's correction is viewed as punishment rather than guidance toward success, and God is perceived as a punishing God. At the same time, shame-bound people believe they deserve punishment, and they expect it. This denies altogether the cross of our Lord Jesus, the love of our Father God, and the power of His Holy Spirit.

Any of these indicators—anger, sarcasm, self-hatred, victim mentality, twisted thinking, lack of vision, hopelessness, or believing you are marked for punishment—tell us shame has captured our thinking. Until we realize truth and begin to think differently, we will never act differently. Remember, merging the lies of hell with our own life-experiences can create in us an unwillingness to believe what God says about us. It is the truth that we know which makes us free. The truth is that Jesus was shamed so that you and I could be free of shame and walk in His glory. He made the way for that divine exchange in our lives, and now we have to begin to live in its reality!

It is truth that makes us free. Truth is not simply a thing to believe, it is a person to know. Here is the first essential truth to overcoming shame: God formed each and every one of us, and He made us in His likeness. God is not ugly, trashy, stupid, no-good, or a liar. We are made in God's image, and that makes us lovely, lovable, beautiful, passionate, wise, gifted, and desirable. That is an essential truth. It is a truth that will make you free.

Many of the things that happened to you as a child were not in God's plan for you. Perhaps you've been shamed by your parents, your friends, leaders in the church, your teachers, and others. Open your heart now to understand and receive truth, and to truly get to know the truth, our Lord Jesus Christ. When we know who He is, then we know who we are, and can begin to walk out of the shame of our past and into His glory. As the Holy Spirit brings to your mind different situations and people, forgive the people and deal with shame as the thief it is. Do not allow shame to steal your true identity any longer. Make yourself vulnerable to God and others, striking a deadly blow to shame as you trust God to free you from fear and shame and release you into love and glory.

Father God, I come before You in the name of Jesus Christ of Nazareth, and I thank You for giving me insight into shame so that I can identify it and begin to remove myself from it. Lord, Your Word says that I am to come out from the unclean thing, and I can see that shame is an unclean thing that has bound me in many areas of my life. I want to be free of shame, Father, and I can't do that without You. Lord, I choose right now to forgive my mother and my father for all the times they shamed me and made me feel worthless and unloved. I forgive all my ancestors for opening the door to shame, and for establishing a pattern of shame in our family. I forgive and release all my ancestors, my parents, my brothers and sisters, pastors and leaders in the church, teachers, classmates, bosses and coworkers, and all others who brought shame into my life, Lord, and I release them into Your hand. I forgive them for the words, the actions, and the attitudes that shamed me and that opened the door for anger, sarcasm, and self-hatred to work in my life. I ask You to forgive me for allow- ing the opinions and words of others to hide Your truth that I am perfectly created in Your image, and I forgive myself for having done that. I ask You to forgive me for any time I brought shame into another person's life, and I forgive myself for having done that. Forgive me, Lord, for participating with anger, sarcasm and self-hatred, and for allowing my thoughts to carry me into a victim mentality, warped thinking, and hopelessness. I real- ize those conditions are not a part of who I am, and I renounce them now. I ask You to forgive me, Father, for allowing shame to rob me of vision and truth, and I ask that vision and truth be restored in me. Forgive me, Lord, for receiving the lie of hell that there is something wrong with me, for believing that lie, and for living it. I receive Your forgiveness, Father, and I forgive myself. Lord, I ask that by Your Holy Spirit You begin to show me the situations of my past where shame came in, so that I can forgive the persons who were used to bring it. I pledge to bring each and every situation before You, Father, and to receive Your truth so that the lies can be dispelled. Thank You, Lord Jesus, for Your sacrifice which enables me to receive truth that frees me from shame. Amen.

Daily Affirmation:

When I am focused on what I don't have, and what I can't do, God has nothing to work with! I must bring Him what I do have and what I can do, and He will multiply it. God prospers me; I do not prosper me! He takes care of my needs for no other reason than that He loves me. One of His names is Jehovah Jireh, which means "God will see to it." So, whatever I need, I can be sure God will supply it because that's who He is. What do I have and what can I do? I will bring God myself, and give Him my life daily in praise and worship. I will recognize Him and exalt Him and speak HIS Word and not the word of the world. I have a voice to worship with, to sing with, to encourage others. I have a mind with which I can choose to agree with God and what He says about me and others. I have a will that I can use to stand against the assignment of the enemy who tries to define my identity, and a will to resolve that only the Lord Jesus Christ has the authority to define my identity. My identity is not in what I can do; it is in what HE can do through me.

Note from the author:

Freedom's Way Ministries has a nine-part CD series on Overcoming Shame, as well as conferences on this and other subjects that can be presented at your church, home group, or community center. Video of this conference is on our website www.freedomswayministries.com. Our prayer ministers make themselves available for telephone or in-person appointments to help God's people come out of shame, fear, bitterness, addictions, anger, relational problems, and mental and physical diseases among other things. If you are interested, please contact the ministry at 904–993–2876 or write to us at Freedom's Way Ministries, P.O. Box 226, O'Brien, FL 32071.

Chapter Seven

Spiritual Deception about Sin

VARIOUS BELIEFS PREVAIL THROUGHOUT THE BODY OF CHRIST, some of which, when examined in the glory light of God's Word, seem lacking in sound doctrine. Some of these beliefs are attempts to address the many major problems prevalent in the Body of Christ: People are hurt, people are hurting, and hurting people hurt people. In our pain, we create doctrines that oppose God's Word and His truth. It's a cycle that comes from hell, and centers itself in three things—self-righteous judgments, pride, and spiritual deception. People make feeble, ineffective, and even downright dumb attempts to "figure out" God. We make things up to explain unexplainable things such as situations we don't understand, or why people are the way they are, or why things happen the way they do, and so on. In doing that, we might create false doctrines that oppose God's Word, and adopt warped views of God and His Word. People have long attributed to God circumstances that are rooted in hell, and at the same time given the devil or the world or themselves credit for things the Lord does. In other words, we are often duped by a counterfeit of the Holy Spirit.

There are four primary areas of deception that have been introduced into most denominational churches, and are well-entrenched in our thinking. These are usually things and beliefs we grew up hearing. They are also spiritual deceptions which may affect our belief system and chip away at our faith in God. These first areas of deception involve the four things that Jesus defeated at the cross, and which we have been instructed by Jesus to defeat in our own lives. They are: sin, sickness, poverty, and death. Let's agree together to be taught of God, and not man, to discover God's heart on these matters, and not what man has told us through human reasoning.

The first step to overcoming a limitation from hell is to recognize it. As you read these things, you may have difficulty believing the Word of God is true because it hasn't proven true in your own life. Remember, God's ways are often the opposite of the obvious. He sees the end from the beginning. He knows what is right and true altogether, and He has a perfect plan to accomplish His purposes.

> FOR MY THOUGHTS ARE NOT YOUR THOUGHTS, NEITHER ARE YOUR WAYS MY WAYS, SAYS THE LORD. FOR AS THE HEAVENS ARE HIGHER THAN THE EARTH, SO ARE MY WAYS HIGHER THAN YOUR WAYS, AND MY THOUGHTS THAN YOUR THOUGHTS. (ISAIAH 55:8–9)

Similarly, if you begin to feel the need to bring correction in a particular area, you may be tempted to justify yourself and by explaining how you understand the issue. Stop and think of what the apostle Paul taught us when he said, "And if any man think that he knows any thing, he knows nothing yet as he ought to know" (I Corinthians 8:2). We should all be aware that hell is continually making a play to stop us from receiving what God has for us. When we oppose God's Word to create a belief that makes sense to us, we are essentially telling God He must be wrong about that particular thing. Take your true identity as an example.

Most of us are living a false identity in some area of our lives. You may not think that's a true statement, but ask yourself this— "Could anyone mistake me for Jesus Christ? Do I reflect Him in every single area of my life?" If the answer is "no, not yet," then there is a place of false identity hiding somewhere within.

As previously stated, the four areas of deception most prevalent in the church, and in our own lives, are sin, sickness, poverty, and death. In each category of deception, we'll give you a few statements of doctrine most of us have been taught, examining each one according to Scripture, and seeking the heart of God. We want the spirit of the Word, which makes alive, not the letter of the law, which kills. As deceptions are exposed, we will all have a decision to make. Are we going to believe what God has to say (which might make us uncomfortable), or would we rather stick with what man has taught us and the things that make us comfortable?

About sin, many of us have been taught that sin is a bad thing that bad people do, and that a Christian cannot have a demon working from within him. About sickness, many have been taught that God doesn't heal everybody, that it's His will for some of us to carry a disease or infirmity so He can teach us something, and that there are some things we "just have to live with" or die from. About poverty, many have been taught that we'll be better Christians if we're poor, that God doesn't want us to prosper financially, that money is a bad thing, and that poverty is godliness. About death, many have been taught that everyone dies a physical death, that there is no way to escape dying, and that we only have a set time on earth of about seventy or eighty years.

Regarding sin, understanding the two natures within us (God's Spirit that perfected our spirits and Satan's spirit that seeks to defile our souls) should give us the freedom to choose which nature we will follow. Every hour of every day, we have the choice to give control to the sin-nature of our wanna-be father, Satan, or the righteous nature of our true Father God and His Christ. What else can we say about the belief that sin is simply bad things that bad people do? The unfortunate conclusion to that belief is this—we all sin, therefore we are all sinners, therefore we all are bad. Keep this in mind: the best lie sounds the most like truth. If the counterfeit did not look real, we would not be fooled by it. Religious-minded and self-righteous people, along with well-intentioned but perhaps not well-studied leaders in the Body of Christ, use several verses from

Scripture to back this belief that sin is simply bad things that bad people do. Here are some of them:

> WHAT THEN? ARE WE BETTER THAN THEY? NO, IN NO WISE: FOR WE HAVE BEFORE PROVED BOTH JEWS AND GENTILES, THAT THEY ARE ALL UNDER SIN; AS IT IS WRITTEN, THERE IS NONE RIGHTEOUS, NO, NOT ONE: THERE IS NONE THAT UNDERSTANDS, THERE IS NONE THAT SEEKS AFTER GOD. THEY ARE ALL GONE OUT OF THE WAY, THEY ARE TOGETHER BECOME UNPROFITABLE; THERE IS NONE THAT DOES GOOD, NO, NOT ONE. (ROMANS 3:9–12)

> FOR ALL HAVE SINNED, AND COME SHORT OF THE GLORY OF GOD. (ROMANS 3:23)

There is truth to this, certainly, but this passage in Romans does not give us the entire truth, and does not fully explain God's heart on the matter of sin. Both aspects of sin— (1) the action and (2) the entity that caused the action—are in these verses in Romans. Sin is not simply bad things that bad people do, as you've already learned. It is also the manifestation of the being behind the action. When He personified sin in His discourse to Cain, God Himself told us there is more to sin than an action of offense. Whatever sin is, if it can crouch and it desires to have you, then sin is something which can move and think.

Paul knew the original language, and so he knew what sin really is. That's why in the passage above, he states that both Jews and Gentiles are "under" sin. This is a positional state of inferiority. There is something Paul calls "sin" which he says has power over us. Again, be reminded a thing cannot have power unless it has life. Paul says people are subject to a being which God named "sin." In other words, rather than doing what God told Cain to do, which was to rule over sin, Cain allowed sin to rule over him! Subsequently, many of us do the same. So, the first reference to sin we just saw (Romans 3:9) speaks of some kind of living being. In the second reference (3:23), "all have sinned" speaks of the action.

This first reference is to the offender, who is not you or me, but an evil spirit from hell on assignment to do the works of hell. This addresses the second doctrinal deception about sin—that a Christian can't have a demon. In actuality, you can have as many as you want to! However, "having" a demon isn't even the right focus. The question is not, "Can a Christian have a demon?" The question is, "Can a demon use a Christian?"

The second reference in this passage is to the offense, which can rightly be attributed to both the offender—that evil spirit on assignment—and the person who agreed with the evil spirit (knowingly or unknowingly). In his or her agreement, the person, under guidance of the demonic being, committed the offense. Having this new understanding, the realization comes that we all are now doubly responsible for the evil actions in which we engage. Clearly, we must be held accountable for the action itself; and now we should be accountable to recognize and break agreement with the entity behind the action as well.

There are plenty of Scriptures which tell us that these evil spirits, sin-beings, are within us. "Hide me from the secret counsel of the wicked; from the insurrection of the workers of iniquity" (Psalm 64:2). This is just one of those Scriptures we need to understand. Insurrections come from within. Insurrection is an uprising against the established order. For instance, we do our best to establish the order of our lives according to the Word and truth of the Living God. Then someone hurts us or our children or someone we love, or maybe the person opposes a view which we hold dear, or perhaps brings an offense against us in some way. Suddenly, the God-ordained order of our lives, which we diligently worked to establish, is upset. We feel something rising up in us. What we feel are those workers of iniquity. They are attempting to bring strife and contention, to cause division and separation, to build walls of rejection and isolation ... or whatever other trouble comes to capture our thoughts or stir our emotions.

The workers of iniquity are inside us, and they hide and work, and hide their work. They hide behind false doctrine that says, "I'm perfected, and there is nothing demonic in me because I have the Holy Spirit in me. An evil spirit can't come into the presence of the Holy Spirit." This flawed thinking that God and the devil can't be at the same place, even in you, at the same time, or that good and evil cannot coexist, is a great limitation in the Body of Christ, and in the individual lives of believers. In the book of Job, the sons of God came to present themselves before Him; and Satan came with them.

> NOW THERE WAS A DAY WHEN THE SONS OF GOD CAME TO PRESENT THEMSELVES BEFORE THE LORD, AND SATAN CAME ALSO AMONG THEM. (JOB 1:6)

In another example of the devil and the Lord together in the same place (and showing also the devil in man), Jesus called Peter "Satan" in the Book of Matthew.

> THEN PETER TOOK HIM, AND BEGAN TO REBUKE HIM, SAYING, BE IT FAR FROM YOU, LORD: THIS SHALL NOT BE UNTO YOU. BUT HE TURNED, AND SAID UNTO PETER, GET YOU BEHIND ME, SATAN: YOU ARE AN OFFENCE UNTO ME: FOR YOU SAVOR NOT THE THINGS THAT BE OF GOD, BUT THOSE THAT BE OF MEN. (MATTHEW 16:22–23)

Jesus heard what came out of Peter's mouth and knew it was the devil speaking. The Lord didn't say, "Peter, you're thinking wrong." He said, "Get thee behind me, Satan!" Was Peter a believer? You bet, and Peter was even the one who had the revelation of Jesus as the Christ and Son of God. The apostle Paul said evil was present with him. Was Paul saved? Yes, I would certainly think so. He knew the Lord so well that God honored Him to be the writer of much of our New Testament. There are dozens of scriptural examples of the Holy Spirit and some unclean spirit operating out of the same person. But the best proof that the Holy Spirit and unclean spirits occupy the same space is in our own lives.

Have you ever been in fear since you were saved? How about feeling heaviness? Have you had an infirmity or maybe even today have some sort of infirmity? Every single one of those things mentioned are spirits named in the Bible, and they did not come from God.

> FOR GOD HATH NOT GIVEN US THE <u>SPIRIT</u> OF FEAR; BUT OF POWER, AND OF LOVE, AND OF A SOUND MIND. (2 TIMOTHY 1:7, EMPHASIS ADDED)

> TO APPOINT UNTO THEM THAT MOURN IN ZION, TO GIVE UNTO THEM BEAUTY FOR ASHES, THE OIL OF JOY FOR MOURN-ING, THE GARMENT OF PRAISE FOR THE <u>SPIRIT</u> OF HEAVINESS; THAT THEY MIGHT BE CALLED TREES OF RIGHTEOUSNESS, THE PLANTING OF THE LORD, THAT HE MIGHT BE GLORIFIED. (ISAIAH 61:3, EMPHASIS ADDED)

> AND, BEHOLD, THERE WAS A WOMAN WHICH HAD A <u>SPIRIT</u> OF INFIRMITY EIGHTEEN YEARS, AND WAS BOWED TOGETHER, AND COULD IN NO WISE LIFT UP HERSELF. (LUKE 13:11, EMPHASIS ADDED)

There are more spirits named in Scripture, but I think you understand. If any of this: fear, heaviness, or infirmity, or any one of the fruits of the other named spirits in the Bible has been or is now in your life, be of good cheer! You can now separate yourself from those sins, and all the others, too, because you can now recognize they are not products of your personality, your character, your imagination, or your true nature. They are limiters from hell. They have been hanging out inside you, right alongside the Holy Spirit. Neither you nor I are better than Paul or John or Peter. If evil was in them, it's in us. Sooner or later, each one of us must come to repentance, acknowledging the truth, and recover ourselves from the snare of the devil. Otherwise, we just go around the same mountain over and over again until we climb it. We get to take the same test over and over again until we pass it.

I don't know what your mountain or your test looks like. Maybe it's a particular person who is difficult to deal with, and you get upset and angry and frustrated. Maybe it's a problem with judging other people, being critical of the way they act, or what they say, or how they believe. Maybe it's a habit of grumbling and complaining that holds in place the very things you complain about. Do you have anger issues? Addictions? Commitment issues? Relationship problems? Do you need approval from people? Do you have to be validated by others? Do you think of yourself as a spiritual giant? Do you think of yourself as a lowly caterpillar? Do you have poor self worth? Exalted self worth? Are you envious or jealous? Do you hold on to bitterness, unforgiveness, and resentment? Victimization? Self pity? Illness or infirmity? Whatever your test, it's up to you to study and pass it. Whatever your mountain may be, it's up to you to make the way plain, to bring the mountains low and lift up the valleys so the King of Glory will have a clear, unobstructed path through you and into the world.

> As it is written in the prophets, Behold, I send my messenger before your face, which shall prepare your way before you. The voice of one crying in the wilderness, Prepare you the way of the Lord, make his paths straight. (Mark 1:2–3)

> And make straight paths for your feet, lest that which is lame be turned out of the way; but let it rather be healed. (Hebrews 12:13)

We have a choice to "let it be healed." God wants to heal us, to free us from the strongholds we've allowed sin to build within us. But we have to choose to let Him do that. If we say we have no sin, we lie and the truth is not in us. We are instructed by Jesus to "go and do likewise."

*He destroyed the works of the devil, and
we must do the same.*

In order to destroy sin, we must recognize it for what it is, and we must go after it.

Cleansing the temple of God is a process that begins within and works its way out. Pressure washing the outside by doing self-righteous acts in our own strength and reasoning only makes us whitewashed sepulchres, full of dead men's bones. These bones might be the traditions of our ancestors, the legalism of our upbringing, or the generational curses which hinder our ministries, our health, or our relationships with others and with God. Those are all dead things and wrong beliefs that interfere with our true identity.

> WOE UNTO YOU, SCRIBES AND PHARISEES, HYPOCRITES! FOR YOU ARE LIKE UNTO WHITED SEPULCHRES, WHICH INDEED APPEAR BEAUTIFUL OUTWARD, BUT ARE WITHIN FULL OF DEAD MEN'S BONES, AND OF ALL UNCLEANNESS. EVEN SO YOU ALSO OUTWARDLY APPEAR RIGHTEOUS UNTO MEN, BUT WITHIN YOU ARE FULL OF HYPOCRISY AND INIQUITY.
> (MATTHEW 23:27–28)

Begin today, right now with this prayer, to cleanse God's temple and become an acceptable dwelling place for the Holy Spirit.

Father God, I am here in the name of my Lord and Savior Jesus Christ of Nazareth to confess my sins before You and to receive Your cleansing anointing that restores me to righteousness. I admit to You that I have agreed with the enemy, many times without realizing what I was doing, and I am sorry. Forgive me, Father, for not recognizing that my true enemy is not me. I am so very grateful that I can now begin to separate myself from the evil spirits that have been rising up to confuse me, to cause me to fall and to fail, to make me give up on myself and even on You, and to destroy me. I can see that the workers of iniquity have been busy working in my heart, bringing me fear and stress, bringing me bitterness and anger, bringing me rejection and heartache, and so many other unclean thoughts and emotions, Lord, that I cannot name them all. Help me, Father, in every situation, to recognize the spirit that wants to control my actions and my attitudes, the thing that wants to have me and carry me into sinning against You and others. I want to stand strong against all assignments of the devil and his henchmen. Give me Your holy boldness to speak to those evil beings with the authority of Jesus, and to put those spirits out of my life forever. I know I cannot do this without You. You alone, Jesus, are my Deliverer, my Messiah, my Risen Lord, and I thank You that You are with me to see this accomplished by the power of Your Holy Spirit. Amen.

Chapter Eight

Spiritual Deception about Sickness

Let's take a look at more spiritual deception in the way we think and view the things of God … who He is, what He does, and how He does it. We tend to want to correct God when we see that His Word and our reality don't match up! We say things like, "Well, it can't be true that God cares about me because if He did, I wouldn't be sick, or I wouldn't be alone, or I wouldn't be poor," or whatever. "It can't be true that God is in control, because if He was we wouldn't have drought and famine and crime and cancer and floods and hurricanes and wars and poverty … and a myriad of other things." Again, we tend to merge the lies of hell and the experiences of our lives, creating a very destructive combination that can make us unwilling to believe that God's Word is true.

Of the four primary areas in which we are spiritually deceived (sin, sickness, poverty, and death), perhaps sickness is the one in which we tend to create more false doctrine than any other. We use our own human reasoning to explain away the "whys." For example, "Why did Aunt Louise, who was a woman of great faith, die from that disease?" "Why do innocent children get cancer or some other life-threatening thing?" "Why does the Word say no plague comes near me, but I got the flu?"

Most of us have a tendency to attempt to explain the unexplainable; and we end up blaming God for the bad stuff. We also have a tendency to give ourselves, or others in the world, credit for the good stuff. If the operation was a success, the doctor is brilliant. If the operation was a failure, God "needed another angel in heaven." That is total deception and an accusation against God. Not only do people NOT become angels; but also, God doesn't take our lives. He does receive us into our new life when our purposes on earth are completed and we're ready to go; but it is a fallacy to think that God has to make us sick to get us to heaven. Beliefs we create to ease our pain in painful situations can become doctrines which then become ingrained in our lives. Some of them are simply abominable to the Lord.

As we look at some of the false beliefs religion has built around the topic of sickness and disease, we recognize that many of us have been taught things which oppose God's Word. For example, we may have been told that God doesn't heal everybody, or that it is His will for some of us to carry a disease or infirmity "so He can teach us something." Many have heard and are expected to believe that there are just some things we "have to live with" or maybe die from. Maybe we were taught that God creates some people defectively, and that healing is not for today, it was only for Jesus and the apostles. We're going to look at each one of these beliefs and do our best to discover God's heart on the matter of sickness and healing.

The idea that God doesn't heal everybody and that He creates defective people comes from life experiences, the lie of the enemy, and a warped understanding of the Word. Religious-minded people, with the help of hell, use Scripture to back up these beliefs. They generally use the passages about Jesus not being able to do much in Galilee and the story of the man who was born blind. Let's look at these Scriptures with a deeper understanding.

> AND HE WENT OUT FROM THERE, AND CAME INTO HIS OWN COUNTRY; AND HIS DISCIPLES FOLLOW HIM. AND WHEN THE SABBATH DAY WAS COME, HE BEGAN TO TEACH IN THE SYNAGOGUE: AND MANY HEARING HIM WERE ASTONISHED, SAYING, FROM WHERE HAS THIS MAN THESE THINGS? AND WHAT WISDOM IS THIS WHICH IS GIVEN UNTO HIM, THAT EVEN SUCH MIGHTY WORKS ARE WROUGHT BY HIS HANDS? IS NOT THIS THE CARPENTER, THE SON OF MARY, THE BROTHER OF JAMES,

AND JOSES, AND OF JUDA, AND SIMON? AND ARE NOT HIS SIS-
TERS HERE WITH US? AND THEY WERE OFFENDED AT HIM. BUT
JESUS SAID UNTO THEM, A PROPHET IS NOT WITHOUT HONOR,
BUT IN HIS OWN COUNTRY, AND AMONG HIS OWN KIN, AND
IN HIS OWN HOUSE. AND HE COULD THERE DO NO MIGHTY
WORK, SAVE THAT HE LAID HIS HANDS UPON A FEW SICK
FOLK, AND HEALED THEM. AND HE MARVELED BECAUSE OF
THEIR UNBELIEF. AND HE WENT ROUND ABOUT THE VILLAGES,
TEACHING. (MARK 6:1–6)

Hmm ... this says Jesus couldn't do mighty works and that He
healed only a few; so, does God heal everybody? Is it His will that
some of us just won't be healed? The reality of our lives tells us that
some people don't get well from their diseases; they actually die. We
all know someone who is in a continual struggle with some kind of
illness, and we all know someone who died in spite of many, many
prayers. This Scripture even tells us Jesus could do no mighty work
in His own country, and He healed only a few sick folks. Why do
you suppose that is? Was the Lord unable to heal everyone? NO!
Was He unwilling? NO!

The evidence would say that because the people thought they
knew Him, they considered Jesus to be essentially a nobody, one
of them, just a regular Joe, nothing great. "Familiarity breeds con-
tempt" is an old saying most people have heard; and in this case, it
seems to be true. The sin of familiarity speaks of how we think we
know something, or someone, so well that we can't get past what we
know and into what is. Many of you can relate to this very thing. I
know in my own life, the people who knew me before I decided to
allow God to mold and shape and correct me have a really hard time
thinking of me as a woman of God. That is one of the drawbacks of
familiarity. Another is that we tend to take for granted the people
we know well. This sin of familiarity is in evidence here in Galilee
when Jesus could do no mighty work.

It wasn't that Jesus was unable to heal, or even that He was unwilling to heal; it was that the people did not think He could, and so they would not come to Him. You can search the Scriptures through and through and be hard pressed to find a single instance when someone was brought to Jesus, or came to Him personally, and was not healed of whatever problem there was. We have not found any word in Scripture where Jesus Christ turned away a sick person. He didn't exactly seek them out, but He never turned them away. First, we have to recognize who Jesus is. One of His common redemptive names is Jehovah Raphah, the Lord our Healer. Next, we have to come to Him.

All healing flows from the cross.

Jesus didn't come down and smear His blood over people. If we want to be healed, we must go to the cross and let His blood drip on us! Everyone who came to Jesus was healed; all who had contact with Him, recognizing Him as King, were healed. That is still true today, according to the Word of God.

> JESUS CHRIST THE SAME YESTERDAY, AND TODAY, AND FOREVER. BE NOT CARRIED ABOUT WITH DIVERSE AND STRANGE DOCTRINES. (HEBREWS 13:8–9A)

If Jesus Christ is the same today as He was yesterday, we need to know what He was like yesterday. Let's go to the book of Acts for the answer.

> THAT WORD, I SAY, YOU KNOW, WHICH WAS PUBLISHED THROUGHOUT ALL JUDEA, AND BEGAN FROM GALILEE, AFTER THE BAPTISM WHICH JOHN PREACHED; HOW GOD ANOINTED JESUS OF NAZARETH WITH THE HOLY GHOST AND WITH POWER: WHO WENT ABOUT DOING GOOD, AND HEALING ALL

THAT WERE OPPRESSED OF THE DEVIL; FOR GOD WAS WITH
HIM. (ACTS 10:37–38)

The prophet Isaiah, the psalmist David, the Apostle Peter and dozens of others testify of the same thing: Jesus healed everyone.

SURELY HE HAS BORNE OUR GRIEFS, AND CARRIED OUR SORROWS: YET WE DID ESTEEM HIM STRICKEN, SMITTEN OF GOD, AND AFFLICTED. BUT HE WAS WOUNDED FOR OUR TRANSGRESSIONS, HE WAS BRUISED FOR OUR INIQUITIES: THE CHASTISEMENT OF OUR PEACE WAS UPON HIM; AND WITH HIS STRIPES WE ARE HEALED. (ISAIAH 53:4–5)

WHO FORGIVES ALL YOUR INIQUITIES; WHO HEALS ALL YOUR DISEASES. (PSALM 103:3)

WHO HIS OWN SELF BORE OUR SINS IN HIS OWN BODY ON THE TREE, THAT WE, BEING DEAD TO SINS, SHOULD LIVE UNTO RIGHTEOUSNESS: BY WHOSE STRIPES YOU WERE HEALED.
(1 PETER 2:24)

Jesus Christ heals everyone who comes to Him. We simply need to get there. Maybe we think we're there, and we're not. Maybe we are withholding from the Lord our hearts or our lives. Maybe we are divided in our loyalties, depending on a "Jesus AND" doctrine. By this, I do not mean we should not seek medical advice or attention. I mean we think we need Jesus and ME—what <u>we</u> can do to be righteous. Many people believe they have to earn God's healing touch by doing something to please Him. This usually means we think we have to be totally upright and righteous (which usually means self-righteous) in order to be healed. Yes, it is important to follow that which is right, and certainly following what is right is beneficial to our lives and our health, but we do not earn our healing from God; it is a part of our salvation package. Jesus already paid for our healing; He made the provision. Health is available to every believer!

> BUT UNTO YOU THAT FEAR MY NAME SHALL THE SUN OF
> RIGHTEOUSNESS ARISE WITH HEALING IN HIS WINGS; AND YOU
> SHALL GO FORTH, AND GROW UP AS CALVES OF THE STALL.
> (MALACHI 4:2)

> AND SAID, IF YOU WILL DILIGENTLY HEARKEN TO THE VOICE
> OF THE LORD YOUR GOD, AND WILL DO THAT WHICH IS
> RIGHT IN HIS SIGHT, AND WILL GIVE EAR TO HIS COMMAND-
> MENTS, AND KEEP ALL HIS STATUTES, I WILL PUT NONE OF
> THESE DISEASES UPON YOU, WHICH I HAVE BROUGHT UPON
> THE EGYPTIANS: FOR I AM THE LORD THAT HEALS YOU.
> (EXODUS 15:26)

In pondering these old covenant Scriptures, we find a very interesting relational truth pertinent to our health. In Malachi, healing is promised to those who fear the name of the Lord. When we have a reverent respect for God, His glory covers us through Jesus Christ who brings healing, new life, and growth wherever and whenever He is revealed in us.

Then in Exodus, the Word is directed to those who have been freed from the bondages of their slavery to the Egyptians. Think about this group for a moment. There were likely about three million people in this throng, and yet the Word tells us there was not ONE feeble person among them when they left Egypt.

> HE BROUGHT THEM FORTH ALSO WITH SILVER AND GOLD:
> AND THERE WAS NOT ONE FEEBLE PERSON AMONG THEIR
> TRIBES. (PSALM 105:37)

What a miracle! Of these three million or so people, there was not one sniffle, one weakness or lameness, nor any pain! Why not? The answer brings their relational position into the light. Before leaving Egypt, the Israelites were given specific instructions regarding a sacrifice to the Lord. The lamb was slaughtered before the door of each house, where there is a bit of a dip before the threshold of the door. The blood of the lamb would have pooled there in that low spot.

As they exited their houses, every person stepped through the blood! That sacrificial lamb, as we have been taught, represented the Lord Jesus Christ. The blood was painted on the doorposts and lintel of the house as a sign of protection from the death angel, who would pass over. It is by the precious blood of Jesus that we are protected, and by which we are healed. The Scripture we quoted above from Exodus, instructing us to listen and obey God, tells us this—"Stay covered by the blood. Stay in relationship with Jesus, always following on to know Him."

Jesus Christ is the same yesterday, today, and forever. He healed everyone who came to Him then, He heals everyone who comes to Him now, and He will heal everyone who comes to Him in the future. His blood is still working, and it is all powerful and effective to rid us of all illness, infirmity, injury, infection, whatever.

Next, we have the statement that God creates people with birth defects. It is true that God created the person, but not the birth defect. He doesn't make babies with missing limbs, brain disorders, blindness, deafness, and so on. Those things are usually the cause of some generational issue in a family. There is always a spiritual legal reason for those kinds of "defects." It is NEVER that God made them that way so He could somehow get glory. That is a religious idea which needs to be slain and buried back in hell where it came from. There is nothing in a "defect" that glorifies God. Perhaps you are questioning, "But what about the blind man?" This is a passage which religious-minded people, with the help of hell, use to prove that God gives us physical problems.

> AND AS JESUS PASSED BY, HE SAW A MAN WHICH WAS BLIND FROM HIS BIRTH. AND HIS DISCIPLES ASKED HIM, SAYING, MASTER, WHO DID SIN, THIS MAN, OR HIS PARENTS, THAT HE WAS BORN BLIND? JESUS ANSWERED, NEITHER HAS THIS MAN SINNED, NOR HIS PARENTS: BUT THAT THE WORKS OF GOD SHOULD BE MADE MANIFEST IN HIM. I MUST WORK THE WORKS OF HIM THAT SENT ME. (JOHN 9:1–4A)

Let us first be reminded that there were no punctuation marks in the original text. We've been taught that the Scripture means the man was born blind because God needed a blind man so He could heal Him and show off His power. That belief is far from true. If we were to move the punctuation, we could say it this way—"Neither has this man sinned, nor his parents. (period) But that the works of God should be made manifest in him. (comma) I must work the works of him that sent me."

Maybe you're thinking, "If the man didn't sin, and neither did his parents, doesn't that negate the idea of a spiritual legal right for Satan to inflict us through a generational curse?" Not at all. Scripture is clear that generational curses can visit a family to the third and fourth generations, and Jesus only mentioned the present and immediately previous one. Scripture also says that God visits mercy on thousands of generations of the righteous. By this we can see that, even though a generational curse may have been present through the actions or attitudes of grandparents or great-grandparents, the righteousness of these two present generations, the man and his parents who had not sinned, enabled this man to be in a position to be healed. It wasn't the sin of the man or his parents which caused his blindness, but it was their righteousness which enabled his healing!

Finally, let's look at one more Scripture on this particular aspect of healing. This one puts to rest the wrong belief that God makes defects in babies in the womb, and therefore being born blind or deaf is an act of God's will.

THE HEARING EAR, AND THE SEEING EYE, THE LORD HAS MADE EVEN BOTH OF THEM. (PROVERBS 20:12)

This verse does not say the ear and the eye, or the deaf ear and the blind eye, or even all conditions of the ear and the eye. It says God made the HEARING ear, and the SEEING eye. Those are the creation of God. If a person is born blind, deaf, deformed, brain damaged, or any way other than perfect, it is a work of hell in the womb. It is not a work of God.

Other false doctrine in this category includes the idea that God gives us a disease or physical infirmity so He can work something out in us, teach us something, or otherwise put us in our place. We adopt this doctrine because it happens oftentimes that people get really sick and find themselves getting close to God. That is our observation, so we might say things like, "God had to get his attention!" or "God gave me cancer so I'd learn to trust Him," or "It's God's will for me to be sick. I deserve it and He's punishing me."

First, let me say that if you really believe it's God's will for you to be sick, then stop trying to get better! It's very hypocritical of a person to think God gave them a disease and then to try to get over it. If God gave it to you, then yield to it and take the consequences of it. Do you see how ridiculous it really is to think that God is the one who made you sick?

Also, do you actually presume to think that God has to make you sick to get your attention? Is that His mode of operation? Does He need to use a disease to speak to us? Hardly! After all, God spoke to a donkey, and through a donkey; and the donkey wasn't sick, and neither was the man riding the animal. "And when the ass saw the angel of the LORD, she fell down under Balaam: and Balaam's anger was kindled, and he smote the ass with a staff. And the LORD opened the mouth of the ass, and she said unto Balaam, What have I done unto you, that you have smitten me these three times?" (Numbers 22:27–28). Do we not think He can speak to us without making us sick first?

Many people think God uses sickness to punish us for our transgressions. That concept is foreign to His nature, and in opposition to His Word. God poured out His wrath for sin on Jesus Christ at the cross. Jesus bore that wrath. He took all punishments for our sins and transgressions, and He took all sickness and disease, so we wouldn't have to. You are either going to believe that and enjoy the benefits of His grace, or you won't.

That being the truth, why do so many people still believe God gives us infections, illnesses, injuries and infirmities? Some use this verse: "I know, O LORD, that your judgments are right, and that you in faithfulness hast afflicted me" (Psalm 119:75). This Scripture has been interpreted to mean that when we don't do everything "right" with God, He will punish us with some sort of affliction. However, if you believe that's what it means, you have to throw out another Scripture that is much more clear.

> TOUCHING THE ALMIGHTY, WE CANNOT FIND HIM OUT: HE IS EXCELLENT IN POWER, AND IN JUDGMENT, AND IN PLENTY OF JUSTICE: HE WILL NOT AFFLICT. (JOB 37:23)

So, if God does not afflict, what does the verse in Psalm 119 mean? Simply this: God is true to His Word. His Word is His faithfulness. In Genesis 3:17, God cursed the ground for man's sake. In other words, we are living in a cursed world where things were made to be difficult. The world was cursed and life in it was made difficult so that we will know we need a Savior. God wanted us to see the need to partner with Him and live a kingdom life, not a worldly life. God is true to His Word. When we are not true to His Word, we are subject to the ways of the world, which are difficult and fraught with affliction.

We will either live in the protection and prosperity and health of God's covering in the kingdom, or we will suffer the afflictions of the world.

It's a choice that each of us must make, often daily. Justice is big with God. When we bring judgment on the lying spirits from hell, we bring justice to the person. Stop believing the lies of the devil which promote doubt of God's goodness, and start believing the truth in order to experience more of the goodness of God. There is another interesting verse in Psalms which tells us that what we believe and declare determines in what condition we will live.

> I BELIEVED, THEREFORE HAVE I SPOKEN: I WAS GREATLY AF-
> FLICTED. (PSALM 116:10)

This Scripture explains clearly that what we believe and declare is an opening for evil to take root in us. For example, if you have a diagnosis from a doctor, and you believe it to be the truth, and then you begin to talk about how bad off you are, you will likely live with the affliction described in the diagnosis. Years ago, I suffered repeated bouts with bronchitis that inevitably turned into pneumonia. Year after year, I spent days in a sick bed, often in the hospital. I was told by my doctor after a particularly ravaging time in the hospital that I was left with chronic acute bronchitis, that my lungs were irreparably damaged and I would never take another clean breath. Those were the doctor's words. I believed them. After all, he was the doctor, and therefore he knew what he was talking about. I began to tell people, "I have chronic acute bronchitis and I can't be around certain smells—smoke, chemicals, perfumes, anything, really." The result of my belief and confession was that year after year, I would be extremely sick at least twice. I believed, I spoke, and I was greatly afflicted.

Then I discovered the truth, and not just the reality I was living because of a doctor's diagnosis and my belief in it. I had ministry around the issues of fear and wrong belief, repented, and headed home again with my husband and my father in a little RV. My husband wanted a cup of coffee, so he pulled off at a diner. I volunteered to go in so we didn't have to juggle my dad in and out of the vehicle. At that time, you could still smoke in restaurants, and the place was absolutely a blue fog with smoke. When I saw the smoke, I had a trace of fear try to jump on me, but I said, "No. I am healed." I went in and they had to make fresh coffee. I stood at the counter with a little old man who was smoking up a storm, and I never even smelled it. I was so excited when I got back to the RV! When I gave my husband the coffee, I asked, "Did you see that?" He leaned toward me and said, "I can't even smell it on your clothes." That experience taught me with certainty that God is a miracle-working God, and also that what we believe and confess makes a huge difference in whether or not we will be afflicted. Since that time, about thirty years ago, I have not suffered with pneumonia.

Another notion to dispel is that there are some diseases or afflictions that God intends for us to live with, or to die from. How did this deception become a doctrine in our churches? This idea, as with other errors, is held in place by our life experiences. Religion digs up a verse or two which people can use to support their error. The most used, or maybe abused, Scripture in this area is that of Paul's thorn in the flesh.

> AND LEST I SHOULD BE EXALTED ABOVE MEASURE THROUGH THE ABUNDANCE OF THE REVELATIONS, THERE WAS GIVEN TO ME A THORN IN THE FLESH, THE MESSENGER OF SATAN TO BUFFET ME, LEST I SHOULD BE EXALTED ABOVE MEASURE. FOR THIS THING I BESOUGHT THE LORD THRICE, THAT IT MIGHT DEPART FROM ME. AND HE SAID UNTO ME, MY GRACE IS SUFFICIENT FOR YOU: FOR MY STRENGTH IS MADE PERFECT IN WEAKNESS. MOST GLADLY THEREFORE WILL I RATHER GLORY IN MY INFIRMITIES, THAT THE POWER OF CHRIST MAY REST UPON ME. THEREFORE I TAKE PLEASURE IN INFIRMITIES, IN REPROACHES, IN NECESSITIES, IN PERSECUTIONS, IN DISTRESSES FOR CHRIST'S SAKE: FOR WHEN I AM WEAK, THEN AM I STRONG. (2 CORINTHIANS 12:7–10)

Paul says he has a thorn in the flesh. He carried this affliction as a badge of honor. Yet, God had made it clear to the Israelites that if they didn't deal with a matter, it would become a thorn in the flesh to them.

> BUT IF YOU WILL NOT DRIVE OUT THE INHABITANTS OF THE
> LAND FROM BEFORE YOU; THEN IT SHALL COME TO PASS,
> THAT THOSE WHICH YOU LET REMAIN OF THEM SHALL BE
> PRICKS IN YOUR EYES, AND THORNS IN YOUR SIDES, AND SHALL
> VEX YOU IN THE LAND WHEREIN YOU DWELL.
> (NUMBERS 33:55)

> AND AN ANGEL OF THE LORD CAME UP FROM GILGAL TO
> BOCHIM, AND SAID, I MADE YOU TO GO UP OUT OF EGYPT,
> AND HAVE BROUGHT YOU UNTO THE LAND WHICH I SWARE
> UNTO YOUR FATHERS; AND I SAID, I WILL NEVER BREAK MY
> COVENANT WITH YOU. AND YOU SHALL MAKE NO LEAGUE
> WITH THE INHABITANTS OF THIS LAND; YOU SHALL THROW
> DOWN THEIR ALTARS: BUT YOU HAVE NOT OBEYED MY VOICE:
> WHY HAVE YOU DONE THIS? WHEREFORE I ALSO SAID, I WILL
> NOT DRIVE THEM OUT FROM BEFORE YOU; BUT THEY SHALL
> BE AS THORNS IN YOUR SIDES, AND THEIR GODS SHALL BE A
> SNARE UNTO YOU. (JUDGES 2:1–3)

Could it be that there was something in Paul's life that he did not deal with? Paul admitted in these verses in Corinthians that God said, "My grace is sufficient." What does that mean? To me, it means the grace of God is what we need to separate ourselves from the "issue" that plagues us, and rid ourselves of it. There may well be a spiritual root which causes the infirmity in our bodies. God's grace is sufficient for healing, and it is sufficient to sustain us if we choose to remain rooted in the infirmity. God's grace is sufficient for us to decide, as Paul did, to live with the thing and let it be a reminder of God's strength in our weakest moments.

Still, it may be, and I believe it is, that God wants us to take action, to rid ourselves of the evil behind our illnesses, to drive out the inhabitants of the land (our bodies), and to make no league with them. We are not to agree with the enemy and become one with it, but if we decide "It's just me," His grace does not leave us.

When God said, "My grace is sufficient," I believe He was telling Paul that His power and presence in Paul's life was the strength he needed to overcome and to cast out the evil that caused the affliction. You have already seen from the Word in Romans chapter seven that Paul knew he had "sin within." Paul chose to remain weak in his infirmity. We can only speculate that perhaps this decision was made because Paul knew himself so well that he may have been unsure of his own steadfastness if he were to be made completely whole. Paul may have questioned whether or not he himself would continue in the way of Christ, depending on the Lord for everything, and trusting Him in all things.

It's not unusual for people to forget God when everything is going well for them. It is also not unusual for those who are strong in the Lord to begin to glory in themselves and not in God for the works they accomplish. Was Paul like that? I don't know. You decide. All I know is that God's grace is sufficient to be the power which removes infirmities, and God's grace is sufficient to be the power which enables people to live with them. It's the choice of each individual as to which way we apply God's grace in our lives. Scripture is clear that it is not God's will that we make the decision to live with illness or infirmity. Jesus healed everything, not just some things. We can see that in several places in Scripture. Here are a few of them:

> AND JESUS WENT ABOUT ALL THE CITIES AND VILLAGES, TEACHING IN THEIR SYNAGOGUES, AND PREACHING THE GOSPEL OF THE KINGDOM, AND HEALING EVERY SICKNESS AND EVERY DISEASE AMONG THE PEOPLE. (MATTHEW 9:35)

> AND JESUS WENT ABOUT ALL GALILEE, TEACHING IN THEIR SYNAGOGUES, AND PREACHING THE GOSPEL OF THE KINGDOM, AND HEALING ALL MANNER OF SICKNESS AND ALL MANNER OF DISEASE AMONG THE PEOPLE. (MATTHEW 4:23)

> FOR THIS IS GOOD AND ACCEPTABLE IN THE SIGHT OF GOD OUR SAVIOR; WHO WILL HAVE ALL MEN TO BE SAVED, AND TO

COME UNTO THE KNOWLEDGE OF THE TRUTH.
(2 TIMOTHY 2:3–4)

The word "saved" in this Scripture is the Greek word "sozo" which encompasses our full salvation package—preservation, soundness, prosperity, deliverance from evil, and healing. God our Savior <u>wills</u> that all people be healed. Yes, it is His will. Healing is in our covenant.

Finally, is healing for today or did it die with the apostles? If you think it's not for today, rip out the page in your Bible which has the verse about Jesus Christ the same yesterday, today, and forever. Jesus heals today. He uses ordinary people to do extraordinary things, including speaking healing into sick bodies, cursing and removing evil spirits which hold sickness in bodies, praying and laying hands on people for healing, and performing lots of other powerful and supernatural acts. As a matter of fact, the book of Acts doesn't have an "amen" at the end of it, because it is still being written! Jesus still heals today; He just uses us to do it. The power of the Holy Spirit comes in and imparts through us the Lord's gift of healing to those in need who come to Him. His grace flows from the cross, His blood cleanses and restores.

HEAL THE SICK, CLEANSE THE LEPERS, RAISE THE DEAD, CAST OUT DEVILS: FREELY YOU HAVE RECEIVED, FREELY GIVE.
(MATTHEW 10:8)

AND THESE SIGNS SHALL FOLLOW THEM THAT BELIEVE; IN MY NAME SHALL THEY CAST OUT DEVILS; THEY SHALL SPEAK WITH NEW TONGUES; THEY SHALL TAKE UP SERPENTS; AND IF THEY DRINK ANY DEADLY THING, IT SHALL NOT HURT THEM; THEY SHALL LAY HANDS ON THE SICK, AND THEY SHALL RECOVER.
(MARK 16:17–18)

Is healing for today? Only if you believe God's Word is true. One of the interesting things about life is that we get to live in what we believe. We can truly and deeply accept God's way, or we can dabble a little in God's way and His kingdom, and a little in the world's way and the system of the world. I don't think any of us is 100 percent in the kingdom all the time, but I'm working my way there. I will not get there by good works which I can manage in my own human strength and wisdom, but by the grace of God to put aside my own human wisdom and strength and give my life over daily to Him. Overcoming sin, sickness, poverty, and death, as Jesus did, calls for a complete surrender of self and yielding to a complete takeover by the Holy Spirit.

My hope is that you now have a better understanding of God's heart about sickness. Perhaps we can all stop blaming Him for making us sick, taking out our loved ones, causing birth defects, and otherwise punishing us. God is not a punisher; He is a rewarder of those who diligently seek Him. That is what you are doing by reading this book, and praying these prayers.

Father God, I appreciate You and Your Word in my life, and I thank You for making Your Word come alive in clarity. Forgive me, Lord, for allowing the opinions of the world, and the lies of hell to influence my beliefs. Help me to become more grounded and established in Your truth, the truth that You are my Healer, Jesus, and that You do not withhold from me. I am sorry, Father, that I have blamed You for not healing, or accused You of bringing illness, infirmity. or injury into my life or the lives of others. I can see I was wrong to think that way about You, and I ask Your forgiveness. I now know clearly that it is not Your will for anyone to be sick or hurt. Forgive me for thinking that You are the cause of birth defects, miscarriages, or barrenness, and that You punish people by giving them these heartaches and tragedies. Thank You for telling me the truth, for giving me ears to hear the truth, for giving me a heart to understand and accept Your goodness and love, and for increasing my faith to say "no" to everything that opposes Your truth, no matter what I see or hear in the world. I declare that the blood of Jesus is all I need to be healed and made completely whole. Amen.

Chapter Nine

Spiritual Deception about Poverty

A NOTHER AREA IN WHICH GOD'S PEOPLE HAVE BEEN deceived is the issue of poverty and prosperity. Some of us spend an inordinate amount of our time trying to figure out why God seems to bless other people, but not us. Or why we do everything we can to move the hand of God to prosper us financially, and it just doesn't seem to happen. Or why our bank accounts dwindle just when things start looking up. As we read earlier, Job tells us: "touching the Almighty, we cannot find Him out." In other words, there are some things about God that are unexplainable and which we likely may not understand. But Job goes on to say, "He is excellent in power and judgment and in plenty of justice; He will not afflict." So, even though we may not understand why some horrific things might have happened to us, we can know with certainty it wasn't God that caused them. Our biggest problems stem from the way we lean toward correcting God when we see that His Word and our reality don't match up. If we pray in faith, and the thing we prayed for doesn't happen, we tend to concoct an explanation that makes sense to our human minds.

This is how false doctrine and doctrines of devils come into the church. Hell works to form a lie about God and bring doubt about His Word. Out of our hurts and woundedness, or our poverty and lack, we create a reason for whatever we see, and oftentimes that reason will oppose the Word of God. The Body of Christ seems to spend a lot of time walking by sight and not by faith. It's really hard not to do that sometimes. Especially when, for example, we've been faithfully tithing and the washing machine breaks down or the car dies. We say, "Wait a minute, God, didn't You say You'd rebuke the devourer? I'm being devoured here!"

Remember, if the counterfeit didn't look real we wouldn't be fooled by it. I remember in the small town where I grew up, there was a really good printer, and for twenty years, he printed counterfeit $20 bills. No one knew it. He was an upstanding member of the community, and had even served as president of the local Chamber of Commerce. He would probably still be printing counterfeit money today if it hadn't been for a couple of young kids who found some of his not-so-perfect bills in the trash bin out back of his shop and started playing with them. Their parents took notice, and asked where they got the play money, and that's how he was finally stopped. That's how it is in the spirit realm. The enemy continues to do what he can to fool us by presenting something that looks very real, and yet won't hold up under careful examination. We are carefully examining some of the counterfeit ideas the devil has instilled into the church, and realizing that they don't hold up in the light of the truth.

What have we been taught, or what do we generally believe about God and the subject of money? Well, for one thing, some have been told that we are supposed to be poor, that we should give up everything to the church and to help others, and that poverty will somehow make us closer to God, and more spiritual. Next is the teaching that God holds it against us and won't bless us if we don't give Him money. There is a lot of coercion in some churches concerning tithing, and I've heard more manipulation from the pulpit about tithing than perhaps any other subject. Again, the best lie from hell can sound like heaven's truth. A lie of the enemy is often a truth of God that has simply been twisted and perverted, or is part truth rather than complete truth. Also, we've likely been told that Jesus was poor, and so to be like Him, we need to be poor, too. These are a few of the off-balance beliefs which we will do our best to correct.

Let's take the first one, that Christians are supposed to be poor. I don't mind declaring that it is a lie from hell that you gain greater spirituality by suffering poverty and lack. So, where does this idea come from? There are a couple of places in the Word that people use to support the warped concept of poverty being a good thing.

> JESUS SAID UNTO HIM, IF YOU WILL BE PERFECT, GO AND SELL THAT YOU HAVE, AND GIVE TO THE POOR, AND YOU SHALL HAVE TREASURE IN HEAVEN: AND COME AND FOLLOW ME. BUT WHEN THE YOUNG MAN HEARD THAT SAYING, HE WENT AWAY SORROWFUL: FOR HE HAD GREAT POSSESSIONS. THEN SAID JESUS UNTO HIS DISCIPLES, VERILY I SAY UNTO YOU, THAT A RICH MAN SHALL HARDLY ENTER INTO THE KINGDOM OF HEAVEN. AND AGAIN I SAY UNTO YOU, IT IS EASIER FOR A CAMEL TO GO THROUGH THE EYE OF A NEEDLE, THAN FOR A RICH MAN TO ENTER INTO THE KINGDOM OF GOD. (MATTHEW 19:21–24)

Many of us know this story of the rich young ruler, and we take it as a directive from the Lord for everyone. Because Jesus says it's difficult for a man to enter the kingdom of heaven if he has a lot of stuff, we think that means nobody who is truly interested in kingdom living should have anything! That belief makes no sense when you really examine it. We cannot give into good works when we have nothing to give. You can't give out of a void. Let's examine what this passage is saying.

First of all, Jesus recognized that the young man didn't have money, money had him. His treasure was in what he had, and therefore his estate held his heart. "For where your treasure is, there will your heart be also" (Matthew 6:21). Jesus wanted his heart. This verse tells us our hearts are linked to something called "treasure." When we think of treasure, most of us think of money. So, we can see that finances get hooked into our hearts without our conscious knowledge. Jesus knew that was a problem with this man.

When the Lord can touch what's important to us, He can begin to capture our hearts, and we all need to realize God wants our hearts. Can we have great possessions and still give our hearts to the Lord? Certainly, we can! At the same time, it is true that the more we have, the more we have to take care of. Having a great estate can take up a lot of our time and energy, which is likely what had happened to this young man. Jesus was saying, "I want to spend time with you, I want relationship with you, but your stuff is in the way!" When He said it is hard for a rich man to enter the kingdom of heaven, He was saying that having to steward a great estate makes it impractical to arise into the realm of happiness, power, and eternity in our daily lives. Is that true? It was for this man, and for many people who have great riches. Some people are so captured by dollar signs that they know the cost of everything, but the value of nothing. They are sometimes unable to separate themselves from the worry of what they have, how they can keep it, how they might lose it, how they can get more of it, and so on. This can be true whether a person has a little, or a lot. When your focus is on how to keep the abundance you already have, or your focus is continually on what you don't have, then money is your priority.

We can safely say that the idea of Jesus wanting us all to give up what we have and live in abject poverty in order to be closer to Him is pure deception. What He wants is our hearts, and if money is the thing that has our hearts, we need to be redirected. God's Word is very clear that He wants us to prosper. But we need to consider that our prosperity does not simply happen. The Lord has set up prosperity principles in the earth, and when we follow them, we will surely succeed. Money is not a bad thing. Loving money more than God is a bad thing. This is the other Scripture which people use to say that God wants us poor.

BUT GODLINESS WITH CONTENTMENT IS GREAT GAIN. FOR WE BROUGHT NOTHING INTO THIS WORLD, AND IT IS CERTAIN WE

CAN CARRY NOTHING OUT. AND HAVING FOOD AND RAI-
MENT LET US BE THEREWITH CONTENT. BUT THEY THAT WILL
BE RICH FALL INTO TEMPTATION AND A SNARE, AND INTO
MANY FOOLISH AND HURTFUL LUSTS, WHICH DROWN MEN IN
DESTRUCTION AND PERDITION. FOR THE LOVE OF MONEY IS
THE ROOT OF ALL EVIL: WHICH WHILE SOME COVETED AFTER,
THEY HAVE ERRED FROM THE FAITH, AND PIERCED THEMSELVES
THROUGH WITH MANY SORROWS. (1 TIMOTHY 6:6-10)

The writer of these verses knew that the spirit of Mammon uses money to entrap and enslave God's people by pulling our focus onto riches and away from God. He says, "They that will be rich fall into temptation and a snare." In other words, those who focus on getting more and more money lose sight of what's really important and end up drowning in destruction and pierced with sorrows. It isn't money that is the root of all evil; it's the <u>love</u> of money. The love of money is an overflowing love that sweeps away the things of God and carries us into hurtful lusts. Remember, God wants our hearts. He doesn't need our money. He knows He has our hearts when we follow His directives. There are eighty-two places in Scripture which use the words prosper, prospereth, prospered, and prosperity. A great number of these verses connect prosperity to obedience, but not one tells us it's good to be poor or God's will that we are poor.

In the book of Genesis, Abraham tells his servant, "The Lord, before whom I walk, will send His angel with you and prosper your way" (Genesis 24:40). In Deuteronomy, Moses told the people, "Keep the words of the covenant and do them, and you will prosper in all you do" (Deuteronomy 29:9). Joshua was told to be strong and courageous and keep the law of Moses, not turning aside from it, so that "you may prosper wherever you go" (Joshua 1:7). King David's advice to his son Solomon was the same:

AND KEEP THE CHARGE OF THE LORD YOUR GOD, TO WALK
IN HIS WAYS, TO KEEP HIS STATUTES, AND HIS COMMAND-
MENTS, AND HIS JUDGMENTS, AND HIS TESTIMONIES, AS IT IS

> WRITTEN IN THE LAW OF MOSES, THAT YOU MAY PROSPER IN
> ALL THAT YOU DO, AND WHITHERSOEVER YOU TURN YOUR-
> SELF. (1 KINGS 2:3)

In the days of King Jehoshaphat, an awesome prophecy of God's grace for battle was given, and he was told there would be no fight, but that the Lord Himself would destroy their enemies. The king then spoke to the people:

> AND THEY ROSE EARLY IN THE MORNING, AND WENT FORTH
> INTO THE WILDERNESS OF TEKOA: AND AS THEY WENT FORTH,
> JEHOSHAPHAT STOOD AND SAID, HEAR ME, O JUDAH, AND
> YOU INHABITANTS OF JERUSALEM; BELIEVE IN THE LORD
> YOUR GOD, SO SHALL YOU BE ESTABLISHED; BELIEVE HIS
> PROPHETS, SO SHALL YOU PROSPER. (2 CHRONICLES 20:20)

The Word of God goes on and on about how prosperity and success are connected to our relationship with God. This is a principle set up by God. He is our provider and our provision; and prosperity in all things comes from Him and Him alone, not from anything we can do on our own. Even those people who don't recognize God, yet prosper in the world, are actually receiving from God, because He is the provider. There is no such thing as a self-made man.

> KNOW YOU THAT THE LORD HE IS GOD: IT IS HE THAT HAS
> MADE US, AND NOT WE OURSELVES; WE ARE HIS PEOPLE, AND
> THE SHEEP OF HIS PASTURE. (PSALM 100:3)

> DO NOT ERR, MY BELOVED BRETHREN. EVERY GOOD GIFT AND
> EVERY PERFECT GIFT IS FROM ABOVE, AND COMES DOWN
> FROM THE FATHER OF LIGHTS, WITH WHOM IS NO VARIABLE-
> NESS, NEITHER SHADOW OF TURNING.
> (JAMES 1:16–17)

We can see a couple of truths so far. God is the One who prospers us, He wants our hearts, and He knows He has our hearts when we follow His directives. The Word says we prosper according to His riches in glory.

But my God shall supply all your need according to his riches in glory by Christ Jesus. (Philippians 4:19)

What does that mean? Perhaps it means we should each ask ourselves, "How rich is He in glory in me? How much Jesus do I reflect?" I believe the more we demonstrate the glory of Jesus in us, the more He can pour out his riches into our lives. When we suffer lack, it is generally because we have concentrated our time and talents and energies on our own domain rather than on His kingdom business. God is certainly not obligated to uphold any kingdom we build for ourselves. The book of Haggai says we have not considered our ways, and have forsaken the house of God.

Then came the word of the LORD by Haggai the prophet, saying, Is it time for you, O you, to dwell in your cieled houses, and this house lie waste? Now therefore thus says the LORD of hosts; Consider your ways. You have sown much, and bring in little; you eat, but you have not enough; you drink, but you are not filled with drink; you clothe you, but there is none warm; and he that earns wages earns wages to put it into a bag with holes. Thus says the LORD of hosts; Consider your ways. (Haggai 1:3-7)

God wants us to prosper, but we have a responsibility in the process. We are to consider our ways. Are we seeking first the kingdom of God and His righteousness? If we are, then we can know for certain that all the things we need will be provided for us.

The next false doctrine about poverty is that being poor will somehow make us more like Jesus. Is that scriptural? First of all, was Jesus poor, the way we think of poverty? I hardly think so. At one point in His ministry, He supported seventy missionaries! The garment the soldiers cast lots for was a prize—they surely would not have wanted the cloak of a beggar.

> THEN THE SOLDIERS, WHEN THEY HAD CRUCIFIED JESUS, TOOK
> HIS GARMENTS, AND MADE FOUR PARTS, TO EVERY SOLDIER
> A PART; AND ALSO HIS COAT: NOW THE COAT WAS WITHOUT
> SEAM, WOVEN FROM THE TOP THROUGHOUT. THEY SAID
> THEREFORE AMONG THEMSELVES, LET US NOT REND IT, BUT
> CAST LOTS FOR IT, WHOSE IT SHALL BE: THAT THE SCRIPTURE
> MIGHT BE FULFILLED, WHICH SAYS, THEY PARTED MY RAIMENT
> AMONG THEM, AND FOR MY VESTURE THEY DID CAST LOTS.
> THESE THINGS THEREFORE THE SOLDIERS DID.
> (JOHN 19:23–24)

By this Scripture, we know this piece of clothing was so well made and valuable that no one wanted to destroy it, and all of them wanted it for themselves. The verse in 2 Corinthians which tells us Jesus became poor is an exaggeration to show us the amazing, divine exchange the Lord made on our behalf. Compared to the riches of heaven, earthly living would seem to be a beggarly existence.

> FOR YOU KNOW THE GRACE OF OUR LORD JESUS CHRIST,
> THAT, THOUGH HE WAS RICH, YET FOR YOUR SAKES HE BE-
> CAME POOR, THAT YOU THROUGH HIS POVERTY MIGHT BE
> RICH. (2 CORINTHIANS 8:9)

Jesus knew the richness of heaven, and He gave it up to be born into the earth as a man, just like us. He had wealth on earth, too, but He gave that up to go to the cross and die. He made Himself obedient to poverty so He could overcome poverty and destroy it. This verse is very clear. We who believe, through His poverty, may be rich. God wants us to be rich, not poor. Being like Him doesn't mean we become poor—it means we become rich through, and in, Him.

Now let's address the issue of God wanting us to give Him money. Again, the Lord set up a principle in the earth. Like the principle of gravity, it's working in the world. God doesn't say, "Don't step off the cliff. If you step off the cliff, I'll punish you." God says, "Don't step off the cliff. If you step off the cliff, there is a principle working. The fall may not hurt you, but that sudden stop at the bottom can be deadly!" It's not a commandment to tithe or to give offerings into the kingdom of God. But there is a clear directive from God to do so.

People may say that tithing (which means giving a tenth of what you gain) is "old covenant" and under the law, and so it's not important for us today. We need to realize that tithing did not start with the law, and it is not a part of the law, other than being incorporated into it. Tithing was a part of the covenant. It was established 430 years before the law. It was established in Abraham. It was a part of God's covenant with Abraham.

> AND MELCHIZEDEK KING OF SALEM BROUGHT FORTH BREAD
> AND WINE: AND HE WAS THE PRIEST OF THE MOST HIGH GOD.
> AND HE BLESSED HIM, AND SAID, BLESSED BE ABRAM OF THE
> MOST HIGH GOD, POSSESSOR OF HEAVEN AND EARTH: AND
> BLESSED BE THE MOST HIGH GOD, WHICH HAS DELIVERED
> YOUR ENEMIES INTO YOUR HAND. AND HE GAVE HIM TITHES
> OF ALL. (GENESIS 14:18–20)

Abram, whose name God changed to Abraham, tithed to Melchizedek. This occurred, as previously stated, 430 years before the law came into being. In addition, we are clearly told that the law cannot destroy the covenant.

> NOW TO ABRAHAM AND HIS SEED WERE THE PROMISES
> MADE. HE SAYS NOT, AND TO SEEDS, AS OF MANY; BUT AS OF
> ONE, AND TO YOUR SEED, WHICH IS CHRIST. AND THIS I SAY,
> THAT THE COVENANT, THAT WAS CONFIRMED BEFORE OF GOD
> IN CHRIST, THE LAW, WHICH WAS FOUR HUNDRED AND THIR-
> TY YEARS AFTER, CANNOT DISANNUL, THAT IT SHOULD MAKE
> THE PROMISE OF NONE EFFECT. (GALATIANS 3:16–17)

Certainly, we can see that tithing is a part of the covenant of God. We also understand that tithing carries a principle of blessing with it. If we consider ourselves covenant children of God, then we give back to the Lord a portion of what clearly belongs to Him. We first give ourselves, and then we release into His kingdom the first fruits of our increase. We don't mix the holy, set-apart things with the common things. We don't give God what's left over after we pay our bills and do what we want to do. We honor Him with the first fruits of our labors, and He honors us for honoring Him.

> HONOR THE LORD WITH YOUR SUBSTANCE, AND WITH THE FIRSTFRUITS OF ALL YOUR INCREASE: SO SHALL YOUR BARNS BE FILLED WITH PLENTY, AND YOUR PRESSES SHALL BURST OUT WITH NEW WINE. (PROVERBS 3:9–10)

Please understand that tithing to the Lord is not for the purpose of getting our needs met by Him. The Lord will take care of us and provide us shelter and food simply because He loves us, and not in return for anything we can do, including tithing.

> CONSIDER THE RAVENS: FOR THEY NEITHER SOW NOR REAP; WHICH NEITHER HAVE STOREHOUSE NOR BARN; AND GOD FEEDS THEM: HOW MUCH MORE ARE YOU BETTER THAN THE FOWLS? (LUKE 12:24)

God meets our needs because He loves us and we are His precious possessions.

However, there is a principle at work in giving. Scripture proves it. When we honor God with the first fruits of our increase, our barns—that's our bank account, the storehouse of our substance—will be filled with abundance. That's good news. Once again, though, we see there is a heart issue involved. We should not tithe because "we have to." If tithing seems to be some sort of drudgery or obligation, then the heart is not right. We should not tithe out of fear, either. If we think by not tithing it will cause us to be financially destroyed, then our hearts are not right. God loves a cheerful giver, not a worried giver, or a fearful giver, or a reluctant giver. He wants our hearts, remember? In other words, we don't give because we want to be blessed, we give because we <u>are</u> blessed. We don't give to have more, we have more because we give.

Paul said it was good to give, not because he needed to receive, but because those who were giving needed to give. In his letter to the church at Philippi he talked about how generous they had been toward him.

> NOTWITHSTANDING YOU HAVE WELL DONE, THAT YOU DID COMMUNICATE WITH MY AFFLICTION. NOW YOU PHILIPPIANS KNOW ALSO, THAT IN THE BEGINNING OF THE GOSPEL, WHEN I DEPARTED FROM MACEDONIA, NO CHURCH COMMUNICAT-ED WITH ME AS CONCERNING GIVING AND RECEIVING, BUT YOU ONLY. FOR EVEN IN THESSALONICA YOU SENT ONCE AND AGAIN UNTO MY NECESSITY. NOT BECAUSE I DESIRE A GIFT: BUT I DESIRE FRUIT THAT MAY ABOUND TO YOUR ACCOUNT. (PHILIPPIANS 4:14–17)

Matters of money matter to the Lord. There are almost ten times as many verses in the New Testament about finances as there are about either faith or salvation! There are 2,084 verses that talk about money and finances, 218 verses concerning salvation and 215 verses about faith. Matters of money really do matter to God. He wants to prosper us, and He wants us to be fully aware that how we feel about money, how we respond to financial situations, and how we treat people in relation to finances can make a big difference in how effective we are in fulfilling our purpose in the kingdom.

People are the stewards of His resources, including financial resources. God wants us to prosper and He wants us to be good stewards of our prosperity. He wants us to recognize the principles He has established in the earth in this area. Giving is only one of them, but it is a big one. Know this—none of us can out-give God!

> GIVE, AND IT SHALL BE GIVEN UNTO YOU; GOOD MEASURE,
> PRESSED DOWN, AND SHAKEN TOGETHER, AND RUNNING
> OVER, SHALL MEN GIVE INTO YOUR BOSOM. FOR WITH THE
> SAME MEASURE THAT YOU METE WITHAL IT SHALL BE MEA-
> SURED TO YOU AGAIN. (LUKE 6:38)

Give and it shall be given unto you. We cannot give if we live in poverty. It stands to reason that if God wants us to give into good works, He also wants us prosperous enough to do so. "And God is able to make all grace abound toward you; that you, always having all sufficiency in all things, may abound to every good work" (2 Corinthians 9:8). That puts to rest the idea we have to be poor to be spiritual. We also saw that Jesus' poverty was a comparative issue. Earthly living can't stand up to heavenly living in any aspect, includ-ing riches. That puts to rest the idea that we have to become poor to be like Jesus.

Finally, we've seen that God doesn't require money to bless us. We want to look at one more Scripture to prove this. We've been told to "sow a seed" into something in order to get something back. There is a truth to that, but it is not the entire truth. The principle of sowing and reaping is a valid principle, but not the way many of us have been taught. Sowing and reaping actually has nothing whatsoever to do with whether or not God meets our needs. Sowing and reaping is not the method of meeting our needs. To think that way is works righteousness. "If I give, God will meet my need." It is wrong and deceptive to believe, "If I do something for God, He'll do something for me." That is actually anti-gospel. That's a strong statement, but Jesus Himself taught against sowing and reaping as a way to meet needs.

> THEREFORE I SAY UNTO YOU, TAKE NO THOUGHT FOR YOUR
> LIFE, WHAT YOU SHALL EAT, OR WHAT YOU SHALL DRINK;
> NOR YET FOR YOUR BODY, WHAT YOU SHALL PUT ON. IS NOT
> THE LIFE MORE THAN MEAT, AND THE BODY THAN RAIMENT?
> BEHOLD THE FOWLS OF THE AIR: FOR THEY SOW NOT, NEITHER

DO THEY REAP, NOR GATHER INTO BARNS; YET YOUR HEAVEN-
LY FATHER FEEDS THEM. ARE YOU NOT MUCH BETTER THAN
THEY? (MATTHEW 6:25–26)

How many times have we heard these words, or something similar,
"Do you have a need tonight? Then GIVE! Give more! Give it all!
God will meet that need as you make your offering. The more you
give, the more you get." "Do you need money? Then GIVE! Sow
into God's kingdom and He will meet your need." In this warped
interpretation of God's principle of sowing and reaping, we are using money to make God do something, when money should be the
means to accomplish the thing God told us to do. It's upside-down
thinking.

When we believe sowing is the way to get our needs met, what
happens? We can't pay the rent, we sow into the offering expect-
ing God to pay our rent, and He doesn't. What does that do to our
faith? What about when we try to tell somebody else, well, if you
were just giving more, you wouldn't have this problem? "I tried that
and it didn't happen for me." Using sowing to meet needs sets up a
situation that often results in a blow to the credibility of the Word
of God and the love of God.

God's provision comes to me <u>not</u> because of what I do.
God's provision comes to me for only one reason—He loves me.
Everything I have comes to me as a gift of His grace, received by
faith. Provision comes because God loves us, not because of anything we can do. The provision we give our children is not based on
what they sow into the household; that is just plain foolish. You can
feel confident to make this confession: "My Father in heaven loves
me, and because He loves me He provides for me. Because He loves
me, He wants to see me prosper in my finances as well as in my
health and in my relationships." When we line up in agreement with
God and understand His heart on the matter of poverty and lack,

we can then destroy it from our lives. Jesus came that we might have abundant life, not meager life.

> THE THIEF COMES NOT, BUT FOR TO STEAL, AND TO KILL, AND TO DESTROY: I AM COME THAT THEY MIGHT HAVE LIFE, AND THAT THEY MIGHT HAVE IT MORE ABUNDANTLY.
> (JOHN 10:10)

Father God, I humble my heart before You and ask Your forgiveness for making my financial condition, money, or the lack of money, an idol in my life. I can see that many times, I've been so focused on what I have and how to keep it, or on what I don't have and how to get it, that I've lost sight of my first love for You. Help me, Lord, to realign my priorities with Your priorities, so that I can truly seek first Your kingdom and Your righteousness. I know that as I do that, I will never lack for anything. Forgive me, Father, for thinking I have to give in order to receive from You, and forgive me for feeling guilty when I prosper. I am sorry, Lord, for having warped views of who You are and the vast treasures You desire to pour into my life, treasures not only of finances, Father, but also of health and joy. Make me a good steward of what I am given, Father, so that I can show myself worthy of Your many blessings in my life, and can be an example of Your godliness to others. I freely give You my heart, Lord, for You are the true treasure. I desire to be the cheerful giver that You love. Help me to trust in You and not in myself or my bank account. Show me Father, the ministries and people You want to bless through me, so that I can advance Your kingdom and not my own agenda. Thank You for these truths. Help me to consider my ways, and not fall back into old patterns and old fears. I want to hold these truths in my heart and be the conduit for good that You created me to be. I know that the sacrifice of Jesus Christ makes this possible, and I thank You. Amen.

Chapter Ten

Spiritual Deception about Death

THERE IS YET ANOTHER AREA OF DECEPTION IN which many of us are snared, and that is the area of spiritual deception concerning death. We've already looked at some of the deceptions Satan has perpetrated toward us in the way we think about God and the way we view the things of God. In addition, we are gaining knowledge about who we are in Christ and learning more and more about the designs and strategies of hell which hinder and plague us. Most of us, in reality, have a tendency to view God the same way we view man. By that, I mean we usually think of God and His power in terms of what man in his own power can do. If there is a situation in which we determine a man, or a superman, could accomplish a certain thing, then we don't have a problem believing God can come through for us. It becomes possible in our minds. However, if it seems impossible for a man to accomplish, then we have trouble believing God can do it, whatever it is.

> AH LORD GOD! BEHOLD, YOU HAVE MADE THE HEAVEN AND
> THE EARTH BY YOUR GREAT POWER AND STRETCHED OUT ARM,
> AND THERE IS NOTHING TOO HARD FOR THEE:
> (JEREMIAH 32:17)

Oh, we know, at least in our heads, that God can do anything and that nothing is impossible with God; but that truth isn't always settled in our hearts. This could be why when we see something in the Word of God that doesn't match our reality, we tend to create a reason for what we see. By doing that, we can "explain" what is happening rather than doing our best to change the situation to align with the Word of God. In other words, we use the situation to define the Word of God, rather than using the Word of God to define the situation.

We all need to know who God is, what He does, and how He does it, and we should have the truth about it, not what we make up in our own human reasoning and wisdom. Remember, Job told us, "touching the Almighty, we cannot find Him out." In other words, there are some things about God that are unexplainable and which we likely will not understand. But we know from Scripture that God will not afflict us.

Sin doesn't come from God. We learned that sin is both the action taken and the evil spirit which manifested the action through a person. Sin is not simply a bad thing that a bad person does. We learned that sickness does not come from God, that He doesn't punish us with illness, infirmity, or injury. And we learned that God's heart is for each of us to enjoy prosperity in our lives and not to live in poverty, that it does not make us more spiritual or more like Jesus to be poor. Through this study of how hell has lied to us, lies that have come even through well-intentioned men and women of God, we've kicked over a lot of sacred cows. Hopefully, these truths are helping us all rid ourselves of a lot of religious ideas which have served to limit our ability to advance the kingdom of God and overcome defeat in our own lives.

The final area we want to look into regarding how deception has entered the church is the subject of death. This one is a little tricky, because very few of us know a single person who has lived on this earth in a human body for longer than a hundred years or so. We know about some people who did—Adam, Noah, Abraham, Joseph, and those people who lived way back then. We also know about a few people who didn't die a physical death—Enoch, Elijah, Moses, and who knows who else. But that was all a LONG time ago. All we have to go on now is what we see: people die physical deaths.

The world and the church both teach us that we must physically die. Death is inevitable. What have we heard all our lives? "The only sure things in this life are death and taxes." That may be true in a sense, but is it the truth? We're going to look at the Scriptures that have been most used to tell us we're going to die a physical death, explore their meanings, and do our best to reveal God's heart on the matter of death. First, let's look at the Scriptures most often used to teach us we must die a physical death. The first one is in Psalms and is the verse upon which so many measure their lives.

THE DAYS OF OUR YEARS ARE THREESCORE YEARS AND TEN; AND IF BY REASON OF STRENGTH THEY BE FOURSCORE YEARS, YET IS THEIR STRENGTH LABOR AND SORROW; FOR IT IS SOON CUT OFF, AND WE FLY AWAY. (PSALM 90:10)

How true is this verse? Threescore years and ten is seventy years. Fourscore years is eighty years. Even today, we know people who have lived past eighty years old. We know people who are alive and vibrant well into their eighties and beyond. A personal friend of mine worked into his nineties in construction. He was climbing up and down scaffolds and pouring concrete and all sorts of other strenuous activities every day, until an accident on the job ended his life at age ninety-six. Every Saturday night, he and his wife, also advanced in age, would go dancing. If it were true that eighty is the top end of our physical existence, my friend and his wife would not have been doing any of that. They would have already been dead and buried. So, what is the meaning of this psalm? We know the Word of God is true, therefore the interpretation or our understanding of the Word must be somehow skewed.

This psalm was written by Moses, who was making a supplication (and bringing a complaint) before the Lord, because the people in the wilderness were dying before their time. Because God told Moses the complainers would not enter the promised land, there was a quickening of death within the camp. An entire generation had to die before the nation could possess their possessions. This verse does not apply to us today, nor did it apply to any generation from Moses forward. It was specific to the nation of Israel in the wilderness. Unfortunately, because people believe any number of years they live beyond seventy or eighty is miraculous, they start getting ready to depart the earth when the years begin to creep upward. Hell has put an <u>expectation</u> of death in us, and a time frame for living on the earth has been planted in our thought lives and in our conversations. Let's not forget that we can have what we say, whether that confession is good or evil. Our words are creative. Take a look at some of the great faith Scriptures, and see what Jesus had to say.

> AND JESUS ANSWERING SAYS UNTO THEM, HAVE FAITH IN GOD. FOR VERILY I SAY UNTO YOU, THAT WHOSOEVER SHALL SAY UNTO THIS MOUNTAIN, BE YOU REMOVED, AND BE YOU CAST INTO THE SEA; AND SHALL NOT DOUBT IN HIS HEART, BUT SHALL BELIEVE THAT THOSE THINGS WHICH HE SAYS SHALL COME TO PASS; HE SHALL HAVE WHATSOEVER HE SAYS. (MATTHEW 11:22–23)

Have faith in God literally translates, "Have God's faith." What does it mean to have God's faith? I think it means to believe what He believes, and to live in that belief. When we believe what God believes, then according to Jesus, we can say to the thing that rises up before us, <u>even if that thing is death</u>, "Be you removed and cast into the sea!" and God's faith will move it out of our way.

Perhaps you are thinking, "Yes, but that doesn't mean death. Everybody has to die. The Word says so." Does it? And in what context does it say we die? We've already shown that in one of those places, the Word was specific to a certain people at a certain time for a certain purpose. God was shortening the days of the lives of the rebellious so that the next generation could move ahead in His plan. That was an expression of mercy to the generations. Don't forget—every person who died before Christ had the opportunity to go with Him into heaven (the realm of happiness, power, and eternity). They were not in the burning flames of hell, but sleeping in their graves when Jesus went into paradise where their spirits were kept. He revealed Himself and told them, "I am the One you've been waiting for, and I'm rising up out of this place. If you want to, you can come with me. Just believe."

Another place people use to say we have to die is in Hebrews.

AND AS IT IS APPOINTED UNTO MEN ONCE TO DIE, BUT AFTER THIS THE JUDGMENT. (HEBREWS 9:27)

On its surface, this looks pretty clear—men are appointed to die once, and then be judged. However, let's dig a little deeper. In its context, the writer is explaining the sacrifice of Jesus Christ on our behalf. He is saying the blood of bulls and goats, offered annually by the high priest was sufficient as an atonement for earthly things. People without the Holy Spirit within them fall into this category; but heavenly things—people who have the Holy Spirit within them—are purified by the blood of our High Priest Jesus Christ, once for all and for all time. Let's look at the entire passage (Hebrews 9:16–28) in its context and see what the Holy Spirit will reveal.

"For where a testament is, there must also of necessity be the death of the testator." In order to give us an inheritance, Jesus had to die. His "last will and testament" is in force because of his crucifixion. Every promise we can see in Scripture now belongs to us. It is up to us to now possess our possessions. "For a testament is of force after men are dead: otherwise it is of no strength at all while the testator lives." Jesus Christ is the only man who ever lived to probate His own will. Because of His resurrection, the inheritance He died to give us can never be revoked by hell.

He defeated death, hell, and the grave by His resurrection; and that gives us the same right.

"Whereupon neither the first testament was dedicated without blood." This, of course refers to animal sacrifices which were a type and shadow of what was to come.

"For when Moses had spoken every precept to all the people according to the law, he took the blood of calves and of goats, with water, and scarlet wool, and hyssop, and sprinkled both the book, and all the people, Saying, This is the blood of the testament which God has enjoined unto you. Moreover he sprinkled with blood both the tabernacle, and all the vessels of the ministry." Everything was covered by the blood, which was another type and shadow of what was coming.

"And almost all things are by the law purged with blood; and without shedding of blood is no remission." Nothing we can do will save us. Good works, the works of our hands, the things we can accomplish in our own human reasoning and our own human strength won't do it. Before the cross, an annual animal sacrifice was made as an atonement for the sins of the people. Today, the remission of sin, and every other aspect of our salvation, is only made possible because of the blood of the Lord Jesus Christ who gave His life once, for all of us. "It was therefore necessary that the patterns of things in the heavens should be purified with these; but the heavenly things themselves with better sacrifices than these." The patterns of things in the heavens, the temple and its instruments and rituals, were made holy by animal sacrifices, but the true heavenly things required a better sacrifice.

"For Christ is not entered into the holy places made with hands, which are the figures of the true; but into heaven itself, now to appear in the presence of God for us." Here is the real meat of this passage. The holy places made with hands are those tangible edifices we call temples, churches, synagogues, fellowship halls, whatever. These are temporary figures of the true. But the true holy places into which Christ enters are not made with hands. This verse says Christ is entered into heaven itself, to appear in the presence of God for us. The word "for" actually translates "over or instead of." The word "heaven" translates "the realm of happiness, power, and eternity." This realm is meant to be where we are because of Jesus Christ. We've been taught that heaven is simply a place we go after we die, to be in the presence of God. That's true, but it isn't the whole truth. Heaven is a spiritual place we can have now, in this life. When Christ enters the temples not made with hands, you and me, He expects to be in the place of happiness, power, and eternity. He sits at the right hand of the Father, and we are seated with Him in that heavenly place. When we go before the Father, Almighty God, we go covered over by Jesus.

"Nor yet that he should offer himself often, as the high priest enters into the holy place every year with blood of others; For then must he often have suffered since the foundation of the world: but now once in the end of the world has he appeared to put away sin by the sacrifice of himself." Jesus doesn't come and go in His temples. He's either in, or He's out. Our spirit does not have a revolving door where Jesus gets caught going round and round, and in and out. My acceptance of His single sacrifice on my behalf, His life for mine, gave Jesus Christ permanent residence in my heart.

"And as it is appointed unto men once to die, but after this the judgment." The word "appointed" means "reserved ... away from something near, stretched out in a prone or horizontal position." We are positioned to die, but what kind of death are we reserved for? Is it a physical death, a spiritual death, or both? Consider this:

the appointed time in which we give up our lives to live His life, on this earth and in our physical body, is reserved for each of us. We will either agree to die to ourselves and live <u>from</u> Christ, or we will experience death in our bodies. When we prostrate ourselves before the Lord and die to our wants and our ways, judgment begins. God comes to purge us of evil. He judges evil spirits and removes them from us, with our agreement and cooperation. His judgment on evil in our lives brings justice to us in every area. It may be painful when God cuts something out of our lives, but what He cuts out is something that wasn't good for us, and so the judgment is merciful. Perhaps this is the death spoken of when we surrender our lives and depart from the things of the world. We know that one day we will stand before the judgment seat of Christ, but we won't be there for punishment. We'll be there for reward. We are to judge ourselves now, in this life, according to the Word. From this we can surmise that our born-again experience is a death to self, and a time to begin to allow God to judge us and cleanse us. The final verse explains this.

"So Christ was once offered to bear the sins of many; and unto them that look for him shall he appear the second time without sin unto salvation." Christ died once. He offered Himself and in doing so He bore the sins of many, including yours and mine. The wages of sin is death. If Jesus bore our sins, we don't get the wages of sin anymore … that is, unless we want them. Death writes a paycheck I don't want. I'm not working for death anymore, I'm working for LIFE! And I'm looking for Christ. When He appears IN ME it is without sin, and I can then move in the resurrection power of the Holy Spirit which dwells within me.

Our hope of glory is the resurrection of Christ <u>in us.</u>

> WHEREOF I AM MADE A MINISTER, ACCORDING TO THE
> DISPENSATION OF GOD WHICH IS GIVEN TO ME FOR YOU, TO
> FULFILL THE WORD OF GOD; EVEN THE MYSTERY WHICH HAS
> BEEN HID FROM AGES AND FROM GENERATIONS, BUT NOW
> IS MADE MANIFEST TO HIS SAINTS: TO WHOM GOD WOULD

MAKE KNOWN WHAT IS THE RICHES OF THE GLORY OF THIS
MYSTERY AMONG THE GENTILES; WHICH IS CHRIST IN YOU,
THE HOPE OF GLORY. (COLOSSIANS 1:25–27)

As ministers of Christ, we are to fulfill the Word of God and reveal
the mystery of the ages, which is Christ in us. Not Christ someday
coming back to earth in bodily form. He will, but there's no mystery in that. He's coming. Before that can happen, Christ must be
revealed from within His believers! The Body of Christ needs to
function as life and truth, not death and deception, which is where
many of us seem to hang out. When will Jesus Christ return? I believe He will return when the world is restored and His enemies are
made His footstool.

AND HE SHALL SEND JESUS CHRIST, WHICH BEFORE WAS
PREACHED UNTO YOU: WHOM THE HEAVEN MUST RECEIVE
UNTIL THE TIMES OF RESTITUTION OF ALL THINGS, WHICH
GOD HAS SPOKEN BY THE MOUTH OF HIS HOLY PROPHETS
SINCE THE WORLD BEGAN. (ACTS 3:20–21)

FOR AS IN ADAM ALL DIE, EVEN SO IN CHRIST SHALL ALL BE
MADE ALIVE. BUT EVERY MAN IN HIS OWN ORDER: CHRIST
THE FIRSTFRUITS; AFTERWARD THEY THAT ARE CHRIST'S AT HIS
COMING. THEN COMES THE END, WHEN HE SHALL HAVE DELIV-
ERED UP THE KINGDOM TO GOD, EVEN THE FATHER; WHEN HE
SHALL HAVE PUT DOWN ALL RULE AND ALL AUTHORITY AND
POWER. FOR HE MUST REIGN, TILL HE HAS PUT ALL ENEMIES
UNDER HIS FEET. THE LAST ENEMY THAT SHALL BE DESTROYED
IS DEATH. (1 CORINTHIANS 15:22–26)

Jesus Christ is reigning now, or should be, from His position of
authority in His temple, which is His body of believers. If you've
got Jesus in you, let Him out! It is our responsibility to allow God
to work through us to accomplish this in its entirety. The last enemy
is called death. We must clearly see death as an enemy and not a
friend. We are His body, and the body has feet; so if death is to be
put under our feet, we're the ones who have to trample it. Jesus came

to earth and demonstrated a kingdom greater than any ever known before or since. He then allowed death to take over His <u>physical</u> body so that He, in His <u>spiritual</u> body, could indwell each and every one of us. Jesus died to give us not only access to the kingdom He brought back to earth, but also possession of that kingdom. He was resurrected and rose again to prove the power of God over death, hell, and the grave, and to make certain the inheritance He died to give us was properly distributed. Look at His coronation celebration:

> I SAW IN THE NIGHT VISIONS, AND, BEHOLD, ONE LIKE THE SON OF MAN CAME WITH THE CLOUDS OF HEAVEN, AND CAME TO THE ANCIENT OF DAYS, AND THEY BROUGHT HIM NEAR BEFORE HIM. AND THERE WAS GIVEN HIM DOMINION, AND GLORY, AND A KINGDOM, THAT ALL PEOPLE, NATIONS, AND LANGUAGES, SHOULD SERVE HIM: HIS DOMINION IS AN EVERLASTING DOMINION, WHICH SHALL NOT PASS AWAY, AND HIS KINGDOM THAT WHICH SHALL NOT BE DESTROYED. BUT THE SAINTS OF THE MOST HIGH SHALL TAKE THE KINGDOM, AND POSSESS THE KINGDOM FOR EVER, EVEN FOR EVER AND EVER. AND THE KINGDOM AND DOMINION, AND THE GREAT-NESS OF THE KINGDOM UNDER THE WHOLE HEAVEN, SHALL BE GIVEN TO THE PEOPLE OF THE SAINTS OF THE MOST HIGH, WHOSE KINGDOM IS AN EVERLASTING KINGDOM, AND ALL DOMINIONS SHALL SERVE AND OBEY HIM.
> (DANIEL 7:13–14, 18, 27)

Jesus Christ ascended into the spirit realm, received His kingdom from the Father, turned around and returned to the natural realm, walked the earth in His resurrected body, and taught His disciples what to do to put the kingdom in order—heal the sick, raise the dead, cast out devils. When Jesus returns in bodily form once again, it will not be to establish His kingdom, because He's already done that, and He expects us to continue what He started. He will return in bodily form to receive His kingdom, which has been put in order through us, by Him. Then He will present the kingdom as a gift to the Father, "Look, Dad, it's been restored, just as You meant for it to be from the beginning. Look at my beautiful bride!" There is indication of a generation which will pass over the grave. Therefore, death is not a certainty for a true believer.

One of the main reasons we haven't achieved the depth of this revelation can be found in God's explanation through the prophet Isaiah. He says we priests think everything is just fine because we are God's chosen people and priesthood. However, we're still subject to the world's ways and death because of our own beliefs in the world's ways and death.

> WHEREFORE HEAR THE WORD OF THE LORD, YOU SCORN-
> FUL MEN, THAT RULE THIS PEOPLE WHICH IS IN JERUSALEM.
> BECAUSE YOU HAVE SAID, WE HAVE MADE A COVENANT WITH
> DEATH, AND WITH HELL ARE WE AT AGREEMENT; WHEN THE
> OVERFLOWING SCOURGE SHALL PASS THROUGH, IT SHALL NOT
> COME UNTO US: FOR WE HAVE MADE LIES OUR REFUGE, AND
> UNDER FALSEHOOD HAVE WE HID OURSELVES: THEREFORE
> THUS SAYS THE LORD GOD, BEHOLD, I LAY IN ZION FOR A
> FOUNDATION A STONE, A TRIED STONE, A PRECIOUS CORNER
> STONE, A SURE FOUNDATION: HE THAT BELIEVES SHALL NOT
> MAKE HASTE. JUDGMENT ALSO WILL I LAY TO THE LINE, AND
> RIGHTEOUSNESS TO THE PLUMMET: AND THE HAIL SHALL
> SWEEP AWAY THE REFUGE OF LIES, AND THE WATERS SHALL
> OVERFLOW THE HIDING PLACE. AND YOUR COVENANT WITH
> DEATH SHALL BE DISANNULLED, AND YOUR AGREEMENT WITH
> HELL SHALL NOT STAND; WHEN THE OVERFLOWING SCOURGE
> SHALL PASS THROUGH, THEN YOU SHALL BE TRODDEN DOWN
> BY IT. (ISAIAH 28:14–18)

God says we've made a covenant with death. Perhaps you don't agree, but there are evidences of our covenant with death in our own lives. For example, people buy life insurance policies and grave plots because we are so aligned with death as to accept its inevitability. We plan our funerals, and we wonder who's going to show up, what songs we want sung, and who we want to serve as our pall bearers. That's a covenant. As the years go by and our bodies wear down from sin or ill-use (which is also sin) many of us say, "I'm just getting old. I'm ready to die." Even later on, as friends die off or we live with chronic pain or heartache, a lot of people begin to ask the Lord to "take me home." The Word says we shouldn't be in haste, but we get that way, or know someone who has. Agreeing with death is easy; agreeing with life is not so easy.

The other part of our covenant with death is considering death a friend rather than an enemy. Some of us tend to think of death as a relief and a blessing, rather than a curse. We have been taught to welcome death rather than to reject it. We've been taught that the only resurrection is one of the physical body, not the spirit man, and that this physical resurrection can only happen at the physical return of Christ. Then and only then can we have a glorified body. Scripture doesn't tell us definitively, but it does tell us that Enoch and Elijah did not die a physical death. To me, that means they must still have a physical body, maybe a glorified body, wherever they are … or perhaps God returned their bodies instantly to dust and extracted their spirits to be with Him.

Either way, if they are examples to us, and they are, then we have hope of stepping over the grave, just as these men did. Enoch's confession was, "I please God." How many of us can say that? I believe that one way to please God is to agree with Him that death is an enemy which has no power over us, and to break our agreement with it. Let's do that now.

Father God, again I thank You for truth. I admit it is difficult for me to accept that there is a possibility of not having to die a physical death. But I do know that Your ways are higher than my ways and I have the desire to live in Your ways. I am sorry that I have accepted death as an inevitable occurrence, and I repent if I have ever wished for it at some point in my life. Forgive me, Father, for making haste, and for not fully realizing that

You have more use for me here and now, in this life and in this world, than in any future life to come. Help me live my life to its fullest, to be my best self in all that I do, and to always look at a future of hope and truth. I want to fulfill my assignments from heaven, which bring life and restoration, and stop agreeing with the assignments of hell which bring death and destruction. Make me aware of my thoughts and my words, Father, so that I can remove those which oppose Your heart. My desire is to think and to speak in such a way that I can expose Your heart, Lord, not oppose it. I want others around me to know what You are like just by my presence. To know that You are Life, and Truth, and Love, and Humility. Jesus, Your Word says that as You are, so are we in this world. You are alive! You've been resurrected, never to die again. Have that be the reality of my life, Lord, that I am resurrected daily in You, and show me how to be a part of the generation that will step over the grave. Amen.

Section Three

AGAIN,
HE MEASURED A THOUSAND,
AND BROUGHT ME THROUGH;
THE WATERS WERE TO THE LOINS.
(EZEKIEL 47:4B)

Chapter Eleven

Identifying Satan's Legal Right to Your Life

Having now delved into some greater understanding of our true identity and explored how we may have been deceived by religion into accepting wrong beliefs, perhaps it is time to explore why the devil can afflict and affect us. If all power belongs to God, and God is on our side, then why does He not always step in and rescue us in the natural world? Why does God stand aside and allow the devil to have his way in our lives? Can it only be because of our wrong beliefs, or is there something more?

> God has spoken once; twice have I heard this; that power belongs to God. (Psalm 62:11)

> And Jesus came and spoke to them, saying, All power is given to me in heaven and in earth. (Matthew 28:18)

> What shall we then say to these things? If God be for us, who can be against us? (Romans 8:31)

Our circumstances do not always testify of the true love and lasting goodness of the Lord. Reasons for this can be many and varied. Satan is a legalist. If there is a place within us that has not been given over wholly and completely to the Lord, the devil will claim it as his. He has the legal right to claim it because, in our ignorance or willful disobedience, we have disagreed with God in that particular area of our lives. Any disagreement with God by default becomes an agreement with Satan, and he begins to work to destroy us. This section will introduce you to the most common means by which Satan stakes his claim, and practical ways to address these legal rights, including prayers to help free yourself from bondage. Although this section contains a solid presentation of spiritual roots and means to freedom from accusations and curses, there may be situations or circumstances in your life that require further exploration. It is often helpful to have a deeper biblical and cultural context surrounding these areas of Satan's legal right. In order to help you gain that understanding, a study guide was created and is available for individual or group study through Freedom's Way Ministries.

Years ago, I came to the realization that the only thing we own, the only thing that is 100 percent our own, is our will. Even the good we do doesn't belong to us. We can't claim credit for doing good because it is the Holy Spirit working in us and manifesting through us that produces good works. If we are doing good works from any other motive than love, the works we do are dead works. They are no more than manifestations of evil spirits called self-righteousness and pride. Our will is the decision-making faculty which we use to determine our responses and actions. We decide, for example, when someone knocks on the door of our home, whether or not to let that person enter. The will determines what we allow in our lives and what we don't. We get to choose. We get to choose which kingdom we will allow to manifest through us.

We have God and we have an enemy. Both want to access and use us.

God wants to express Himself through us. He wants us to die to ourselves and what we want so that He can work His works in the earth. Satan and his demons also want to express themselves through us. Two of the primary ways they accomplish this are through deception and fear. If the devil can keep you in fear, you're his to use as he wishes (knowingly or unknowingly on your part). Through fear, the devil snares us, but there is a way out. We must recognize the sin of fear, repent for it, and remove it from our minds and hearts.

> AND THE SERVANT OF THE LORD MUST NOT STRIVE; BUT BE GENTLE UNTO ALL MEN, APT TO TEACH, PATIENT, IN MEEKNESS INSTRUCTING THOSE THAT OPPOSE THEMSELVES; IF GOD PERADVENTURE WILL GIVE THEM REPENTANCE TO THE ACKNOWLEDGING OF THE TRUTH; AND THAT THEY MAY RECOVER THEMSELVES OUT OF THE SNARE OF THE DEVIL, WHO ARE TAKEN CAPTIVE BY HIM AT HIS WILL.
> (2 TIMOTHY 2:24–26)

We must agree with God that we were not given a spirit of fear, but that we have all the fullness of the Godhead in us because of Jesus and His finished work on the cross.

> FOR GOD HAS NOT GIVEN US THE SPIRIT OF FEAR; BUT OF POWER, AND OF LOVE, AND OF A SOUND MIND.
> (2 TIMOTHY 1:7)

We have the Spirit of God in its entirety and therefore should never entertain fear of any kind, for any reason, at any time. In the verse above, power represents the Holy Spirit, who empowers us to overcome adversity and to be lifted up through humility. Love represents God the Father who gave His only begotten Son that we might be reconciled back to Him and have relationship with our Father. The sound mind represents Jesus Christ, who gives us wisdom through the Word to cleanse and refresh us. Once we grasp the truth that God really is bigger than the boogie man, and that He really cares about us and can do a better job with our lives than we can, fear won't have a chance to mess us up. There will no longer be an open door to fear when you have, living and working in you, the perfect love of God that casts out all fear.

Take note that God has given us power. If you read on in Matthew 28, you'll see that after Jesus declared that all power had been given to Him, He said, "Now you go!" He handed over authority to use the power of God, the heft of heaven itself, to His disciples. That includes you and me, if you are a born-again believer.

> AND JESUS CAME AND SPOKE TO THEM, SAYING, ALL POWER
> IS GIVEN TO ME IN HEAVEN AND IN EARTH. GO YOU THERE-
> FORE, AND TEACH ALL NATIONS, BAPTIZING THEM IN THE
> NAME OF THE FATHER, AND OF THE SON, AND OF THE HOLY
> GHOST: TEACHING THEM TO OBSERVE ALL THINGS WHAT-
> SOEVER I HAVE COMMANDED YOU: AND, LO, I AM WITH
> YOU ALWAYS, EVEN UNTO THE END OF THE WORLD. AMEN.
> (MATTHEW 28:18–20)

Another noteworthy weapon Satan uses is deception, which we've already looked at in four areas often misinterpreted by religion (sin, sickness, poverty, and death). God does not want us ignorant of the devil's ways. Ephesians says God wants us to stand ready and equipped to withstand the wiles of the devil.

> PUT ON THE WHOLE ARMOR OF GOD THAT YOU MAY BE ABLE
> TO STAND AGAINST THE WILES OF THE DEVIL. (EPHESIANS 6:11)

Today's description of "wiles" would be "schemes or tricky methods." From careful study of the word, we can reason that the wiles of the devil are ever moving around us, accompanying us in our travels, and that they carry a purpose and have a method. Their purpose, of course, is to gain our agreement. The devil knows we have the authority to use God's power, and wants our agreement (knowingly or unknowingly) to surrender it to him. If Satan can get us to hand over the power, he's in. His method is deception.

If the devil came to you in his red suit and pitchfork and said, "Hey, I'm here to ruin your day!" You'd say, "Oh no, you're not!" and you would stand against him in the power of God. But he doesn't come that way. Satan comes with deception, whispering another gospel into your spirit, hissing like the serpent hissed to Eve, and instilling doubt into your thinking. "What if" is his favorite question. "What if God doesn't heal you? Look—it hasn't happened. What if you're not really saved? What if God doesn't love you after all? What if you're not worthy? What if this happens, or that happens?"

The "what ifs" that pop up in your thinking are almost always thoughts instilled in your mind by the devil. They are meant to cause doubt concerning the things of God and throw you into fear of the future. "What ifs" can also drag you back into the past and keep you in self-pity. "What if I hadn't married that guy or that girl? What if I'd had different parents? What if I hadn't gone to this doctor, or participated in that practice? If only I had…." These types of "what ifs" and "if onlys" defeat God's people as easily as the ones that project into the future, because God does not want us in our past. He is the God of now. He is I AM, not "I used to be," or "I never was," or "I will be some day." He is interested in what you do now with what you know. God says, "How will you respond now to my ability?" That is the phrase that defines our responsibility in this life: we are to respond to God's ability. Whenever you hear "what if" you need to take that thought captive and examine it. You may likely discover the devil is at work to trap you into disagreeing with God.

As stated, any disagreement with God is an agreement with the enemy. Perhaps you're not ready to receive that as truth. If you don't agree with me, that's okay. It isn't important that we agree with each other. It is important that we each and every one agree with God. If you want to think those thoughts originated in your own head, then take the credit. It will only make it more difficult for you to separate yourself from that way of thinking. Because if a thought doesn't line up with what God said, no matter where it came from, we are to cast it down!

(FOR THE WEAPONS OF OUR WARFARE ARE NOT CARNAL, BUT MIGHTY THROUGH GOD TO THE PULLING DOWN OF STRONG

> HOLDS;) CASTING DOWN IMAGINATIONS, AND EVERY HIGH
> THING THAT EXALTS ITSELF AGAINST THE KNOWLEDGE OF
> GOD, AND BRINGING INTO CAPTIVITY EVERY THOUGHT TO
> THE OBEDIENCE OF CHRIST. (2 CORINTHIANS 10:4–5)

In addition to wrong beliefs and traditions of religion, there are still more veils of deception that prevent us from realizing how the devil sneaks in. Knowing the truth is what makes us free, so let's get free. We've found five areas where Satan takes occasion by way of his legal right to bring curses into our lives and to take ground from us. These are:

Word curses,

Our own personal sins,

Sins of our fathers—generational iniquities,

Involvement in others' sins—associational sins,

Witchcraft or incantation.

All of these are open doors for various evil spirits to come in and influence our lives—many times through curses which are already in the earth. In our seminars, we expose all of these areas, in order to clearly reveal the wiles of the devil. Also, we show how so many, through ignorance as well as willful disobedience, can fall victim to assignments of the enemy and live under a curse. Proverbs tells us that "the curse causeless shall not come," so we know if there is a curse ongoing or recurring in our lives, there is a reason for it.

> AS THE BIRD BY WANDERING, AS THE SWALLOW BY FLYING, SO
> THE CURSE CAUSELESS SHALL NOT COME. (PROVERBS 26:2)

This verse doesn't mean the curse will never touch you, or won't slap you as it passes. It means the curse will not come to rest on you. It's not going to make its home with you and continually torment or afflict you. Yes, there can be intrusion by the enemy through no fault of your own.

> FOR, LO, THEY LIE IN WAIT FOR MY SOUL: THE MIGHTY ARE
> GATHERED AGAINST ME; NOT FOR MY TRANSGRESSION, NOR
> FOR MY SIN, O LORD. (PSALM 59:3)

Even though we may not have opened the door, Satan will do his best to interrupt your righteousness in Christ and cause a crack in your armor. If his intrusion can create the slightest crack or weakness, it's probable that the devil will come bursting in. Still, more than likely, when the curse comes into our lives, we have stepped out from under the protection of the Father in one of the five named areas of Satan's legal right to afflict.

Let's start with word curses, an area greatly affecting God's people. Too many times, we curse ourselves and others without being aware of opening that door. The spoken word is perhaps the most creative force in the universe. Consider just a couple of important points:

First of all, the worlds and everything in them were created by the spoken Word of God. Think about these words. The words God spoke were carried on His breath. God's breath is in man. You and I are breathing with God's breath. It is His creative, life-giving breath that carries our words.

> AND THE LORD GOD FORMED MAN OF THE DUST OF THE
> GROUND, AND BREATHED INTO HIS NOSTRILS THE BREATH OF
> LIFE; AND MAN BECAME A LIVING SOUL. (GENESIS 2:7)

It's God's breath in us that gives us life, and that gives life to our words. There are many, many Scriptures that speak of the creativity of our words, and this is the reason why. Our words are carried on God's breath. Satan likes nothing better than for us to use God's breath against Him by creating evil. Here's a verse you may not have considered in this light:

> HE SHUTTETH HIS EYES TO DEVISE FROWARD THINGS: MOVING HIS LIPS HE BRINGETH EVIL TO PASS. (PROVERBS 16:30)

How can this be? The Word tells us that angels "hearken" to the voice of the Word of God. Hearken means they are listening to obey. So when we speak a word in agreement with what God says, the angels are on alert to capture that word and make it happen. They perform it; they work the word for its intended purpose in God. The opposite is also true. When we speak a word that opposes God and what He says, Satan's demons are on alert to capture that word and make it happen. They perform the word for its intended purpose in Satan, which is to thwart the advancement of the kingdom of God and to bring evil into our lives.

> BLESS THE LORD, YE HIS ANGELS, THAT EXCEL IN STRENGTH, THAT DO HIS COMMANDMENTS, HEARKENING UNTO THE VOICE OF HIS WORD. (PSALM 103:20)

Truly realizing the power of our words helps us to close this open door to the devil and keep curses out of our lives and the lives of our loved ones. Know, too, that words spoken in jest are still creative in the atmosphere. Satan doesn't care if you "didn't really mean it." You said it, and that's good enough for him.

Another area that opens doors to the devil and his curses is our own personal sins. These are the actions and attitudes of our lives which oppose God's ways, His Word, and His will. We already know that sin is more than simply the action or attitude, and that the devil has a hand in all of it. But clearly, each one of us is accountable for allowing the evil spirit to express itself through us in any area. We are also clearly responsible for the action or attitude that resulted from that evil influence.

Certainly, it isn't necessary to define all the aspects or specifics in sinful actions and attitudes. Most of us recognize and understand when we have sinned. You may get a little twitch in your stomach or a sick feeling in your gut, and you know. All of the sins we commit will ultimately fall under one or more of three categories: Fear, Pride, or Deception. These are the primary aspects of Satan's nature, which still works within us even after we are born again and reconnected to our true nature, the nature of God. Deuteronomy 28 outlines curses that result from not keeping God's commandments. Now that we are in a better covenant, God's commandments are simple: love the Lord your God with all your heart, mind, soul, and strength and love your neighbor as yourself.

I assure you, if you are walking in love and forgiveness toward yourself and others, it is impossible to break any of God's previous commandments. In Romans we are told, "Whatsoever is not of faith is sin" (Romans 14:23b).

There are sins of omission as well as sins of commission.

> THEREFORE TO HIM THAT KNOWETH TO DO GOOD, AND
> DOETH IT NOT, TO HIM IT IS SIN. (JAMES 4:17)

It seems that the way to close the open door of sin in our lives, we need only to trust God and to walk in love. It's simple, but it isn't always easy, is it? From a practical, "What can I do?" standpoint, keep directing your thoughts back to your true identity. Recognize when fear, pride, and deception are stalking you and remember who you are. Remember that you have the heft of heaven in your spoken word that agrees with God. Refuse Satan entrance through your thoughts and emotions, and keep short accounts with the Father. When you mess up, 'fess up! Confess and repent. Then do your best to identify the evil spirit, reject it, and remove it from your life. We will all commit sins, not because we are sinners, but because we are easily deceived, made to feel fearful, and snared into the pride of "self." Thank God we have a Savior!

> IF WE SAY THAT WE HAVE NO SIN, WE DECEIVE OURSELVES,
> AND THE TRUTH IS NOT IN US. IF WE CONFESS OUR SINS, HE

IS FAITHFUL AND JUST TO FORGIVE US OUR SINS, AND TO
CLEANSE US FROM ALL UNRIGHTEOUSNESS. IF WE SAY THAT WE
HAVE NOT SINNED, WE MAKE HIM A LIAR, AND HIS WORD IS
NOT IN US. (1 JOHN 1:8–10)

Moving into the area of generational iniquities, most people realize that generational traits are passed from father to son, from mother to daughter, etc. But not everyone realizes that these traits may be more than just a tendency or propensity for a certain thing. They could easily be evil spirits that travel from one generation to the next to destroy families and individuals. We need to put aside what we think we know, and look to the truth as revealed by the Holy Spirit.

AND IF ANY MAN THINK THAT HE KNOWS ANY THING, HE
KNOWS NOTHING YET AS HE OUGHT TO KNOW.
(1 CORINTHIANS 8:2)

Some believe and teach that generational sins are no longer in effect, and refer to the verses from Ezekiel 18. The passage basically states that fathers don't die for the sins of their sons and sons don't die for the sins of their fathers. However, careful study reveals this: a son need not continue in the sins of his father, but rather can choose life by turning away in repentance and forgiveness of his ancestors and restoring the principles of God into the family line. It also has to do with the present tense. If a son commits a crime, for instance, the father would not be the one arrested and made to serve a prison sentence, and vice versa. We have only to look around us to see that generational curses are still in effect in the world today.

The medical profession recognizes this door to the devil, only they name it your "family history." Doctors can foretell what you may experience health-wise by the diseases that "run" in your family. These are some of the generational cords of iniquity that bind us. Then we have the tendency to fall into the same iniquities. People often receive this as their lot in life, and do not believe that anything can change. "It is what it is," is a saying that holds iniquities and their resulting consequences in place.

> HIS OWN INIQUITIES SHALL TAKE THE WICKED HIMSELF, AND
> HE SHALL BE HOLDEN WITH THE CORDS OF HIS SINS. HE SHALL
> DIE WITHOUT INSTRUCTION; AND IN THE GREATNESS OF HIS
> FOLLY HE SHALL GO ASTRAY. (PROVERBS 5:22–23)

> AND IF THEY BE BOUND IN FETTERS, AND BE HELD IN CORDS
> OF AFFLICTION; THEN HE SHOWS THEM THEIR WORK, AND
> THEIR TRANSGRESSIONS THAT THEY HAVE EXCEEDED. HE OPENS
> ALSO THEIR EAR TO DISCIPLINE, AND COMMANDS THAT THEY
> RETURN FROM INIQUITY. IF THEY OBEY AND SERVE HIM, THEY
> SHALL SPEND THEIR DAYS IN PROSPERITY, AND THEIR YEARS IN
> PLEASURES. BUT IF THEY OBEY NOT, THEY SHALL PERISH BY THE
> SWORD, AND THEY SHALL DIE WITHOUT KNOWLEDGE.
> (JOB 36:8–12)

There are several Scriptures confirming that God's people perish for lack of knowledge. Without instruction, we die. You are receiving knowledge and instruction, that you may recover yourself from the snare of the devil. Perhaps you believe it's not fair that you should have to repent for something your grandfather did, either in action or attitude. It wasn't your fault. Still, chances are that in some way you have entertained some of the same thoughts and participated in some of the same activities. Even if you haven't, consider this: someone has to own a thing before it can be given away. Your ancestors or those who opened these doors of iniquity—the ones who went their own way and departed from the Word of God—aren't here to own it. We must repent on their behalf. Stand in the gap to forgive them, take responsibility for the curse, and then give it to the Lord Jesus who is your curse bearer.

The next area of Satan's legal right is associational sin. This is one area where most of us are very susceptible to the wiles of the enemy, and often are unaware of how we set ourselves up for curses. We are susceptible because we like people or we love someone and don't want to see our loved one suffer. Perhaps we want to be approved and accepted by others. Maybe we simply go along to get along, so that we don't risk being rejected. Need for approval and fear of rejection are two reasons why people fall into associational sin. In order to define associational sin and its resulting consequences, read the account of Ananias and his wife, Sapphira, in Acts 5.

Briefly, members of the church were selling their possessions and bringing the proceeds to the church. Each one was taking care of another so that no one went without and all were cared for. Ananias sold a property and decided to keep back a portion. He decided to withhold something, and he apparently told his wife what he was doing. In the culture of the day, you will see that a woman did not avail herself of those decisions. The man was in charge. It was HIS sin, not hers. But when her husband didn't come back home after a reasonable time (the Word says it was about three hours), Sapphira came looking for him.

When Peter asked her if the land was sold for what Ananias gave them, she covered for him and lied about it. She thought she was being a good wife by covering for him and hiding his sin, and she was then made subject to the same consequence of the sin. It became as much her sin as it was her husband's. What these two did may seem to be understandable. Consider. Perhaps they had a piece of property and thought it was worth a certain amount. So they pledged to give the money to the church, "We're going to sell our property and give the money to you!" Then, when they sold it, they found it brought more than they thought it would, so they gave the amount that was in their heads at the first. That kind of withholding would be tempting for anyone to do. After all, they likely never pledged a certain amount, just the proceeds from the sale.

Many people are tempted to cover for others in their sins, because they may believe there is a benefit in it for them. Maybe they will be better-liked, or the other guy will return the favor at some time in the future, or perhaps covering for another will give them a "bargaining chip" in the relationship. However, when we cover another's transgression, we open the door for curses to affect us. A person can fall into agreement with associational sin through co-dependency. This is where we end up calling evil good for the sake of love. We might cover for a spouse or a loved one out of love, and end up under the same curse as they have, or a similar one. We might give our children money, knowing they are using it for drugs or riotous living, or poor stewardship, or something else that may not be pleasing to God. When that happens, we justify the action because it seems to be the right thing to do. Maybe we don't want to see them in trouble, evicted from where they're living, or going to jail for writing bad checks—any number of what we think are good reasons to help them out—so we bail them out one more time. But, by helping them continue along the wrong path, we may be participating in associational sin and holding curses in place in their lives as well as inviting curses into our own lives.

There are many other examples of associational sin in the Bible, and many of us have our own testimonies as well. Once we realize the impact that other people's sins can have on us, we will find it easier to separate ourselves from it. The Holy Spirit in us will lead and guide us, when we stop and listen to His voice and not to the voices that tell us we'll lose a friend if we refuse to go along with what they're doing. Or that it's okay to tell a little white lie so no one gets hurt. Most people know when they're doing something wrong. The Holy Spirit in us gives us a little nudge in the gut. You also need to keep in mind that the moment you confessed your sin was NOT when God found out about it! People who think they can get by with something are sadly mistaken. Now we can see that people who think they won't be affected by what someone else is doing are also sadly mistaken. If you cover another's sin, it will become your own sin. Then Satan will have a legal right to afflict you.

Here is a cautionary word about associational sin. Because you see someone doing something wrong doesn't mean you are supposed to tell them, or others, about it. Do your best NOT to condemn others for what they are doing. That kind of judgmental or self-righteous attitude opens a wide door for the devil in our own lives. We are to pray for those who have been snared and seek God's protection and guidance for them while they are under the control of the enemy. Pray that the Lord visits them with His love and truth that will free them from the evil influences of hell. Pray 2 Timothy 2:24–26, that God would grant to those who are going astray His gift of repentance to the acknowledging of the truth. But always be aware it could easily be you!

> WHEREFORE LET HIM THAT THINKS HE STANDS TAKE HEED
> LEST HE FALL. (1 CORINTHIANS 10:12)

Before we move into the area of witchcraft and incantation, let's break off a few curses. When you pray this prayer, don't simply read or pray it in your mind. This is a deliverance prayer. The reason we pray out loud is that only God can read your mind. Angels hearken to the <u>voice</u> of the Word of God, so you want them to hear your voice so that they can minister to you and enforce your agreement with God. On the other side, demons also need to hear that you break agreement with them and they no longer have a legal right to afflict or affect you. As you pray, you may experience a manifestation of some kind, or there might be nothing discernible. Many people yawn, or sneeze, or cough. You might feel a tightness in your chest or throat, a headache or band around your head, a pain in the neck, or a sick feeling in your belly. These things are normal, and not to be feared. The devil just wants to distract you or cause you fear so that the evil spirit can stay. Let it go!

Father God, in the name of Jesus Christ of Nazareth who is come in the flesh, I pull down from the heavens all evil words spoken and I crush their curses under the feet of Jesus. I command those words to die and I declare they will no longer bear fruit in my life. I now break and loose myself and my family from word curses spoken by any person, living or dead. With the sword of the Spirit of God, I sever the cords of word curses that would bind them to me. I declare I am redeemed by the blood of the Lamb. I take back all the ground I yielded to Satan through my participation in word curses, knowingly or unknowingly, and I establish myself in faith in the Lord Jesus Christ. I claim the blessing, rather than the curse. I will speak the blessing, and not the curse, over my life and the lives of others. You are my deliverer, Lord Jesus. You are my curse bearer. I confess You with my mouth, and I confess that the power of every word curse over my life is now BROKEN in the authority of Your name, Lord Jesus. I break all agreement with every spirit and spirit guide connected to word curses and ask to be delivered of them now.

I humble my heart before You, Father. I confess Jesus Christ as my Lord, and I believe He is risen from the dead. I declare I have been bought by the blood of Jesus and I am not my own. I am bought with a price and I belong to You. Father, I choose as an act of my will to forgive my ancestors who may have participated with sin. I forgive them and release them from responsibility for any curse that has attached itself to me because of their actions or attitudes. I take responsibility for those curses, and I give them to Jesus Christ, who is my curse bearer. Father, I repent to You for having cursed myself and others with my words. I ask You to forgive me, and I ask that these word curses be broken. Father, I forgive every person who has spoken a curse over me, including myself, and I release them from responsibility for those curses.

(Stop here for a moment to think of those people and the things they said. Forgive them and release them. As time goes on, I am certain the Holy Spirit will bring to your remembrance other things that were spoken, and you will know how to free yourself through repentance and forgiveness.)

I confess my sins and the sins of my fathers. I ask forgiveness for any time I participated in the iniquity of going my own way in any area, for disregarding Your Word. I repent for all sexual sins and iniquities, ungodly order in the home, and disorder in the family. I am sorry, Lord, that I honored my children or spouse over You. I am sorry, Lord, for cursing my parents, and for any time I did not honor them with my words or my actions. I ask You to forgive me, Lord, for any time I failed to properly minister to You or to Your people, for any time I touched Your glory or tried to take credit to myself, for any time I have robbed You by not fully giving myself to You. I repent for not paying my vows to You and for not cooperating with You in Your work. Please forgive me, Father. I ask that the curses connected to these actions and attitudes be BROKEN off my life now, in the name of Jesus.

Show me, Heavenly Father, every evil work, sin, perversity, fault or iniquity, generational or present, that has kept me from complete liberty in the Lord Jesus Christ. I appropriate forgiveness for myself and my family, and remit those sins. I stand in the gap for all my ancestors who rejected Your ways and followed their own ways, being led into paths opposed to Your Word. I forgive them, and I release them now from responsibility for any curse that has attached itself to me. Lord, I ask You to forgive me for my own participation in the sins of my fathers, and for entertaining the thoughts of the enemy, for dwelling on those thoughts, and imagining those acts, even if I never engaged in them personally. Lord, You said even the thought of foolishness is sin, and I ask to be forgiven for foolish thoughts and actions. I am sorry, Lord, that I allowed generational curses to continue in my family. I am sorry that I have been negligent in bringing judgment on the enemy and justice to my family. I break and loose myself and my family from generational curses. I accept Your forgiveness, Father, and I thank You for cleansing me and my family from all unrighteousness by the blood of Jesus Christ. I choose life and freedom through living by the principles of every word that proceeds from Your mouth.

In the name of Jesus Christ of Nazareth, who is come in the flesh, I command every evil, unclean spirit that has come through these doors to leave me NOW! I speak to every demon and demonic root of word curses, general iniquities, personal sins and iniquities, the iniquity of going my own way, disregarding Your word, family disorder, ungodly order in the home, and disorder in the church and I cast You out. I send You to the pit, bound to be burned. Loose me and let me go! By the blood of Jesus and the power of the Holy Spirit, I cast out every unclean, ungodly spirit or spirit guide that has prevented me from taking up the sword and drawing blood in spiritual warfare. I dig up and cast down every demon and demonic root of generational iniquities that would cause physical problems in my body. I speak to every evil familiar spirit that has followed my family line to bring guilt, shame, condemnation, or ungodly grief and I say, <u>leave me now</u> in the name of Jesus and by His blood. I declare I am a mighty warrior, armed and unafraid; and these lying spirits can no longer deceive me into avoidance of my destiny in God. I send all of you evil spirits into the pit. Thank You, Lord God, for being my covenant-keeping God, my Redeemer, my Messiah, my Risen Lord, my Deliverer!

Father, I humble my heart before You. I confess Jesus Christ as my Lord, and I believe He is risen from the dead. I choose as an act of my will to forgive all those who have offended me, who have led me in paths away from Your truth and I forgive those who were used by the devil to ensnare me. I forgive them and release them from responsibility for any curse that has attached itself to me through associational sin. Father, I recognize that I have participated with the wiles of the devil in this area, and I ask that You forgive me. I ask that the curses of associational sin be broken off my life by the power of the blood of Jesus and Your Holy Spirit. I ask that You reveal to me, Father, any and all times and circumstances where I entertained associational sin, so that I can repent to You of every instance. And I ask that You keep me alert to recognize this door so that I will not open it again in the future.

(Stop for a moment and repent for any specific associational sins the Holy Spirit has revealed to you, then continue.)

In the name of Jesus Christ of Nazareth who IS come in the flesh, I now break and loose myself and my family from the curses of associational sins from any person, living or dead. With the sword of the Spirit of God, I sever the cords of associational sin that would hold those curses in place in my life, or that would reattach them to me. I declare I am redeemed by the blood of the Lamb. I take back all the ground I yielded to Satan through my participation, knowingly or unknowingly, in associational sin, and I establish myself in faith in the Lord Jesus Christ. I claim the blessing, rather than the curse. I will speak the blessing, and not the curse, over my life and the lives of others. You are my deliverer, Lord Jesus. You are my curse bearer. I confess You with my mouth, and I confess that the power of every curse of associational sin is now BROKEN in the authority of Your name, Lord Jesus. I break all agreement with every spirit and spirit guide connected to associational sin and ask to be delivered of them now. In the name of Jesus Christ of Nazareth, who is come in the flesh, I command every evil, unclean spirit that has come through the door of associational sin in my life to leave me NOW! I speak to every demon and demonic root of associational sin and I cast You out. I send You to the pit, bound to be burned. Loose me and let me go!

(If there is any specific name or thing that comes to your mind, speak it out and command it to leave you. It will go by the authority in the name of Jesus.)

Father God, I pray that You extend Your healing anointing to flow through me in every place where a curse of associational sin, generational iniquities, personal sins, and word curses has caused infirmity, weakness, illness, pain, deformity, or disease. I ask in the name of Jesus Christ that You follow Your Word with signs and wonders, freeing me from the bondages of curses and turning them into the blessings of health in every area of my body and my mind. I thank You, Lord God, for a mighty testimony to Your glory and power coming forth from me as I begin to do things I couldn't do before. Thank You, Lord, there is none like You. To God be the glory! Amen.

Chapter Twelve

Witchcraft and Incantation

WE CAN NOW MOVE INTO THE FINAL MAJOR area of Satan's legal right, which is witchcraft and incantation. When we know how we got into something, we can get out of it! Most of us would gladly stop what we're doing that messes up our lives if we knew how to go about stopping. Uncovering the root causes and subtleties of these areas of sin exposes the wiles of the devil and how he can deceive us. That knowledge empowers us to cleanse ourselves of all filthiness of the flesh and the spirit.

> HAVING THEREFORE THESE PROMISES, DEARLY BELOVED, LET US CLEANSE OURSELVES FROM ALL FILTHINESS OF THE FLESH AND SPIRIT, PERFECTING HOLINESS IN THE FEAR OF GOD. (2 CORINTHIANS 7:1)

Our hope is to give you a general understanding about witchcraft in order to get out of it, to not fall into it, to avoid being fooled by it, and to stay out of it. This is not an exhaustive study, and much more is revealed in our seminars and study guides. Before we get into this thing called witchcraft, perhaps we should say that the more we recognize what opened the doors, the easier it will be to keep those doors closed. It's important to emphasize that it is essential to do something righteous, as well as to not do something unrighteous. The righteous thing we are to do is to bring judgment on the evil spirits that cause curses and manifest sin in our lives. We are called to repent for the sin, bring judgment on the evil spirit behind the sin, break the curse and give it to Jesus. In that way, we bring justice to ourselves and on our family line.

Equally important to victory is not doing the unrighteous thing. Certainly, it is possible for a person to discern a spirit without having knowledge of the action or behavior that gave it the right to manifest. So, we can cast out demons just because we have discerning of spirits and can recognize them. At the same time, it does little good to remove an evil spirit if we continue to open the door to that spirit by what we're doing, or by what was done somewhere back up our family line. That is the primary reason we need to know what actions and attitudes God considers a cause for curses to come. When our actions and attitudes fall into one of these areas of curses, they are often considered "open doors." Witchcraft is a very large open door in most Christians lives, even though few recognize it for what it is.

> AND SAMUEL SAID, HAS THE LORD AS GREAT DELIGHT IN BURNT OFFERINGS AND SACRIFICES, AS IN OBEYING THE VOICE OF THE LORD? BEHOLD, TO OBEY IS BETTER THAN SACRIFICE, AND TO HEARKEN THAN THE FAT OF RAMS. FOR REBELLION IS AS THE SIN OF WITCHCRAFT, AND STUBBORNNESS IS AS INIQUITY AND IDOLATRY. BECAUSE YOU HAVE REJECTED THE WORD OF THE LORD, HE HAS ALSO REJECTED YOU FROM BEING KING. (I SAMUEL 15:22–23)

You may find this interesting: Rebellion translates "bitterness, to be bitter, to make bitter, to provoke, to disobey." The first definition for rebellion in this verse is "bitterness." So, if rebellion is as the sin of witchcraft, so is bitterness. If there is a root of bitterness in your heart, rebellion is very near, and so is witchcraft! That is dangerous ground, which may be why the Word tells us bitterness springs up and defiles many, not just the one who is bitter.

> FOLLOW PEACE WITH ALL MEN, AND HOLINESS, WITHOUT WHICH NO MAN SHALL SEE THE LORD: LOOKING DILIGENTLY LEST ANY MAN FAIL OF THE GRACE OF GOD; LEST ANY ROOT OF BITTERNESS SPRINGING UP TROUBLE YOU, AND THEREBY MANY BE DEFILED. (HEBREWS 12:14–15)

Bitterness, rebellion, and witchcraft are closely related. They are intertwined and intermingle with each other, working together to bring destruction and heartache. Participating with these spirits, knowingly or unknowingly, will very likely prevent you from walking in freedom and living a victorious life.

> THEREFORE THUS SAYS THE LORD; BEHOLD, I WILL CAST YOU FROM OFF THE FACE OF THE EARTH: THIS YEAR YOU SHALL DIE, BECAUSE YOU HAVE TAUGHT REBELLION AGAINST THE LORD. SO HANANIAH THE PROPHET DIED THE SAME YEAR IN THE SEVENTH MONTH. (JEREMIAH 28:16–17)

These verses in Jeremiah refer to rebellion as apostasy and a crime. For those who may not understand the word "apostasy," it means turning away from the true God, and backsliding out of the way of righteousness. Simply put, we turn away from God and turn to something else, usually to our own way of thinking or doing things, or someone else's. It is the opposite of repentance, where we stop what we're doing, turn away from it and turn back to God. In apostasy, we are turning from God, not back to God. Any time we do that, we are dangerously close to being snared by witchcraft.

This final category of Satan's legal right to hold curses in place in our lives, witchcraft and incantation, warrants a closer look. First, we will define witchcraft and incantation and then show you how they seem to be operating in the church. It's very easy to open ourselves to curses from witchcraft, since we all want control of something. We either want to control our own lives or someone else's, and witchcraft is all about control. The first step in overcoming anything is to recognize what it is. Following are some words that make up the definitions for witchcraft and incantation.

In Strong's Concordance, we find two Hebrew words and one Greek word in which "witchcraft" is a part of the definition. The first is "magic or sorcery" and the root word means "to whisper a spell, to enchant or practice magic, a sorcerer or witch." The second

Hebrew word means "a lot, divination and the fee for it, an oracle." The root word in this case means "to distribute, to determine by lot or magical scroll, to divine, use divination, soothsayer." Divination in its simplest terms is the need to know. This need to know opens the door to a need to control, which is what witchcraft is, in its simplest terms.

The third place we find witchcraft used as a part of the definition is in the Greek, and it means "medication, pharmacy, literal or figurative magic, sorcery." The root word means "drug, spell-giving potion, druggist, poisoner, magician. [and again] sorcerer." The only place the word "witchcraft" is used in the New Testament is in Galatians 5:20, where Paul is listing the works of the flesh, which we have identified previously as manifestations of evil spirits. The works of the flesh are the sins that become ours when we allow an evil spirit to express itself through us.

There are three Hebrew words that have incantation as a part of their definitions. The first word means "to whisper in a bad sense of whispering, as opposed to whispering a private prayer." It also means "amulet," which is a lucky charm of some kind: "charm, earring, enchantment, orator, prayer." The root meaning is "whisper or mumble a spell (as a magician), charmer, and whisper together." (Think conspiracy.) The second word means "covered or secret, enchantment, covertly, privately, softly." The root meaning is "muffled, silent, soft, or wrapped." The third word means incantation or augury (which is an omen or divination) and comes from the root meaning "to hiss or whisper a magic spell."

Basically, we are back in the garden again, where Satan is hissing to Eve, enchanting and ensnaring her. His intent was control. His method was witchcraft. He wanted the dominion God had given to mankind. Every time he tricks us into participating with the spirit of witchcraft, Satan gets to use our dominion against God and against us. Witchcraft is a powerful spiritual force. It draws its power from our agreement with it, whether willful or innocent, and it opens the door for curses in our lives and in our generations. How does God feel about witchcraft?

YOU SHALL NOT SUFFER A WITCH TO LIVE. (EXODUS 22:18)

People have many questions about witchcraft, especially what is called Christian witchcraft, which some call "charismatic" witchcraft. The single most-asked question we get on the subject is this: "Can another person's incantations affect me?" In other words, does witchcraft really work? The answer is yes—and no. Allow me to explain. Again, witchcraft is a powerful spiritual force. It is powerful because it is worked through people.

AND GOD SAID, LET US MAKE MAN IN OUR IMAGE, AFTER OUR LIKENESS: AND LET THEM HAVE DOMINION OVER THE FISH OF THE SEA, AND OVER THE FOWL OF THE AIR, AND OVER THE CATTLE, AND OVER ALL THE EARTH, AND OVER EVERY CREEPING THING THAT CREEPS ON THE EARTH. (GENESIS 1:26)

The word "dominion" means "tread down, subjugate, crumble, come to have dominion, make to have dominion, prevail against, reign, bear rule, make to rule, rule over, take." Please notice—God did not give dominion to Christians. He gave dominion to mankind. Witches are simply moving in the God-given dominion of man. They tap into and operate in the spirit realm, which is where we are all supposed to be. The difference is that witches are moving in the darkness of the spirit realm, and we are called out of darkness and into His marvelous light. Witches recognize their dominion and use it to fulfill their own lusts, and in so doing are feeding the demonic realm and giving them a base of control in the earth. Do witches have dominion? Yes. That said, do not entertain fear of evil. Settle this truth in your heart: your authority in Jesus Christ supersedes, overrides, treads down, subjugates, overwhelms, and defeats the dominion of a witch.

The incantations of a witch have creative power, and they create evil. Remember one of the definitions for witchcraft is oracle, an orator, a spokesman, a mouthpiece. Just as Christians are supposed to be the oracle of God, or the mouthpiece for good in the earth, witches are the mouthpiece for evil and the oracle of Satan. The words spoken, either by a saint or a witch, all have creative power. Here's a reminder as to why:

> AND THE LORD GOD FORMED MAN OF THE DUST OF THE GROUND, AND BREATHED INTO HIS NOSTRILS THE BREATH OF LIFE; AND MAN BECAME A LIVING SOUL. (GENESIS 2:7)

God breathed into man's nostrils the breath of life. Breathed means "inflate" and breath, as in breath of life, means "VITAL breath, divine inspiration, intellect, soul and spirit." We all, witches and saints alike, as people created by God, are breathing with the breath of God. If we should leave this planet before Jesus manifests in the earth, God's breath will return to Him.

> YOU HIDE YOUR FACE, THEY ARE TROUBLED: YOU TAKE AWAY THEIR BREATH, THEY DIE, AND RETURN TO THEIR DUST. (PSALM 104:29)

> HIS BREATH GOES FORTH, HE RETURNS TO HIS EARTH; IN THAT VERY DAY HIS THOUGHTS PERISH. (PSALM 146:4)

When these bodies of ours are of no use any longer, God's breath that sustains them will be gathered up and returned to Him. But for now, every breath we take is breathed with the very breath of God Almighty. This means every word we speak is carried on the breath of God, which is creative and eternal. That is why our words, and the words of every other human being on the earth (saved and unsaved alike), are creative. The worlds were formed by the Word of God, carried on the breath of God. That is why the incantations, the hissing and whispers, of a witch can take effect.

Still, that did not entirely answer the question of the effect of incantations, so here's the other part. Witchcraft is effective and powerful, but witchcraft cannot affect you unless there is an open door for it. Generally speaking, the open door for witchcraft is witchcraft. Satan cannot cast out Satan.

> AND JESUS KNEW THEIR THOUGHTS, AND SAID TO THEM,
> EVERY KINGDOM DIVIDED AGAINST ITSELF IS BROUGHT TO
> DESOLATION; AND EVERY CITY OR HOUSE DIVIDED AGAINST
> ITSELF SHALL NOT STAND: AND IF SATAN CAST OUT SATAN, HE
> IS DIVIDED AGAINST HIMSELF; HOW SHALL THEN HIS KINGDOM
> STAND? (MATTHEW 12:25–26)

When we participate with spirits of control and manipulation, we are open targets for those same witchcraft spirits.

Using emotional pressure to manipulate others is witchcraft.

Here are examples: "If you really loved me you'd tell me if you're going to be late for supper." "If you really loved me you wouldn't do that." "If you had respect for me, you would blah blah blah blah." I think you get the picture. Some sales techniques, super-hype, high pressure, even in soliciting service for the kingdom of God, are witchcraft. Manipulative tactics are witchcraft.

False prophecies and false prophets are rooted in witchcraft. You can tell the difference because false prophets use their gifts for themselves, to advance their position, power, or personal gain. True prophets give themselves to the people in service. Intercessors motivated by a spirit of control or manipulation are almost always praying witchcraft prayers. Any time we pray for someone to change some action or attitude in their lives, we are practicing witchcraft, because we could easily be going against the will of the person.

When we try to use God to change the person, it is a witchcraft prayer. Essentially, we want to control God by telling Him how He should do things!

Putting our focus on the Lord and not on what we think we know is vital to walking in freedom. We have briefly concentrated on sin and evil spirits, but that does not mean this should be the focus of our attentions. God does not intend for us to be in constant battle against the enemy, but rather, to be in constant praise of Him, reminding ourselves of His greatness. The battle is the Lord's, the victory is ours! It is important to understand that the reason for any study of darkness is to gain knowledge so that we may step into and stay in the light. We need to know how to go about cleansing ourselves of all filthiness of the flesh and the spirit, but we don't need to concentrate on the evil. Evil is only overcome by good.

> BE NOT OVERCOME OF EVIL, BUT OVERCOME EVIL WITH GOOD. (ROMANS 12:21)

One of the ways Satan snares us into participation in witchcraft is through prayer that leads into what is known also as "charismatic" witchcraft, and through what is commonly called "white" magic. Black magic is what we all think about as being witchcraft—casting spells, concocting potions, sacrificing living beings, participating in ungodly rituals, controlling the forces of nature, manipulating the will of people, and that kind of thing. There is no need for heavy study of black magic for a couple of reasons. First, we don't need to know anything more than that it exists and has power; and second, if we focus on the evil and not the good, we can never overcome the evil because evil is what we know. We won't know the good. Our main focus must be on the Lord and His goodness, not on the devil and his deceptions.

It is simply a matter of spiritual authority. We all are created with a desire to move in spiritual authority, to have what we call supernatural power. This desire is fulfilled as Christians operate in the authority of God through the gifts of the Holy Spirit. Still, many of us were taught that the gifts of the Spirit are not for us, and that has left Christians openly vulnerable to the counterfeit spiritual authority of witchcraft. This is especially evident as presented through New Age practices, manipulation, mind control, pharmekia (prescription as well as illegal drugs), gossip, and even prayer.

The highest form of black magic is Satanic ritual, especially as it pertains to human sacrifice. Most of the church turns its head, closes its ears and refuses to believe "that kind of thing" goes on; or if it does, it's not in OUR neighborhood. The tragic truth is, human sacrifice is being made all over the world, and in every state in America. Neither is it new. The shedding of blood, particularly the innocent blood of a child, empowers Satanists and elevates them to a higher spiritual level in the demonic realm. They get to give themselves over to more demons and accomplish more evil, which gives them more control and authority over others.

There is a progression to the levels of spiritual, mental, and emotional affliction of witchcraft. Generally, the first arrow drawn from the quiver of witchcraft is discouragement. When we allow this arrow to pierce our spirit man, it is followed by confusion, which settles in our minds, and depression, which deflates our emotions. Following these arrows, we may then suffer loss of vision, wherein we simply give up on ever attaining our goals. Afterward, more arrows are sent forth … disorientation, withdrawal, despair, and defeat. Every one of these piercing arrows is a curse, and every one has a spirit behind it. Most of us have experienced some or all of this at one time or another in our lives, and so we need to close the doors to spirits of witchcraft. As we recognize the doors, we can close them through the power of God, and seal them shut with the blood of Jesus. God closes doors that no man can open.

AND TO THE ANGEL OF THE CHURCH IN PHILADELPHIA WRITE;
THESE THINGS SAYS HE THAT IS HOLY, HE THAT IS TRUE, HE

THAT HAS THE KEY OF DAVID, HE THAT OPENS, AND NO MAN
SHUTS; AND SHUTS, AND NO MAN OPENS. (REVELATION 3:7)

Let's look at this progression of witchcraft, starting with discouragement. Being discouraged does not always mean witchcraft is evident. However, if we are increasingly or frequently feeling discouraged for no apparent reason, spirits of witchcraft are a possible source. When situations are basically normal in our lives, yet we feel overwhelmed by them, there is likely a spiritual attack in progress. Not being able to handle everyday stresses and feeling discouraged by them can be an indicator of witchcraft. When we agree with the spirit of discouragement, the progression continues. Discouragement will invite its friend confusion, and now real trouble is on its way.

Confusion is often a sign that a person has been a victim (or a student) of mind control manipulations. Indicators of mind control include being unable to focus, to make a decision, to concentrate on the Word or anything else being read, or to accomplish what should be simple tasks, because you just can't keep your mind on what you're doing. Mind control can also result in a fragmented soul, where pieces of your mind, your true acuity or personality, have been stolen by witchcraft. In this case, it may seem that you have lost all clarity about what you are called to do, and that can cause even more discouragement, which then leads to depression.

When spirits of discouragement and confusion enter and begin working together against someone, a kind of dread comes over the person. There's no particular reason for it, but that person just doesn't want to move. People in this stage of witchcraft don't want to do anything, and may dread even talking to people. Fear sets in and they begin to doubt God, and to doubt their own purpose in God. It is at this point that the ones affected may lose all thought of having vision or purpose in the kingdom of God. They begin to suffer a loss of vision. Next, they begin to think that what God said about them and what they are to do must have been wrong. There is no longer any way for these people to hold their course through adversity because they have lost sight of the destination. At this point these people don't really know where they're going, so it's nearly impossible to make headway toward getting there. Now they're just going in circles, and life seems pointless. Without a vision, how can there be pro-vision? Pro means "for" —for the vision. If the devil can entrap us into losing our vision, he can effectively prevent provision from flowing into our lives.

When you don't know what it is you want, or where you're going, and you just don't care anyway, all the provision that flows to you from the mercy of God gets trapped. It's imprisoned as an unwanted thing because you don't care! Let me explain from an early edition of Webster's unabridged dictionary. Are you familiar with the word "limbo?" Many people have used this word, even in describing themselves. Have you ever said, "I feel like I'm in limbo?" Do you know where you put yourself? Here is what Webster's has to say about limbo:

1. In some Christian theologies, a region bordering on hell, the abode for the souls of good men who died before the coming of Christ and the souls of unbaptized infants. (Now, we are definitely not of the theology that unbaptized infants go to hell, or that baptism is necessary for salvation. The Word is clear that baptism in water is not necessary for salvation. I'm simply giving you the definition from the dictionary.)
2. A prison or imprisonment.
3. A place or condition of neglect or oblivion to which unwanted things or persons are relegated.

Limbo is a place described as being located outside the gates of hell where blessings and provisions are held up. They are stolen in the spirit realm and sent there, guarded by the spirit of limbo. Why were the blessings and provisions taken into limbo? Because the people they were meant for fell into the trap of discouragement, confusion, depression, and loss of vision, which made them unable to receive what God had for them. They did not fight against the lies, and did not keep on course. It seems that when this progression of witchcraft begins to come on us, and the first arrow is released from the devil's bow, one of the first things many of us do is neglect the Word. The deep desire for the things of God is not so deep anymore and we don't feel like reading the Word. It is in that moment that we need to recognize what has happened, stand, and fight. 2 Kings gives an example in which Israel did not stand and fight, and so they forfeited the victory. They didn't lose the battle; they forfeited the victory. They gave it up.

In Joshua 10, we see a similar picture with a different result. This is the story in which the king of the city of Gibeon, seeing that the Israelites were on the move and conquering everything in sight, had made an alliance with Joshua. He didn't want his city burned and his people killed, so he tricked Joshua into agreeing they would be allies. Then the five kings of the cities surrounding Gibeon got mad and said, "Look what Gibeon did. Now they're our enemy, so let's go destroy Gibeon." They were five against one, so they figured they could take revenge, but Gibeon appealed to Joshua—"Hey, now we're allies, so you've got to help me!" Joshua responded and the armies of the five kings were defeated by Israel. The five kings had hidden themselves in a cave, and were trapped there. Read what Joshua did and what he said to the people:

THEN SAID JOSHUA, OPEN THE MOUTH OF THE CAVE, AND BRING OUT THOSE FIVE KINGS TO ME OUT OF THE CAVE. AND THEY DID SO, AND BROUGHT FORTH THOSE FIVE KINGS TO HIM OUT OF THE CAVE, THE KING OF JERUSALEM, THE KING OF HEBRON, THE KING OF JARMUTH, THE KING OF LACHISH, AND THE KING OF EGLON. AND IT CAME TO PASS, WHEN THEY BROUGHT OUT THOSE KINGS TO JOSHUA, THAT JOSHUA CALLED FOR ALL THE MEN OF ISRAEL, AND SAID TO THE CAPTAINS OF THE MEN OF WAR WHICH WENT WITH HIM, COME NEAR, PUT YOUR FEET UPON THE NECKS OF THESE KINGS. AND THEY CAME NEAR, AND PUT THEIR FEET UPON THE NECKS

OF THEM. AND JOSHUA SAID TO THEM, FEAR NOT, NOR BE DISMAYED, BE STRONG AND OF GOOD COURAGE: FOR THUS SHALL THE LORD DO TO ALL YOUR ENEMIES AGAINST WHOM YOU FIGHT. (JOSHUA 10:22–25)

What a wonderful promise! The Lord Himself will put His foot on the neck of the enemies against whom you fight. If you lie down and roll over, that's what it will be ... over. The point is this, when the arrows of witchcraft have hit your heart, and symptoms begin to be revealed—symptoms of discouragement, confusion, and depression—don't lose your vision! Having thoughts or feelings such as these indicate it's time to fight, not time to quit. That way, we can keep limbo from stealing our blessings. It is easier to prevent those blessings from being taken into limbo than to go in after them.

If we've already been hit with the next sting of witchcraft, disorientation, we not only have forgotten what course we were on, but also, we don't know how to read a compass. The Word doesn't speak to us. We can't seem to get anything out of even the most anointed message. God seems far, far away, and we feel spiritually incapacitated and unable to function. We feel as if we are in a state of spiritual paralysis, and that withdrawal is the easiest thing to do.

Yielding to and following that feeling could result in a total retreat from our purpose in ministry and from fellowship in the church. There are those who have even withdrawn from family and friends and refuse to be comforted. Next comes despair. In this state, many believe there is no hope. Without hope, there can be no faith. Hope can be compared to the thermostat in your home. It sets the goal to change the atmosphere around you. Faith is comparable to the compressor which kicks in to accomplish the set goal. Without hope, we are easy prey for the enemy. He can take us out of the picture, through temptation into sin, sickness, poverty, or even death. This is the final arrow of witchcraft, defeat.

The goal of witchcraft is control. If Satan cannot control us, then he uses witchcraft to weaken and defeat us. He may trick us into participating with him in it. The good news is that every arrow of witchcraft was taken by our Lord Jesus Christ on our behalf so that we don't have to be affected by them. We overcome witchcraft and every symptom of it when we step into Christ. Having Jesus in us, and our being in Him, are two different things. The significance of being Christian is NOT when we get Jesus, it's when He gets us!

> FOR THIS CORRUPTIBLE MUST PUT ON INCORRUPTION, AND THIS MORTAL MUST PUT ON IMMORTALITY. SO WHEN THIS CORRUPTIBLE SHALL HAVE PUT ON INCORRUPTION, AND THIS MORTAL SHALL HAVE PUT ON IMMORTALITY, THEN SHALL BE BROUGHT TO PASS THE SAYING THAT IS WRITTEN, DEATH IS SWALLOWED UP IN VICTORY. O DEATH, WHERE IS YOUR STING? O GRAVE, WHERE IS YOUR VICTORY?
> (1 CORINTHIANS 15:53–55)

We can overcome witchcraft as we close the doors we opened by using controlling spirits to get our own way, and by praying controlling prayers. Yes, we can cast off witchcraft curses. How do we overcome? The Word of God tells us there are three things we must do in order to walk in overcoming victory.

1. We believe on the Lord Jesus Christ, His forgiveness of sins through sacrifice of His own life, and His resurrection from the dead.
2. We speak the Word of God as truth, and tell others of His love.
3. We do not cling to our lives but instead recognize that our lives are not our own, so we die to our own will and adopt the will of the Father.

> AND THEY OVERCAME HIM BY THE BLOOD OF THE LAMB, AND BY THE WORD OF THEIR TESTIMONY; AND THEY LOVED NOT THEIR LIVES UNTO THE DEATH. (REVELATION 12:11)

Let's examine Christian witchcraft prayers. This is one of the common deceptions that may open the door to witchcraft curses. Basically, a witchcraft prayer is an attempt through prayer to change a person's actions or attitudes. Essentially, when that happens, we are using God to control another person, as if God is on call for us. There are a lot of Christians who seem to act like God was created for them, instead of them being created for Him. "What can God do for me today? And if He doesn't do it, I'm angry." Here are a few examples of the types of prayers which are considered witchcraft. Some people call them "soulish" prayers.

"Oh, Lord, make my husband love me."

"Oh, Lord, make my daughter stop seeing that guy."

"Oh, Lord, make the pastor notice me. Have the worship leader invite me to sing."

"Oh, Lord, speak to the prophet to give me a word."

"Oh, Lord, don't let the teacher call on me."

"Oh, Lord, let our team win. Have my son hit a home run. Score a touchdown."

Perhaps we all have prayed something along these lines at one time or another. They don't seem so bad, but they open the door for witchcraft to affect us. The reason is that each is designed to manipulate another person's will, their actions, or their attitudes. Before we pray, we should consider, "Am I about to ask God to comply with something I want which might oppose another person's will? Is this prayer about me and my own selfish desires?" The Word tells us we have not because we ask amiss.

> YOU ASK, AND RECEIVE NOT, BECAUSE YOU ASK AMISS, THAT YOU MAY CONSUME IT UPON YOUR LUSTS. (JAMES 4:3)

Other types of witchcraft prayers are gossip posing as prayer. Perhaps we are in a prayer meeting and somebody starts praying for Old Joe to stop beating his wife. These prayers are especially dangerous, as they not only invite spirits of criticism and accusation, but spirits of murder as well to begin their work in our lives.

Whenever we expose another's sin under the deception of praying for them, we are participating in witchcraft.

Other spirits of witchcraft are seducing spirits, especially the spirit of Jezebel, which truly desires to destroy spiritual leaders and take their God-given authority to herself or himself. Yes, Jezebel is a spirit, and can work through men as well as women. There is almost always a spirit of Jezebel in the church that falls into sexual sin. The spirit of Jezebel is at work whenever there is a stressful church split, or when a pastor or leader is subverted or overthrown. The kinds of controlling prayers behind this are witchcraft and perversion. We think we are setting ourselves up in a position of power, and in a way we are, but it is a counterfeit spiritual authority.

There is always more to discover about witchcraft and the specific spirits that work in concert with it as the Holy Spirit begins to reveal things in your life. Ask the Lord to show you open doors in your own life and generations. No one needs to dig around, or to fear. Our Lord is faithful to reveal, and to heal.

Father God, I come boldly to You and ask to be delivered from the deception of witchcraft. I ask that You remove the veil of darkness that has prevented my recognition of the subtleties of this spirit. Tear down its strongholds over me, and those that have been built in my heart to control and manipulation. I thank You, Lord, that You are my deliverer, You are my Messiah, my Redeemer, my Risen Lord, and You are all powerful and effective to free me from the snares of witchcraft. I declare my need for You, Father. Without You, I can do nothing, but with You, nothing is impossible. In the name of Jesus Christ and by the power of the Holy Spirit, I bind the strongman of witchcraft and I say:

I am here in name of Jesus Christ of Nazareth. I declare I belong to You, Lord, and to no other god. I was bought with a price, paid in blood by my Savior, Jesus Christ, and I thank You. I confess my sins before You, Lord, and I confess the sins of my fathers. I recognize that in myself and in my generations I've allowed evil spirits of witchcraft to manifest and cause sin and curses in many areas of my life. Lord, I recognize and I repent to You for allowing the enemy to afflict me with the arrows of witchcraft. I ask You to forgive me for yielding to spirits of discouragement, depression and confusion. I repent for agreeing with them and not You, Father. I ask Your forgiveness and I ask that the curse be broken. I repent to You for loss of vision, for disorientation, and for withdrawing from You and Your people. I ask You to forgive me, and I ask that the curse of these evil spirits be broken. I repent for entertaining spirits of despair and defeat, Father. I am neither desperate nor defeated. Because of the blood of Jesus Christ I am joyful and victorious. I am victorious in HIM, and I am sorry I allowed the enemy to convince me otherwise. Please forgive me, Lord and take these curses from me now. I break all agreement with every arrow of witchcraft and the spirits behind them, including rebellion and bitterness.

I now renounce any and all legal holds or grounds which spirits of mind control may have on me. Forgive me, Father, for any time I used these spirits of control and manipulation on others to get my own way, allowing mind control to operate through me. In the name of Jesus Christ, I renounce every contact with mind control, those I know about, and those I don't know about. Specifically, I renounce any mind control holds or evil soul ties on me from family members, past and present friends, doctors, psychologists, psychiatrists, psychics, religious leaders, therapists, pastors, preachers, hypnotists, and counselors. I renounce any mind control holds or ties created through Jewish mysticism, rejection, fear, associational sins, generational sins, a false messiah, spiritual error, Satanic ritual abuse, Islam, anti-Christ teachings, the New Age, Sibaba, Dr. Herwitz. I renounce any mind control holds or ties from the occult, witchcraft, karate, Eastern religions, transcendental meditation, yoga groups, the military, cults or churches teaching false doctrine, individual musicians, or groups. Father, I claim my freedom from all these things in the name of Jesus Christ because of HIS resurrection victory over all the power of the enemy. I claim Jesus Christ as my curse bearer, and I roll all curses connected to these evil spirits over onto Jesus now. In the name of the Lord Jesus Christ, I break all bondage over my conscious and unconscious mind. I ask that any piece of my soul that has been stolen by witchcraft, Communism, Masonry, Catholicism, false religions, rock music, drugs, or any other means to be returned to me. I renounce all evil soul ties that I have ever had with abusers or adulterers, and I revoke all ungodly binding agreements or covenants. I declare them destroyed by the blood of Jesus. Thank You, Father, for sending Your Word to free me.

In the name of Jesus Christ of Nazareth who is come in the flesh, I speak to spirits of discouragement, confusion, and depression. Loose me and let me go! Leave from every cell in my body right now. Spirits of loss of vision, disorientation, and withdrawal, I cast you out by the power of the Holy Ghost and the blood of Jesus. I speak to despair and defeat and I cast you out. You no longer have a legal right to affect my life and I command you to leave. I send all of you to the pit to be burned. I declare I am loosed from the bondage of witchcraft and bound to the Spirit and love of God. In the name of the Lord Jesus Christ, I come against and cast out every spirit of mind control from any source named or unnamed, generational or present. Loose me and let me go! I cast you out and I send you to the pit, that burning coals fall on you and you cannot rise again. I break agreement with spirits of Jezebel and Ahab and send them into the consuming fire of our Living God.

With the sword of the Spirit of God, I sever the cords of generational iniquities that have held these sins in place in my life. I sever all ungodly soul ties that were created in my life with abusers and adulterers, and I revoke every ungodly covenant and binding agreement that would allow the arrows of witchcraft to be released toward me, or that would open the door for any attack of the enemy in my life. I loose myself from all demonic subjection to any person, living or dead who has dominated me in any way contrary to the will of God. I ask You, Father, to loose angels from the third heaven against all demon and demonic roots in my life—to uncoil, untangle, dig out, and break loose from me these ungodly things. I send angels of burning judgment and destruction against the enemy to cut, sever, and remove all demons and demonic roots, all fetters, bonds, bands, coils, tangles, serpents, cords, metals, wires, hairs, snares, gins, nets, and webs. Father, I ask that You send Your angels to the four corners of the earth and the heavens to gather and restore all fragments of my broken soul, and to utterly break off any bindings that have been put on my soul, with or without my knowledge. Free my soul, Father, from all bondage. I ask that the curses that resulted from these things be broken off my life and my family. I ask that You close the door to the devil in these areas, and that You continue to reveal to me other open doors. I stand in agreement to cooperate with You, to work with You as You purge me of my sins and the iniquities of my forefathers. Thank You, Lord God, for being my covenant-keeping God! Thank You, Father, for filling me now with Your love and peace and joy and patience and faith and every other fruit of Your Holy Spirit. Fill me with more of YOU, Lord God. Let Your glory fill the earth, and let it start with me. Keep me full of You, Lord. Keep me in Your will and Your way. In Jesus name. AMEN.

Section Four

AFTERWARD, HE MEASURED A THOUSAND,
AND BROUGHT ME THROUGH;
AND IT WAS A RIVER THAT
I COULD NOT PASS OVER:
FOR THE WATERS WERE RISEN,
WATERS TO SWIM IN, A RIVER
THAT COULD NOT BE PASSED OVER.
(EZEKIEL 47:5)

Chapter Thirteen

Becoming a SON of God

WHEN THE ARROWS OF WITCHCRAFT PENETRATE THE HEART, they can cause a person to feel more like a deflated balloon than anything else. The resulting lack of business interests and associations can slow the economy of life and cause personal income to plummet. Some years ago I lost someone dear to me, and experienced this kind of withdrawal. My lack of motivation in the face of this arrow left me without cash flow, a condition to which I was unaccustomed and not very disciplined to enjoy. So, I began to discipline myself to listen to successful business people on webinars and YouTube speeches and so on, as a part of effectively re-entering the workplace in a meaningful and financially prosperous way.

During this time of "retraining" for the business world, I was led to a presentation by one of the premier sports coaches of many years ago, speaking at a convention of religious broadcasters. He presented a twelve-point list of attitudes and actions that set apart the winners from the losers in sports, or business, or just life itself. As I heard him speak, I kept thinking of how much of what he was saying could apply to our lives as Christians and the success or failures we experience in our Christian walk and callings, whatever they may be. I started to think of his points as a twelve-step program of discipleship.

Our business mission as Christians is to overcome the world and advance the kingdom of God. We are His hands and feet and mouthpieces in the earth today, led by the Holy Spirit to operate the family business as fully mature sons of God. Our Father, through the Lord Jesus Christ, has given us an inheritance, and we have to grow up and learn to develop the attitudes and actions that will allow Him to release our inheritance to us. In Jewish culture and custom, the inheritance of the first-born son was leadership of the family business. To this end, he was apportioned double what the other sons received. He needed the extra portion, not to squander on himself, but to run the business. There is insight about this in the book of Galatians.

> NOW I SAY, THAT THE HEIR, AS LONG AS HE IS A CHILD, DIFFERS NOTHING FROM A SERVANT, THOUGH HE BE LORD OF ALL; BUT IS UNDER TUTORS AND GOVERNORS UNTIL THE TIME APPOINTED OF THE FATHER. (GALATIANS 4:1–2)

According to custom, the time appointed of the father was the day in which the son had learned everything he needed to know about the family business, and was considered mature enough to handle it and keep it prospering. Then, and only then, was his inheritance given to him, along with its inherent responsibilities. Jesus is the first born; He is in us. Therefore, we are now the inheritors of the double portion, for use in the establishment and advancement of the business of our Father God. This was in my mind as I listened to these attributes of winning in business. I began to realize how much accomplishing kingdom business is similar to businesses in the world, because God works within the kingdoms and systems of the world. There is a lesson in taking what we learn in the world and then discovering God's perspective in order to translate and apply what we learn in the world into our Christian journey.

The first thing we all need to adopt into our attitude and actions is to **Be Excited!** If you want people to be excited about what you're doing, and in what you believe, then you have to be excited about it yourself. The word "excitement" means "a feeling of great enthusiasm and eagerness." This brought to mind "the zeal of the Lord." In looking up synonyms for zeal I found "eagerness and enthusiasm" and concluded that zeal could be described as excitement on steroids.

FOR UNTO US A CHILD IS BORN, UNTO US A SON IS GIVEN: AND THE GOVERNMENT SHALL BE UPON HIS SHOULDER: AND HIS NAME SHALL BE CALLED WONDERFUL, COUNSELOR, THE MIGHTY GOD, THE EVERLASTING FATHER, THE PRINCE OF PEACE. OF THE INCREASE OF HIS GOVERNMENT AND PEACE THERE SHALL BE NO END, UPON THE THRONE OF DAVID, AND UPON HIS KINGDOM, TO ORDER IT, AND TO ESTABLISH IT WITH JUDGMENT AND WITH JUSTICE FROM HENCEFORTH EVEN FOR EVER. THE ZEAL OF THE LORD OF HOSTS WILL PERFORM THIS. (ISAIAH 9:6–7)

Paul the apostle was a man full of zeal for God. His eagerness and enthusiasm to please God had him out rounding up Christians for persecution! Zeal, excitement on steroids, drove him to action. Admittedly, it was wrong action, even though it may have been rightly motivated. Still, Paul wasn't punished by God for his enthusiasm and excitement. Actually, once understanding was imparted to him, Paul was promoted by God to greater things.

Each and every day when we wake up, we need to be excited! Excited to be alive, excited for a new day, and anticipating great things. Perhaps you don't think you have much to be excited about, but if that's your mindset, it needs changing.

God our Father was excited to provide us a Savior and we should be excited about Him *every day of our lives, full of the joy of our salvation!*

Instead, many of us are grousing and complaining that we didn't get enough sleep, or that nobody helps us out, or that we're stuck in a dead-end job. We might dwell on the negatives: how our husbands or our wives or our children don't contribute enough to our emotional or financial wellbeing, or how miserable we are and all the things that we don't have and can't do. In that state of mind, a person isn't eager or enthusiastic about helping other people succeed, or contributing time or energy into other people's lives or endeavors. But according to the words of Jesus, helping others succeed in their goals opens the door for our own success.

> AND IF YOU HAVE NOT BEEN FAITHFUL IN THAT WHICH IS ANOTHER MAN'S, WHO SHALL GIVE YOU THAT WHICH IS YOUR OWN? (LUKE 16:12)

The reverse is also true. If you are faithful in what belongs to another, God will give you your own. Do you work for someone else? Then, if you want success for yourself, be excited to help the person in authority over you succeed. Be the first to volunteer for the little things, to work overtime to finish the project, with or without extra pay. Stop complaining, and start praising God for the opportunity to be faithful wherever you are. He has given you life, and Jesus came that you would have not just any old life, but you would have abundant life.

> THE THIEF COMETH NOT, BUT FOR TO STEAL, AND TO KILL, AND TO DESTROY: I AM COME THAT THEY MIGHT HAVE LIFE, AND THAT THEY MIGHT HAVE IT MORE ABUNDANTLY. (JOHN 10:10)

The Greek word for "life" in that Scripture is "zoe," which literally translates "life the way God lives it." If you can't get fired up about that, then your wood's too wet; and if your wood's too wet, you soon will be in a very dry place. It is there, in those dry places and seasons of our lives, that God can dry out our wood and get it ready to start a flame for His kingdom purpose. The more you cry and whine and complain about being in a dry place, the longer it will take for the wood that is your humanity to be made suitable for building a fire.

The next attribute we need to develop is to **Be a Dreamer.** In thinking this one over, I was reminded of two different kinds of dreams. There are the dreams and visions in the night, those that come in sleep, and then there are dreams and visions that become goals or objectives in life for us to work toward and accomplish. These two aspects of dreaming are both physical and spiritual. Many of the characters in the Bible were dreamers. Job was a dreamer. Daniel was a dreamer. Joseph, Isaac's son, was a dreamer. Joseph, Mary's husband, was a dreamer. Even Nebuchadnezzar was a dreamer—and there are many more. Here are some biblical references of dreams and visions in the night:

> NOW A THING WAS SECRETLY BROUGHT TO ME, AND MINE EAR RECEIVED A LITTLE THEREOF. IN THOUGHTS FROM THE VISIONS OF THE NIGHT, WHEN DEEP SLEEP FALLS ON MEN. (JOB 4:12–13)

> THEN WAS THE SECRET REVEALED TO DANIEL IN A NIGHT VISION. THEN DANIEL BLESSED THE GOD OF HEAVEN. (DANIEL 2:19)

> AND JOSEPH DREAMED A DREAM, AND HE TOLD IT HIS BRETHREN: AND THEY HATED HIM YET THE MORE. (GENESIS 37:5)

> BUT WHILE HE THOUGHT ON THESE THINGS, BEHOLD, THE ANGEL OF THE LORD APPEARED TO HIM IN A DREAM, SAYING, JOSEPH, YOU SON OF DAVID, FEAR NOT TO TAKE UNTO YOU MARY YOUR WIFE: FOR THAT WHICH IS CONCEIVED IN HER IS OF THE HOLY GHOST. (MATTHEW 1:20)

We can establish from these examples that physical dreaming is also spiritual. There is a message in dreams and visions of the night. The dream isn't because of the pizza, or the movie we watched before going to bed. God can use those things as a catalyst for His message to us, but there is a spiritual message in our dreams. If you are interested in dreams and dream interpretation, there is plenty of material available, but we caution you to check with the Holy Spirit about what you are to read and conclude, because there are no formulas. The Holy Spirit of God is the only true dream interpreter, and you cannot depend on a mental understanding or detection by formula. The formula may not apply in many cases. It takes discernment.

That being said, there are a few things to keep in mind about your dreams, and everyone dreams. If you don't remember your dreams it's probably because you've dismissed them as unimportant. Consider this: if the dream is in color, you can be pretty sure the dream is from the Lord. If your dream is in black and white, it's probably from the kingdom of darkness. Also, the people in your dream are oftentimes not really the people of the message, and dreams are very seldom literal in nature. They are symbolic. Dreams from God are personal to you; they are about you, and not someone else. For example, if you dream about your dead relative, the dream is usually not about that person. That person is simply a representation of something, perhaps a generational issue, or perhaps a feeling or attitude. The dream can be a confirmation, a warning, or just a little "heads up" from God about something coming that should be dealt with. Generally speaking, cars and other forms of transportation (even shoes) represent ministry or spiritual calling. Pregnancy and children generally represent gifts. Colors all have meaning and significance. Do your best not to fall into the trap of mentally interpreting your own or someone else's dreams according to a "dream book" or a class taught by man. The Holy Spirit is the interpreter of dreams, and no one else can give an accurate interpretation.

If you want to begin to remember your dreams, repent for disregarding them and tell the Lord you want to remember. Ask Him to help you remember. Keep a pen and paper by your bedside, and when you wake up write down what you dreamed, even if it's the middle of the night. That proves you are serious about hearing from God, and interested in what He has to say to you, even while you sleep. If you wait until the morning, the dream may evade you as it did Nebuchadnezzar, who called for his magicians to tell him what he had dreamed, in addition to its interpretation!

> THE KING ANSWERED AND SAID TO THE CHALDEANS, THE
> THING IS GONE FROM ME: IF YOU WILL NOT MAKE KNOWN
> TO ME THE DREAM, WITH THE INTERPRETATION THEREOF,
> YOU SHALL BE CUT IN PIECES, AND YOUR HOUSES SHALL BE
> MADE A DUNGHILL. BUT IF YOU SHOW THE DREAM, AND THE
> INTERPRETATION THEREOF, YOU SHALL RECEIVE OF ME GIFTS
> AND REWARDS AND GREAT HONOR: THEREFORE SHOW ME THE
> DREAM, AND THE INTERPRETATION THEREOF. (DANIEL 2:5-6)

The other aspect of being a dreamer lies in the visions you have for your life, both the smaller, short-term ones and the long-term goals you set for yourself. It's been rightly said, "You have to see it before you see it!" In other words, you need to envision yourself having already achieved the goal, won the prize, received the promotion, whatever. You can't put negative images of failure in your head and expect a positive result in your circumstance. I remember the story of Cassius Clay, who changed his name to Mohammed Ali. As a poor, scrawny little black kid, twelve years old in a rundown neighborhood, he'd be skipping rope and proclaiming for all the world to hear, "I'm the heavy weight champion of the world!" Who believed him? Nobody but him. He had a vision for his life, and he believed it, and he worked toward it, and he made it happen. This is a sure principle. It works, no matter where a person is positioned spiritually. A person who has a vision, believes in his vision, and works diligently toward his vision, will see it come to pass.

Do we have a vision for our lives as Christians? Do we believe it? Are we working toward it? Those are certainly questions to consider.

The third thing on the list of attributes for success is **Never Say "Can't."** At some point in your life, if you grew up like I did, you probably said, "I can't," and somebody answered you with, "Can't never could." That is absolutely true. As long as we confess a belief in failure, we will be afflicted with failure. There is a progression to how things come about in our lives.

I BELIEVED, THEREFORE HAVE I SPOKEN: I WAS GREATLY AF-FLICTED. (PSALM 116:10)

The words "I can't" are words of the enemy of God who seeks to destroy us, because the truth is: we CAN. We can accomplish because of God, no matter what the task. We can do all things through Christ which strengthens us. The Christ in us, the anointing of God, is the enabler for our success in whatever we set our hands and our minds to do. There can never be enough said about the power of our words, or their creativity. We create good, and we create evil, by the fruit of our mouth. Following are a few "I can't" statements many of us make, and God's answer to them. These are taken from a book titled *Who's Using Your Tongue?*

"I can't be forgiven."

IF WE CONFESS OUR SINS, HE IS FAITHFUL AND JUST TO FOR-GIVE US OUR SINS, AND TO CLEANSE US FROM ALL UNRIGH-TEOUSNESS. (1 JOHN 1:9)

"I can't bear the pain."

WHEREFORE LIFT UP THE HANDS WHICH HANG DOWN, AND THE FEEBLE KNEES; AND MAKE STRAIGHT PATHS FOR YOUR FEET, LEST THAT WHICH IS LAME BE TURNED OUT OF THE WAY; BUT LET IT RATHER BE HEALED. (HEBREWS 12:12-13)

"I can't go on."

WHEREFORE SEEING WE ALSO ARE COMPASSED ABOUT WITH SO GREAT A CLOUD OF WITNESSES, LET US LAY ASIDE EVERY WEIGHT, AND THE SIN WHICH DOES SO EASILY BESET US, AND LET US RUN WITH PATIENCE THE RACE THAT IS SET BEFORE US. (HEBREWS 12:1)

THEN HE SAID TO THEM, GO YOUR WAY, EAT THE FAT, AND DRINK THE SWEET, AND SEND PORTIONS TO THEM FOR WHOM NOTHING IS PREPARED: FOR THIS DAY IS HOLY UNTO OUR LORD: NEITHER BE YOU SORRY; FOR THE JOY OF THE LORD IS YOUR STRENGTH. (NEHEMIAH 8:10)

Attribute number four is **Stand for Something.** In any business, what we stand for is vital to the success of our actions. It's been said that if you don't stand for something, you'll fall for anything, and that is oh-so-true! Christians who are not grounded in sound doctrine are easily swayed by the next slick-talking charmer sent by hell to draw us off track and into compromise, complacency, and confusion. These are three conditions in the lives of many Christians who have lots of "I can'ts" in their vocabularies. What should we stand for as Christians seeking to operate the family business? The big three are Love, Truth, and Humility. Falling under one or more (likely all) of those categories will come Honor, Integrity, and Courage.

When we don't STAND for the truth of the Word of God, when we don't STAND in the face of evil, when we don't STAND in uprightness as Christians, we end up being those compromised Christians who give God a bad name. Standing is a stationary position. We don't move away from where we are if we are standing. There is a steadfastness associated with standing. As Christians, standing for something means to "stand fast" for what we believe, without wavering through uncertainty or doubt, and not wandering over into other beliefs and mingling Christianity with occultism. Every cult claims Jesus, because to do so gives them credibility; and every world religion recognizes Jesus, but not the resurrection of Jesus.

What we stand for is easy: we stand for Jesus the Christ, the anointed One of God, and His anointing. In order to do that, we need to understand the core character of our Lord, which is love, truth, and humility. When we are steadfast in love, we are standing for Jesus. When we are steadfast in truth, we are standing for Jesus. When we are steadfast in humility, we are standing for Jesus.

> ONLY LET YOUR CONVERSATION BE AS IT BECOMES THE GOS-
> PEL OF CHRIST: THAT WHETHER I COME AND SEE YOU, OR ELSE
> BE ABSENT, I MAY HEAR OF YOUR AFFAIRS, THAT YOU STAND
> FAST IN ONE SPIRIT, WITH ONE MIND STRIVING TOGETHER FOR
> THE FAITH OF THE GOSPEL. (PHILIPPIANS 1:27)

How do we stand? Like men, not like children. Like soldiers, not like civilians. That means, again, we have to grow up before we can realize our full inheritance in the Lord. We are to stand in strength, and in preparedness.

> WATCH YOU, STAND FAST IN THE FAITH, QUIT YOU LIKE MEN,
> BE STRONG. (1 CORINTHIANS 16:13)

> FINALLY, MY BRETHREN, BE STRONG IN THE LORD, AND IN THE
> POWER OF HIS MIGHT. PUT ON THE WHOLE ARMOR OF GOD,
> THAT YOU MAY BE ABLE TO STAND AGAINST THE WILES OF
> THE DEVIL. (EPHESIANS 6:10–11)

In order for us to stand properly, we have to stand IN Christ, and in the freedom of our salvation, not in the heavy yoke of religious orders and the law of man. God's law is love.

> THEREFORE, MY BRETHREN DEARLY BELOVED AND LONGED
> FOR, MY JOY AND CROWN, SO STAND FAST IN THE LORD, MY
> DEARLY BELOVED. (PHILIPPIANS 4:1)

> STAND FAST THEREFORE IN THE LIBERTY WHEREWITH CHRIST
> HAS MADE US FREE, AND BE NOT ENTANGLED AGAIN WITH
> THE YOKE OF BONDAGE. (GALATIANS 5:1)

If you want to be successful in kingdom business, as in any other, you have to stand for something, and that something is the same yesterday, today, and forever.

JESUS CHRIST THE SAME YESTERDAY, AND TO DAY, AND FOR
EVER. (HEBREWS 13:8)

The next attribute we all need can sometimes overlap with standing
for something. It's called **Be Controversial**. When I say that, I don't
mean that we should be contentious or disagreeable. Those traits
only serve to turn people away from Christ. I mean we have to stop
compromising to be liked, accepted, or approved.

---

*We have to put down the fear of
offending someone by our belief, and
stop being afraid of controversy.*

What did Jesus say?

THINK NOT THAT I AM COME TO SEND PEACE ON EARTH: I
CAME NOT TO SEND PEACE, BUT A SWORD.
(MATTHEW 10:34)

Is everyone going to love you? No. Is everyone going to respect you?
No.

HE IS DESPISED AND REJECTED OF MEN; A MAN OF SORROWS,
AND ACQUAINTED WITH GRIEF: AND WE HID AS IT WERE OUR
FACES FROM HIM; HE WAS DESPISED, AND WE ESTEEMED HIM
NOT. (ISAIAH 53:3)

IF THE WORLD HATES YOU, YOU KNOW THAT IT HATED ME
BEFORE IT HATED YOU. IF YOU WERE OF THE WORLD, THE
WORLD WOULD LOVE HIS OWN: BUT BECAUSE YOU ARE
NOT OF THE WORLD, BUT I HAVE CHOSEN YOU OUT OF THE
WORLD, THEREFORE THE WORLD HATES YOU. (JOHN 15:18–19)

Is everyone going to listen to you? No.

> BECAUSE I HAVE CALLED, AND YOU REFUSED; I HAVE STRETCHED OUT MY HAND, AND NO MAN REGARDED; BUT YOU HAVE SET AT NOUGHT ALL MY COUNSEL, AND WOULD NONE OF MY REPROOF. (PROVERBS 1:24–25)

> AND BECAUSE I TELL YOU THE TRUTH, YOU BELIEVE ME NOT. (JOHN 8:45)

Is everyone going to be nice to you? No.

> REMEMBER THE WORD THAT I SAID TO YOU, THE SERVANT IS NOT GREATER THAN HIS LORD. IF THEY HAVE PERSECUTED ME, THEY WILL ALSO PERSECUTE YOU; IF THEY HAVE KEPT MY SAYING, THEY WILL KEEP YOURS ALSO. (JOHN 15:20)

> AND I WILL VERY GLADLY SPEND AND BE SPENT FOR YOU; THOUGH THE MORE ABUNDANTLY I LOVE YOU, THE LESS I BE LOVED. (2 CORINTHIANS 12:15)

When we are truly like Jesus, we will likely be reviled, not loved by many. We will likely be rejected and abandoned, not accepted in many places. We will likely be ignored and disregarded, not respected and admired by the masses. None of that can ever be allowed to cause us to become weary in well doing, or draw us away from truth. Truth is controversial, love is controversial, and humility is controversial. BE CONTROVERSIAL!

The sixth thing we need to examine and adopt into our lives in terms of our quest to take over the family business of the kingdom of God is to **Make a Total Commitment**. If you start a business, and you aren't totally committed to making it successful, you will have a business that is mediocre at best, and a drain on your life, rather than a blessing. If you enter a marriage and you aren't totally committed to its covenant, you will have a miserable marriage that will likely end in divorce. If you aren't totally committed to walking as a mature son of God, preparing yourself every day to take over the family business, then you will become one of those Christians that nobody wants to be around. Those are the Christians who seem to have more failures and defeats in their lives than they do victories. They are the ones who go around with complaint on their lips, rather than praise, and who look like they've been sucking on lemons. Who wants that? Nobody is going to be interested in being like you if that's you. Nobody is going to be interested in what you have to sell if that's you!

What does it mean to be truly and totally committed to something? Let's take breakfast as an example. The chicken is involved in breakfast, but the pig is totally committed. Did you understand that? The chicken is involved in breakfast, but the pig is committed! I will go on record and say that there are a lot of chicken Christians out there. They will contribute, but they are not truly committed. They may buy in, but they aren't sold out. We all need to realize that to follow Christ, there is a price to pay. It will cost us our lives as we know them.

> BUY THE TRUTH, AND SELL IT NOT; ALSO WISDOM, AND IN-
> STRUCTION, AND UNDERSTANDING. (PROVERBS 23:23)

We may not have to give up our lives in the physical sense—I do not believe we are all called to become martyrs to be sacrificed for our faith, though many are. But we all must put ourselves on the altar of God and allow Him to burn away the dross of our lives. We all must be willing to abandon the things of the world for the things of the kingdom. Jesus said, "Take up your cross and follow Me." What's on your cross isn't your deadbeat husband or your drug-addicted children. "Oh, my son so-and-so is my cross to bear"—OH, NO—what's on your cross is YOU.

> THEN SAID JESUS TO HIS DISCIPLES, IF ANY MAN WILL COME
> AFTER ME, LET HIM DENY HIMSELF, AND TAKE UP HIS CROSS,
> AND FOLLOW ME. (MATTHEW 16:24)

The word "deny" in this verse means to utterly and completely deny, to disown. It does not mean to deny and then change your mind. It doesn't mean we deny ourselves today, and indulge ourselves tomorrow. We're the pig at breakfast—completely committed. In our attempts to hold on to our lives, we can lose them!

> FOR WHOSOEVER WILL SAVE HIS LIFE SHALL LOSE IT; BUT WHO-SOEVER SHALL LOSE HIS LIFE FOR MY SAKE AND THE GOSPEL'S, THE SAME SHALL SAVE IT. (MARK 8:35)

True commitment means you do whatever it takes to succeed, even if it means giving up your life. We overcome by the blood of the Lamb, the word of our testimony, AND we love not our lives unto the death. Our covenant commitment with God is mutual. Jesus gave up His life. He sacrificed His life for us, and we must sacrifice our lives for Him. This means we must put our souls on the altar—our minds, our wills, our emotions, and our desires.

> GOD IS THE LORD, WHICH HAS SHOWN US LIGHT: BIND THE SACRIFICE WITH CORDS, EVEN TO THE HORNS OF THE ALTAR. (PSALM 118:27)

This is a strange Scripture, if you think about it. The animals which were thrown onto the altar in sacrifice to God were slain before they were put on the altar. There would be no need whatsoever to "bind the sacrifice with cords." A dead animal is not going anywhere. The only reason to tie something to the altar is if that something were still living. That's a picture of us, the living sacrifice. We say we give our lives to the Lord, but when it gets hot, we have a tendency to crawl off the altar. To make a total commitment to Christ and kingdom business means we lay down our ways and take up His way. We train our minds to think in kingdom language and kingdom purpose. We train our hearts to come into alignment with the heart of the Father so we can feel His emotions. We train our wills to conform to the will of God. We lay down our desires for what He desires for us to have.

The next attribute for successfully running God's kingdom is simple: **Treat People Well**. That does not apply only to people you like, and those who treat you well. If you want to grow up to be like your Father, this is a principle that must apply to everyone you meet, the good, the bad, and the ugly, as they say. There is so much Scripture written about how we are to treat people that it would be impossible to include it all here, but we'll give a sample directly from our Lord Jesus:

> YOU HAVE HEARD THAT IT HAS BEEN SAID, AN EYE FOR AN EYE, AND A TOOTH FOR A TOOTH: BUT I SAY UNTO YOU, THAT YOU RESIST NOT EVIL: BUT WHOSOEVER SHALL SMITE YOU ON YOUR RIGHT CHEEK, TURN TO HIM THE OTHER ALSO. AND IF ANY MAN WILL SUE YOU AT THE LAW, AND TAKE AWAY YOUR COAT, LET HIM HAVE YOUR CLOKE ALSO. AND WHOSOEVER SHALL COMPEL YOU TO GO A MILE, GO WITH HIM TWO. GIVE TO HIM THAT ASKS YOU, AND FROM HIM THAT WOULD BORROW OF YOU TURN NOT YOU AWAY. YOU HAVE HEARD THAT IT HAS BEEN SAID, YOU SHALL LOVE YOUR NEIGHBOR, AND HATE YOUR ENEMY. BUT I SAY TO YOU, LOVE YOUR ENEMIES, BLESS THEM THAT CURSE YOU, DO GOOD TO THEM THAT HATE YOU, AND PRAY FOR THEM WHICH DE-SPITEFULLY USE YOU, AND PERSECUTE YOU; THAT YOU MAY BE THE CHILDREN OF YOUR FATHER WHICH IS IN HEAVEN: FOR HE MAKES HIS SUN TO RISE ON THE EVIL AND ON THE GOOD, AND SENDS RAIN ON THE JUST AND ON THE UNJUST. (MATTHEW 5:38–45)

Treating people well and with respect, whether or not you think they deserve it, is a condition of trusting the Lord. If you truly trust God, then you know that whatever wrongs the person has perpetrated against you or others will be dealt with by God Himself. The Lord is just and will right all the wrongs. The sooner we stop trying to judge whether others are worthy of decent treatment, or trying to make them be the people we want them to be, the sooner we can become the people God wants us to be! Treat people well.

Number eight on our list is to **Establish Right Priorities**. This one is also easy to understand, but more difficult to follow. It's hard to do, because we are all somewhat guilty of letting the urgent get in the way of the important. In order to establish right priorities, we all must understand what a priority is in the first place. The definition of "priority" is this: the fact or condition of being regarded as more important. In order to establish priorities, you look at the things in your life and rank them in order of importance. The simplistic picture of right priorities is this: God first, then family, then work, then your home. The absentee father (or mother) who puts his or her job ahead of family is out of order. The top priority in our lives as a whole and in our everyday lifestyle should always be God, and He establishes all other priorities in our lives.

> YOU SHALL HAVE NO OTHER GODS BEFORE ME.
> (EXODUS 20:3)

Family comes next, and then your job. The Word tells us to establish ourselves in work, and then build our house.

> PREPARE YOUR WORK WITHOUT, AND MAKE IT FIT FOR YOUR-
> SELF IN THE FIELD; AND AFTERWARDS BUILD YOUR HOUSE.
> (PROVERBS 24:27)

Ask yourself if your big picture priorities are in proper order. Do you greet the Lord with a "Good morning" and a prayer before your feet hit the floor in the mornings, or do you stumble your way to the coffee pot? If your desire is to get your priorities right, you will develop the habit of saying "Good morning" to God and setting the tone of your day with a thank you prayer. Same thing with family. Your loyalty after God is your husband or your wife, then your children. Develop a habit of speaking a blessing over them before you go about your day. Then stop worrying so much about your house and where and how you live, and concentrate more on establishing yourself in whatever work your hands and mind find to do.

When all that is in order, then you can begin to segment each category of priorities into smaller chunks. Learn what God's priorities are, and follow His precepts and His statutes. You will find that God's priorities are always people and relationships. God's precepts have to do with how and what He thinks, and His statutes have to do with how and what He directs us to do. When these things are in order, the rest will fall into place. You won't be drawn off course with the insignificant things that eat up your time and don't advance your life or kingdom business.

The next attribute to develop is to **Have the Will to Win**. Maybe you think that sounds simplistic, but it isn't. More times than not, most of us are willing to settle for less than the best.

> KNOW YOU NOT THAT THEY WHICH RUN IN A RACE RUN ALL, BUT ONE RECEIVES THE PRIZE? SO RUN, THAT YOU MAY OBTAIN. AND EVERY MAN THAT STRIVES FOR THE MASTERY IS TEMPERATE IN ALL THINGS. NOW THEY DO IT TO OBTAIN A CORRUPTIBLE CROWN; BUT WE AN INCORRUPTIBLE.
> (1 CORINTHIANS 9:24–25)

This is not to say you have to <u>be</u> the best, or that you should go for the win no matter what the cost, but it means that you should <u>do</u> your best. To do this, you have to remove the words "I'll try" from your vocabulary. "I'll try" speaks to your will and gives it an excuse not to do whatever it is you said you'd try to do. "I will" speaks to your will and tells it to accomplish the thing because you said you would. Keeping your word is a huge part of winning in any business, especially in the business of the family of God.

Many of these attributes complement each other. It would be difficult to develop a will to win if you haven't written your vision, and made a total commitment to working to achieve it. Train your will to comply with the will of God, which always wins and never fails!

> NOW THANKS BE UNTO GOD, WHICH ALWAYS CAUSES US TO
> TRIUMPH IN CHRIST, AND MAKES MANIFEST THE SAVOR OF
> HIS KNOWLEDGE BY US IN EVERY PLACE.
> (2 CORINTHIANS 2:14)

The tenth attribute is this: **Pay the Price, and a Little More.**
Hearing this one brought to mind Joseph of Arimathaea. This is the
man who went to Pilate and begged for the body of Jesus on the day
the Lord was crucified.

> AND NOW WHEN THE EVENING WAS COME, BECAUSE IT WAS
> THE PREPARATION, THAT IS, THE DAY BEFORE THE SABBATH,
> JOSEPH OF ARIMATHAEA, AN HONORABLE COUNSELOR, WHICH
> ALSO WAITED FOR THE KINGDOM OF GOD, CAME, AND WENT
> IN BOLDLY UNTO PILATE, AND CRAVED THE BODY OF JESUS.
> AND PILATE MARVELED IF HE WERE ALREADY DEAD: AND
> CALLING TO HIM THE CENTURION, HE ASKED HIM WHETHER
> HE HAD BEEN ANY WHILE DEAD. AND WHEN HE KNEW IT OF
> THE CENTURION, HE GAVE THE BODY TO JOSEPH. AND HE
> BOUGHT FINE LINEN, AND TOOK HIM DOWN, AND WRAPPED
> HIM IN THE LINEN, AND LAID HIM IN A SEPULCHER WHICH
> WAS HEWN OUT OF A ROCK, AND ROLLED A STONE UNTO THE
> DOOR OF THE SEPULCHER. (MARK 15:42–46)

This is one of the best examples of paying the price and a little bit
more that I have seen. This man came before Pilate, the Roman
ruler who had authority over him. That in itself had to be a price to
pay, in terms of setting yourself up for rebuff or rejection or worse.
He begged the governor to give him the body of Christ. He showed
up, and he spoke up! How many of us are willing to face the au-
thorities of the world and beg for the Body of Christ today? Then
he took his own money, which was certainly a personal sacrifice,
to buy the best. He bought fine linen, not rags or discards, to wrap
around the bloodied, battered, unrecognizable body of Christ. How
many of us are willing to contribute our hard-earned cash to take
care of the Body of Christ today? As if that weren't enough, Joseph

of Arimathaea then placed that body in his own tomb. How many of us are willing to give up something we've carved out for ourselves to shelter the Body of Christ today? If you want to succeed in the kingdom, pay the price, and a little bit more.

Next on the list is **Be Tough and DO NOT QUIT**. No one ever fails unless they quit. There is a song from many years ago: "So let the sun shine in—face it with a grin—winners never quit—and quitters never win—so let the sun shine in—face it with a grin—open up your heart and let the sun shine in." Consider this: after His resurrection, Jesus told His disciples and apostles to wait in Jerusalem for the promise of the Father. Scholars say there were about 500 of these people who witnessed the crucifixion and could testify of Jesus' resurrection. These followers are supposedly those who were told to wait. Not all of them waited.

These same followers had seen Jesus when He came back to give them the kingdom He received from His Father (Daniel 7). They were taught by Him as He walked the earth for 40 days. We don't know for certain when they received the directive to wait, or how long they had to wait, but we do know that on the day of Pentecost, there were only 120 who remained steadfast, who did not give up on the word, who didn't quit. Those who waited were rewarded with something so amazing it's hard to conceive. They were there, live and in person, for the outpouring of the Holy Spirit!

> AND WHEN THE DAY OF PENTECOST WAS FULLY COME, THEY WERE ALL WITH ONE ACCORD IN ONE PLACE. AND SUDDENLY THERE CAME A SOUND FROM HEAVEN AS OF A RUSHING MIGHTY WIND, AND IT FILLED ALL THE HOUSE WHERE THEY WERE SITTING. AND THERE APPEARED UNTO THEM CLOVEN TONGUES LIKE AS OF FIRE, AND IT SAT UPON EACH OF THEM. AND THEY WERE ALL FILLED WITH THE HOLY GHOST, AND BEGAN TO SPEAK WITH OTHER TONGUES, AS THE SPIRIT GAVE THEM UTTERANCE. (ACTS 2:1–4)

It was tough to wait. It's hard to imagine this indefinite waiting when we live in such a microwave, instant gratification, want-it-hot-and-want-it-now world. I wonder how many of us would have waited for something so nebulous and undefined? Especially in the face of the rest of the world saying "you've got to be crazy," and so many of our friends and fellows having already left? Yet, 120 of them did not quit. That's less than 25 percent of the original group. In today's world of instant gratification, it would likely be even fewer. Ask yourself, "Would I have waited, or would I have quit and gone home?" None of us can say for sure, because we aren't faced with that situation. No one knows with certainty what he or she would do in any given situation until faced with it. Think of how bad those quitters must have felt! If you want success in kingdom business, be tough and don't quit.

The last point to make is this: **Be a Leader**. Maybe you don't think you're a leader, but you are. Jesus Christ was a leader. He didn't have to market Himself, build a website, pass out flyers or anything else. When he spoke, people listened. They didn't always follow Him, but they all recognized Him as a Leader. It's one of the main things that had the Pharisees and other religious people so worried that they had to bribe the soldiers who guarded His tomb to tell a lie.

> NOW THE NEXT DAY, THAT FOLLOWED THE DAY OF THE PREPARATION, THE CHIEF PRIESTS AND PHARISEES CAME TOGETHER UNTO PILATE, SAYING, SIR, WE REMEMBER THAT THAT DECEIVER SAID, WHILE HE WAS YET ALIVE, AFTER THREE DAYS I WILL RISE AGAIN. COMMAND THEREFORE THAT THE SEPULCHER BE MADE SURE UNTIL THE THIRD DAY, LEST HIS DISCIPLES COME BY NIGHT, AND STEAL HIM AWAY, AND SAY TO THE PEOPLE, HE IS RISEN FROM THE DEAD: SO THE LAST ERROR SHALL BE WORSE THAN THE FIRST.
> (MATTHEW 27:62–64)
>
> NOW WHEN THEY WERE GOING, BEHOLD, SOME OF THE WATCH CAME INTO THE CITY, AND SHOWED TO THE CHIEF

PRIESTS ALL THE THINGS THAT WERE DONE. AND WHEN THEY
WERE ASSEMBLED WITH THE ELDERS, AND HAD TAKEN COUN-
SEL, THEY GAVE LARGE MONEY TO THE SOLDIERS, SAYING, SAY
YOU, HIS DISCIPLES CAME BY NIGHT, AND STOLE HIM AWAY
WHILE WE SLEPT. AND IF THIS COME TO THE GOVERNOR'S
EARS, WE WILL PERSUADE HIM, AND SECURE YOU. SO THEY
TOOK THE MONEY, AND DID AS THEY WERE TAUGHT: AND
THIS SAYING IS COMMONLY REPORTED AMONG THE JEWS
UNTIL THIS DAY. (MATTHEW 28:11–15)

First, these men tried to prevent the truth from coming forth, then
they perpetrated a lie to cover it up, hoping to maintain their own
<u>false</u> leadership over the people. Having Jesus in you makes you an
<u>authentic</u> leader. You will face opposition, but be encouraged to con-
tinue to lead in truth, love, and humility, maintaining your integrity
regardless of the outcome.

Jacob was a leader, and the following account serves as a type, or
symbol, of Christ. In this story, Jacob is searching for a bride.

AND HE LOOKED, AND BEHOLD A WELL IN THE FIELD, AND, LO,
THERE WERE THREE FLOCKS OF SHEEP LYING BY IT; FOR OUT
OF THAT WELL THEY WATERED THE FLOCKS: AND A GREAT
STONE WAS UPON THE WELL'S MOUTH. AND THERE WERE ALL
THE FLOCKS GATHERED: AND THEY ROLLED THE STONE FROM
THE WELL'S MOUTH, AND WATERED THE SHEEP, AND PUT THE
STONE AGAIN UPON THE WELL'S MOUTH IN HIS PLACE. AND
HE SAID, LO, IT IS YET HIGH DAY, NEITHER IS IT TIME THAT
THE CATTLE SHOULD BE GATHERED TOGETHER: WATER YOU
THE SHEEP, AND GO AND FEED THEM. AND THEY SAID, WE
CANNOT, UNTIL ALL THE FLOCKS BE GATHERED TOGETHER,
AND TILL THEY ROLL THE STONE FROM THE WELL'S MOUTH;
THEN WE WATER THE SHEEP. AND IT CAME TO PASS, WHEN
JACOB SAW RACHEL THE DAUGHTER OF LABAN HIS MOTHER'S
BROTHER, AND THE SHEEP OF LABAN HIS MOTHER'S BROTH-
ER, THAT JACOB WENT NEAR, AND ROLLED THE STONE FROM
THE WELL'S MOUTH, AND WATERED THE FLOCK OF LABAN HIS
MOTHER'S BROTHER. (GENESIS 29:2–3 AND 7–10)

All these shepherds are just sitting around and waiting for the group to come to consensus on watering the sheep. When Jacob suggested they water the sheep they said, "We can't!" Nobody wanted to be the first to go against tradition and break routine. "It's always been done this way!" Then Jacob steps up and opens the well. He didn't let anything stand between him and his objective, because he was a leader. If we are to be successful in kingdom business, then we, too, need to take the lead. Get it done! When you see something to do, just do it. Be a Leader.

When you continue on in the story of Jacob and this first encounter with Rachel, you learn two important lessons about our Lord. First of all, He opened the well for His bride. He did the heavy lifting, but when he did, it was open for everyone to drink. Second, he kissed Rachel before he even told her who he was. He expressed his love for her in an intimate demonstration that everyone witnessed; and <u>then</u> after he had kissed her, he let her know who he was. It was when he revealed himself to her, when she knew who he was, that Rachel knew who she was and that her future was secure.

That is assuredly a picture of us today. We will not know our true identity until the Lord reveals Himself and tells us who He is. Knowing the Lord is an essential key to knowing ourselves. Then following these twelve attributes of success in business will bring us certainty that our true and loving Father will release us into our full inheritance of authority in His kingdom. We will become the overcomers we were created to be, enabled and empowered to rise to the level of our intended creation.

It is now time for us to step into the depths of the river of God and swim eternally in its flow.

Other Books by Vicki Smith Berdit
(formerly White)

- *The Counterfeit Kingdom … A false principality with a powerless king*
- *Freedom Is for Such a Time as Now: Discovering God's plan for restoration and our part in it*
- *The Thursday Gift: A legacy of Jerry White*
- Yet to be released: *Higher Faith, Greater Power, Deeper Peace*

If this book has blessed you, please contact Freedom's Way Ministries to receive other valuable resources to help you move into your destiny and fulfill your purpose in God. Pastors Phil and Vicki Berdit are available for personal appearances to teach kingdom principles, and also for personal ministry to help you come into your true identity and be released from the lies of hell and the labels of the world.

Permission is given to use the materials in this book for study and teaching to advance the kingdom of God. Donations to Freedom's Way Ministries are gratefully accepted and much appreciated. Contact us at 904–993–2876, or for more information and to order the study guide for this book, please visit our website: www. freedomswayministries.com.

Freedom's Way Ministries
P.O. Box 226
O'Brien, Florida 32071

Spread the Word!

IF THIS BOOK HAS IMPACTED YOUR LIFE, PLEASE help me spread the word! Here's how:

- Recommend this book to your book club or life group leader.
- Post a 5-Star review on Amazon.
- Write about *Where the River Flows* on your social media.
- Use an excerpt from the book in your blog, and link it to our website: www.FreedomsWayMinistries.com (You have my permission to do this, as long as you give proper credit and backlinks.)
- Tell your friends to buy this book, and to read it! Word-of-mouth is still the most effective advertising method.
- Gift the loved ones in your life with a copy of their own.
- And finally, provide the venue and invite me to present other life-changing materials in one of our dynamic seminars!

    Disarming Satan's Strongest Weapon

    Growing in Kingdom Power

    Understanding and Moving in the Anointing of God

    Learn to Live and not Die

    Going on to Perfection

- Contact me at 904-993-2876 for availability and to request full descriptions of these event topics.

Thanks and God bless you! Vicki Berdit